Property Metamorphosis: From rat race to property developer and educational business owner

Jay Munoz

All rights reserved. No part of this publication may be reproduced, stored in a retrieval system, or transmitted in any form or by any means, without the prior permission in writing of the publisher, nor be otherwise circulated in any form of binding or cover other than that which it is published and without a similar condition including this condition being imposed on the subsequent purchaser.

Text © Jesus Munoz 2021

The right of Jesus Munoz to be identified as the author of this work has been assented by them in accordance with the Copyright Designs and Patterns Act 1988.

Editing and proof reading: Andrew Dawson
Typesetting: Adam Hollier
Book cover design: Luke Jarvis

Dedications

I dedicate this book to my daughters Antonia, Luisa and Carlotta who are the light of my life. I hope that one day they will apply this knowledge and hopefully teach others so they can also change their lives for the better.

I would also like to express my deepest gratitude to my wife Dr Rosamond Munoz, who put up with me getting up at 4 a.m. to write this book for several months. She has been my rock and support from when I used to rent a single room in a House of Multiple Occupation in West Byfleet, Surrey, back in 2006.

Finally I would like to dedicate this book to our Assets For Life Academy members, mentors, all our members of staff and all those who have contributed suggestions for the content of this book.

Acknowledgments

I am forever grateful to all those who helped me to write and edit this book.

To my wife Dr Rosamond Kate Munoz and our three little manguitos Antonia, Luisa and Carlotta Munoz who allowed me to work on this project during silly hours and gave me the strength and persistence to continue.

To my dear mamá Diva Mireya and my papá Luis Gonzalo Munoz and my brother Martin, and sisters Lorena and Julieta who all live in Colombia who have always been there for me.

To my business partner Liam Ryan who has been amazingly supportive and instrumental in my entrepreneurial journey since we started building our amazing Assets for Life familia.

To our devoted AFL staff members David Morgan, Nigel Mansley, Seb Brantigan, Nick Staab, Kavell Coatman, Tyler Simms, Ludovic Stephenson, Lauren Collins, Hayley Mitchell, Austin Behan, Frances Moss and several mentors and community who have truly made this book dream possible. They inspire me to be my personal legend every day and we would not have been where we are if it wasn't for every single member of this amazing familia.

And to all my readers, for their interest, precious time and comments. If a book sits on a shelf and no one reads it, does it make a sound?

As noted in the Introduction, this book has been written in conversation with our AFL community and LinkedIn network. Many chapters were composed in response to questions I was asked during Facebook Lives and conversations. I would therefore like to thank you for participating and giving up your precious time whilst voting or commenting.

Kilonewtons of love.

Contents

Introduction		8
Chapter 1	Mindset is the key to your success	15
Chapter 2	Property investments concepts	49
Chapter 3	Active vs passive property investment	51
Chapter 4	Property market types	53
Chapter 5	The AFL rules for market selection	57
Chapter 6	The only formula you need to know in property development	71
Chapter 7	Layout is King	72
Chapter 8	Property economics	92
Chapter 9	The step by step process	128
Chapter 10	Case study six	171
Bibliography		269

Introduction

In a fast-paced world, built upon the mindset of previous generations ('go to university so you can graduate and get a good job'), we might not even notice or question whether there is another way. Most of us can't even afford the luxury of considering it, because we have more pressing things to do: we have to go to work at the crack of dawn (almost five years ago, this included me), feed our kids, or look after elderly parents.

Unfortunately, history doesn't give discounts. If the future of humanity is decided in your absence because you are too busy feeding and clothing your offspring, you, and perhaps they, won't be exempt from the consequences. This may be unfair, but unfortunately this is the reality. Not having the right tools at the right time to make informed decisions about our lives makes me utterly sad. This is why I decided to embark on a journey to write this book. I hope it will empower you to think differently and, at the same time, give you the tools that you need to start your own property development journey, to improve your life and the lives of your loved ones just as it did for me and mine, as well as all the families that we help through our annual charity events at Assets for Life (AFL).

I can't give everyone a roof over their head, food or clothes, but with this book I can offer some clear steps and clarity on how I made this difficult transition, thereby helping to level the global playing field. If this book empowers even a handful of people outside our Assets for Life Academy to join us on our entrepreneurial journey, I will feel that I have done my job.

My first publication - *My AFL Journey* (2018) - is helping me and others appreciate and manage their time more effectively. The methods in it helped me to write this book systematically and efficiently.

In this book, I wanted to step back and zoom in on how I managed to free up the most precious asset and the most level playing field that we all have - time. There are 24 hours or, to be more pedantic, 1,440 minutes in a day, and how many of those you spend awake makes a big difference. If we're lucky, at the end of each day we get another 1,440 minutes. The key then is what we spend that time doing, making, building, feeling, and sometimes just simply being. Only five years after my career transition, I am able to do pretty much whatever I want, whenever I want, and I feel like I have created a life that I can't wait to wake up to every day. For me, that's the real meaning of success.

Introduction

My agenda here is mostly focused on the UK. However, some people wanted me to give a broader view; therefore, as well as advocating a mindset which is globally applicable, I am also providing basic concepts to help anyone, anywhere, eager to make a change in their lives on this beautiful planet.

I am sharing my journey from the time that I arrived at Gatwick airport in the UK - back in 2000, with a suitcase full of dreams, including the desire to learn English to be able to communicate with you - until now, in 2020, when I am running multimillion-pound companies and truly helping to change other people's lives for the better. As you can appreciate, it has not been all rosy. Previously, I also proudly did newspaper deliveries at 4 a.m., cleaned toilets, delivered pizzas, worked in factories, and did other unskilled, poorly paid jobs to pay for my studies and my living costs.

This book was written in constant interaction with the public. Many of the chapters were composed in response to questions I asked during Facebook Lives, LinkedIn Pools and general conversations with our amazing AFL community. Earlier versions of some sections have already been posted on Facebook or Instagram, which gave me the opportunity to receive feedback and hone my arguments. Some sections focus on mindset, some on numbers, and others on simple steps to work towards your own dream. But, at the end of the day, it's down to you to take a leap of faith and make the necessary changes in your mindset and subsequent actions to make your dream happen.

I am passing along this knowledge because I am now at the stage in my life where I want to help others to be successful, rather than to be more successful myself. Because these steps have helped me and others so much, I want to share them with you. It is up to you to decide how valuable they really are and what, if anything, you want to do with them.

This book begins by giving you clear suggestions on how you should talk to yourself first, what you should be focusing your energy on day-in and day-out, and then gives clear steps, fundamental concepts, and simple formulas and tools to be able to analyse if a property development deal is feasible or if you should walk away from it.

My hope is that reading this book will prompt you or help you to change your corporate mindset and, if you have been hesitant on giving property development a chance as a new way forward, this may be the catalyst for you to take the leap. As well as reading further, I would also recommend you start investing in yourself and hiring mentors that are ahead of you, who can save you precious time that you will never get back.

Please do choose wisely, look at their values and principles as a person, and choose those that are most in line with your own. In general, it is clear that when you enter into a relationship with others your principles and their principles will determine how you interact. People who have shared values and principles get along. People who don't will suffer constant misunderstandings and conflicts. Think about the people you are closest to right now: are their values and principles aligned with yours? Do you even know what their values and principles are? I very often see business relationships in which people's principles aren't aligned. This is particularly problematic, and in 99 out of 100 cases the business will fail as a result. Being crystal clear about your principles, values and what you really want from your life is the most important thing, and I at least want to give you the opportunity to choose a different path – one that you may not even have thought possible, as I did not so many years ago!

Kinaesthetic learning

This book has been designed to help you turn theory into action. The science of learning has shown that retention of new ideas increases dramatically when new information is immediately recalled (either verbally or via writing), as well as when it is practically applied to your life. To help with this, I have left dotted lines for you to write down the areas that apply to you so you can learn the concepts more effectively and apply them as you read.

A bit about my journey

I was born in Colombia and had a privileged upbringing. My parents started their lives together as teachers with very little, but through sheer hard work and re-training they changed careers. My dad became a successful homeopathic doctor and my mother got into property development. I'm sure it was growing up in this environment that shaped my own work ethic, as well as my love for building.

I had an amazing life as a kid; I was able to have pretty much whatever I wanted. My dad bought a small house in the hills near my hometown and has extended it over many years so it is now able to accommodate the whole extended family. I went to one of the best private schools in town, and had the best clothes etc.

One day, when I was only 14 years old, someone asked me: 'Jay, may I ask you a personal question?' I was puzzled, but I said yes. The question was very simple: "Are you happy?" But it was not actually easy for me to answer. In fact, I took several minutes to think about my answer. This made me realise that, despite all the materials things that I had access to, I was indeed not happy with my life at the time. This made me step back and reflect on my life journey until then. I decided to find the cause of my unhappiness and soon realised that I was being selfish, and only thinking of myself; I was not giving enough back. I came to the conclusion that I was then ready to start working on projects to help others, such as volunteering to look after elderly people and working with local orphanages.

When I finished school, I saw civil engineering as a way of improving lives: transport connections, power supplies, and buildings all make a contribution to how people lived. So, I enrolled at the University of Cauca and did a BSc (Hons) in civil engineering. This qualification was very demanding and I spent several years eating, drinking, and sleeping books to be able to achieve it. You have to study very hard for five years and do a dissertation on top of all your modules. However, the reality is that you have to specialise at some point and so you end up forgetting all the theoretical knowledge and never get to apply it.

Once I finished university, I worked for a construction firm delivering affordable housing units. Here I learned a modular construction technique that was very popular in the 1990s and is still a popular option today. This technique is based on panels that get filled up with concrete and is very efficient, as you can build a two-storey house in a week.

I was happy working in Colombia, but I was hungry to continue to learn more about my chosen career. For this reason, I decided to come to the UK to learn English. I am here writing this book due to the fact that I have an Abundance Mindset and, at the time that I was looking for English courses, I spoke a lot to someone I knew in Canada who was also looking for an English course abroad. She gave me the contact details of a friend of hers who was going to the UK for a very similar cost. This guy, Gabriel Yepes, is still a good friend of mine now. At first, he would not answer the phone but finally, after five attempts, he answered and mentioned that he was going to live in Eastbourne. Immediately after that I decided to investigate and found out that the town was a popular destination for retired people and getting jobs would be a bit difficult. I therefore decided to take another course in Brighton where there were more opportunities to find jobs. As a matter of fact, I found my first job in McDonalds. I was over the moon because my English was very poor and the fact that I somehow managed to get a job in the first week was a real achievement for me.

My goal at the time was to be able to pass the Test of English as a Foreign Language (TOEFL) exam within six months and go on to do an MSc at Florida International University but, once I arrived in sunny Brighton, I decided to stay. Initially I decided to extend my visa by six months, as I was not feeling ready to continue with my MSc studies after only six months. I must say that learning English was a real challenge. I remember waking up in the middle of the night, looking at the ceiling, and thinking "what the hell am I doing here?" Perhaps you have been in my shoes and have also experienced the same feeling, where you are completely out of your comfort zone? But I knew that I had to be resilient. Consistency is key, and I decided to persevere until I accomplished my goal.

The most frustrating thing when you are a foreigner is not being able to communicate, and not being able to learn at the speed that you anticipate. I was getting rather frustrated until one day I decided to step back and reflect for a moment on what was going on. I realised that if you just translate from your first language to a second language, you are never going to be fluent. It was key for me to not be translating everything in my head. The best way to tackle this was by following these simple steps:

- Relax and approach the learning process as a game.
- Believe that everyone else is happy for you to learn. If you want something from the shop, you need to go there, ask nicely, and they will give it to you.
- Have a target of learning at least 50 new words a day – both pronunciation and spelling.

Once you know the words and understand the grammar, you are in for a winner.

In your head, narrate your day. For instance, 'I just woke up and I am taking my pyjamas off to go to the shower'. If you do this mentally several times a day, you will become fluent and the magic starts to happen.

Once I was able to communicate a little better, I could start making friends to help me perfect the language. To start with, I have to confess I was going out with people whose company I didn't even enjoy. But, I had to do this to fulfil my goal of being fluent.

As well as learning English, I also wanted to travel around Europe. To do this I was working about 15 hours a day at McDonalds and saving money to go to Europe, which I did for several weeks. I had the opportunity to visit Spain, Italy, Switzerland, Germany, and France before my visa expired and I had to go back to Colombia, 11 months after I arrived in the UK.

When I arrived, Colombia was in a real political mess. When you have had the opportunity to live in and experience another culture, it is impossible not to compare the two. It made me realise how lucky I was to be able to explore other cultures. I came to the conclusion that the country that was most in line with my values and principles was the UK, so I knew I had to go back there at some point. To achieve my goal, I applied to several MSc courses and decided to enrol at the University of Surrey when I got back to the UK. Before that, I had to earn some money to pay for my education as well as my bills and housing. I found a job in Colombia which was in a consultancy company in charge of building civil infrastructure. The company was responsible for making sure that works were carried out according to the specification and drawings.

After a few years in the construction industry, I left Colombia and decided to emigrate permanently to the UK. In 2003, I started doing an MSc at the University of Surrey. I was determined to achieve this qualification while supporting myself. I negotiated staged payments of the course fees, and I worked full time doing jobs such as cleaning toilets and delivering pizzas to fund it all.

With perseverance and my new qualification, I set out to find myself a job. I was very conscious that UK nationals would be far higher up any pecking order, followed by Europeans, leaving the 'kid' from South America at the bottom of the pile. I knew I had to do something special, so I sent out 30,000 CVs! And it worked; the result was five job offers.

I worked on some great projects during my career, including:
- The London Underground
- The Wallbrook and other iconic structures in central London, worth £1.5 billion
- EDF new nuclear power station at Hinkley Point C, worth £20 billion.
- Extension of Puerto Caucedo in the Dominican Republic

I achieved Chartered Civil Engineering status and was highly ranked while working in the corporate environment, and I thought I was absolutely in the right place. This was until I read the book *Rich Dad, Poor Dad* by

Robert T. Kiyosaki. This set my head spinning, and I knew I had to have my own business. This moment in my life is the perfect example of what they call a 'satori moment' where your past, your present and your future aligns and you realise that you have been empowered with knowledge to change your life for the better and it is now up to you to make it happen.

And then I met Liam. This cheeky Essex lad came knocking on my door. There was something infectious about his energy and purpose. We started our property journey by investing £25k for mentorship using our credit cards and yes, it was scary to do so but reflecting back it has been one of the best decisions we have taken as we have been able to transform our lives and the ones of many others for the better which make this investment one of infinite returns.

I love Assets for Life. It ticks all my boxes – I can share and help other people, I can improve lives through building and development, and I have the wealth to have choice and freedom, which means I can give my best to my family too.

In the chapters to follow you will learn the tools to start your own property metamorphosis so watch this space.

This was also my driver to write this book so I do hope that after reading it you will have your own satori moment and are able to start your own property metamorphosis.

Chapter One

Introduction

In this chapter you will learn how to switch your mindset from rat race to business owner and start your own metamorphosis....

Mindset is the key to your success

A. Change your tools or sharpen them

> 'Self reflection orbits around self development' - Jay Munoz

My option is that there is no 'reality' as such - there is only how we individually interpret reality. Adopting a mindset of success is the best tool you can have in order to effectively conquer life's biggest obstacles.

As Ray Dalio says in his book *Principles*, in order to have the best life possible you have to first know what the best decisions are, and second, have the courage to make them.

I would expand on these two points and say that in order to accomplish the above, we have to:

1. Have clear SMART (Specific, Measurable, Achievable, Realistic, and Time-bound) goals
2. Eliminate the possibility of failure
3. Find mentors that are ahead of you and learn from them so you get to where you want to be quicker
4. Turn your 'failures' into advantages
5. Thrive in discomfort
6. Accept conflict as a part of your journey, and
7. Focus on what matters most every single day, and avoid the rest

Go to a mindset seminar, any seminar, and you'll see journals full of big plans and commitments – every attendee ready to conquer the world. And that's fine, necessary even, but it's not the end of the story.

Real success comes when the sun has gone down when everyone else is in bed. It's not a specific tactic or hack – it's a mindset.

Or, to be more precise, it's a series of mindsets. Success comes from changing the tools with which we see the world. Some 'experts' call this the Law of Attraction – but there's more to it than a simple law. You need to be equipped with the right tools. You need to change how you think. Change how you perceive the world.

Think of this analogy. In 2014 while on vacation with my brother and dad in Brazil for the football world cup, I would never have thought of starting a fight with the security guard before he or she even let me in the stadium, right? Why not? Because this is not who I am. It's not even an option. I am fundamentally not someone who would do this. I don't have to motivate myself not to offend anyone while on vacation.

Which is why changing who you are is more than motivation – it's about literally changing who you are.

The world was one way – and now it's another. Permanently. Forever. No going back.

Now, let's do some kinaesthetic learning:

Can you think of a time recently when you 'committed' to a particular new habit or goal and then stopped halfway through?

As an example:

I committed to starting a relationship with commercial agents a month ago but ... well, let's just put it this way ... I'm ... I am afraid of making the first phone call.

Write your own example below:

Now think about what happened? Why did you give up?
As an example:
I committed to the habit - did it five times, but when it became difficult, when my motivation faltered...I just stopped. I hadn't changed the core of who I am. I didn't expand my zone of comfort and step towards becoming my personal legend.

Write your own reason below:

What mindset shift would have made it so you were still following that 'commitment'?

As an example:
Well, I could have said "I'm not a person who eats sugar" the same way I now say "I'm not a person who eats dog". I could just make it a part of who I am.

Write your own below:

B. Look at regret from a different perspective

'No matter where you are in the process, stop playing small, the time is now, otherwise WHEN?' - Jay Munoz

After reading many books about regret, I discovered that it can be one of the most hopeful and powerful emotions we can feel. This is because, while regret can be painful, it can be used to make better decisions in the future - what is called negative visualisation.

There's no loss when you actually go for it. When you step into your bold decisions, new doors will open and you will encounter new, like-minded people. When you look back at your life, you'll regret the things you didn't do more than the things you did.

To take a leap of faith is not an easy decision to make. Nevertheless, bold decisions have to be made in order to become your Personal Legend (which means ultimately, ultimately being the best ever version of yourself in every way and being your own competitor, always hungry for more). You know you have to do it, but you're hesitating and not actually bringing it to life.

There are multiple types of leaps, ranging from business to relationships. Leaps can also vary in size; from a massive, life-changing decision to leave my native and beloved Colombia, to a career change I took a few years back when I gave up my highly paid Chartered Civil Engineer job to concentrate on property, to a smaller one, like reading a new book collecting dust on our shelves.

Today, four years later, I am eternally grateful I took those leaps. I spent more than a decade working for someone else as a Chartered Civil Engineer and fulfilling someone else's dreams.

I don't regret this, as I was improving many people's lives building much-needed infrastructure. The reality is that we spend most of our lives at work. The problem with most people is that they're disengaged with their work, or experience a toxic environment while they're there. This is because they lack excitement about their career, or there are other colleagues that contaminate their environment.

When there's no alignment between our job and life, work becomes a monotonous chore.

I encourage you, if you are not happy with your current life, to take a leap and make your dreams come true. Take a leap and turn that idea into your own business, and live your life on your own terms. If a proud South American kid needing a visa to come to the UK can do it, so can you.

What happened before is unimportant compared to what will someday happen. Our lives are affected by our past, but only insofar as we let the past define our present reality. It all lives in our head.

And once we understand that reality, it's easier to consciously choose our future, rather than allow it to be defined by our past. But what future will it be? Will your future self be proud of what you're doing right now?

Let's do some kinaesthetic learning, and have a conversation with yourself in the future.

Picture this. Imagine that you take your future self out for a nice Colombian coffee. Imagine you and your future self having a little chat.

Will your future self say:

1. *Thank you for getting me here – I'm glad and grateful that you made it this far and took that leap of faith, didn't take no for an answer, were obsessed with success and now run your own business and, as a result, have positively impacted so many lives during your journey.*

Or will he/she say:

2. *What are you doing sitting on the same warm seat, doing the same mundane job that you don't enjoy and used to do three years ago!?*

It's important to note that imagining too far into the future is not helpful, nor is focusing too much on the present moment. The sweet spot, then, is about three years from now. It's close enough that you can feel yourself making progress, but it's not so far away that you can't even imagine getting there.

What's one of your three-year goals, in either your personal or professional life?

As an example:

I'd like to have a greater positive impact on other people's lives by starting my own property metamorphosis.

Now, time to write your own goal:

Now, rather than negative visualisation, use positive visualisation to imagine yourself three years from now, sitting across from you, having a conversation with current you about what they did today.

What would he or she say? How are you doing?

Are you taking active steps towards reaching the goal you wrote above?

Here's an example:
I did alright. I gave up my job and started my property development journey full time. It was not easy but now I have a life that I can't wait to wake up to.

Now imagine your own conversation with your future self:

C. Get rid of your safety net

> *'If you are going to make a difference, you have to take risks in life'*
> *- Jay Munoz*

It was not an easy or straightforward decision to make, being the very risk-averse person that I am, but sometimes, in order to accomplish your dreams, the decisions that we need to make are binary – all or nothing.

As I've told you, I made a transition from the corporate world, where I was highly paid as a Chartered Civil Engineer to the entrepreneurial world. The monkey on my shoulder and my peers were telling me: 'Don't quit your job! How are you going to keep your lifestyle? How are you going to feed your kids? You will never ever make it on your own!' And however many other excuses you can imagine. If I discussed my ideas with my peers and colleagues, they would laugh at me, saying that I was completely mad. This is when the people that are most influential to you come into play. If I didn't have the woman that is behind me, and has been through thick and thin, I probably wouldn't be writing this book for you.

My wife said to me: 'You are far better than that Jay!'

She gave me all the courage in the world to cut my safety net, sack the boss and embark on one of the biggest leaps in my life.

Stepping back and analysing these events in detail, I can conclude that if I didn't have the courage to get rid of the monkey on my shoulder and listen to the right people, this dream of becoming an entrepreneur and business owner would never have materialised.

The only way to do this was to cut that safety net called a job and jump into the freedom of running my own business, living life to the full and having the ability to control the way I spend my time which, in essence, is the real currency of life.

Before I took the leap, I had some steady income coming from a property portfolio, so I was able to survive on that and invest that precious time in educating myself financially before going into property full time.

Please do make sure that, before you quit your job, you have a plan of survival during the time that the nice steady income that you once had doesn't come. I would suggest you have at least one year of expenses saved so you can take a leap and go all in.

Besides this, my wife was employed, and we were able to share the cost of living together. This also helped me to go full steam ahead with property development full time.

I love analogies, as you probably know if you have heard me talking at AFL training events, so let me give you one as an example:

Juan Valdez arrived in London too young, green, and without a single client. However, within three years he was able to found and grow a thriving business.

But how did Juan manage to achieve that?

Let's put it this way: if I asked you to run the London marathon right now, could you do it? You may say that you can't – but what if I told you that your life, or the life of someone that you love, depends on it? Now would you? I bet that now you would do it. What is the moral of this analogy?

Sometimes it takes jumping off the ledge to learn how to fly.

Now, let's apply that with some kinaesthetic learning.

What's the biggest obstacle in your way right now? What is stopping you from going 'all in' with your goals?

Here's an example:

Well, I have a side business that's doing alright, but I've kept my full-time job because it brings in more money. Though if I quit my job it would certainly force me to push myself harder...

Now write your own below:

Reminder: go for it; make it happen! Get closer to being your Personal Legend! If not now, when?

D. Seek perspective from someone more experienced than you

'The opposite of success is not failure but ignorance' - Jay Munoz

One of the key decisions that I made before embarking on my full-time property journey was to seek the perspective of someone that was ahead of me in their career. When I met Liam Ryan, my wonderful business partner, the first thing I said to him was that we needed to get mentors who were the best of the best in the same line of business. Even though I had well over a decade of experience working on projects in central London, I felt that I needed someone to hold my hand through the process, since I knew it was going to be completely different from being a contractor, designer, or client.

Before we embarked on our journey, we spent £25,000 on our first mentorship programme. To date, it has been one of the best investments that we have made, and we recovered our investment back in less than 12 months. We also decided to go big and pay extra for the best two mentors rather than getting other, less qualified (in our view) mentors who were cheaper but did not have the vision and big picture that is in line with our core values and principles as a company now.

To put it simply, the reason that we have mentors in our lives is to save us time and to get us to where we want to be quicker. In order to skip costly mistakes in your learning process, you need to be okay with being wrong, be prepared to listen, and take action sometimes even though it is not in line with your line of thought. Most importantly, you need to find a mentor who will push you to your limits in all ways.

I must stress that the secret to a successful relationship with your mentor is: follow up! If my mentor told me to read a book, I read it within a week, wrote to the author of the book, asked them questions, did a review on Facebook and Instagram about the book, applied the knowledge of the book immediately, and taught others to complete the cycle. If you consistently respond to your mentor's advice with such enthusiastic action, they will introduce you to more people when you ask them a very simple but powerful question: 'Who do you know who ...?'.

Don't wait to test your follow-up skills. Take immediate action: make a plan before you meet your mentor where you outline what advice you're seeking, who you're going to ask, and when you're going to ask them. Afterwards, document what advice they gave, and what your follow-up plan for that advice is. I created a spreadsheet like the one below that may also help you with your journey.

You can also use *My AFL Journey* for this.

Before
After
Advice you seek
Mentor to ask
When?
Advice they gave
Your follow-up plan
Their reaction

How to be in the best shape for charity calendar photo shoot?

Eugenio Caicedo
August 17
Follow agreed work out routine
Follow the exercises every day
Upload photos to Facebook describing my improvement, write a thank-you card to Mr Eugenio Caicedo
Very impressed!

How to get ground investigation reports right
Institution of Civil Engineers – possible full day training
June 17
Follow up with a live project
Bought a piece of land that had planning permission to build seven flats and two houses, and carried out site investigation report. Documented the whole thing, prepared a presentation and did a webinar to all my students after this.
Extremely grateful and impressed.

Property Metamorphosis

Mentors are not the only source of information; you should also consciously push all your boundaries, read the right books, talk to other experts, listen to the best podcasts, and pay attention to the best writers. Think of the quality of this content as nutrition, the building blocks of the future Personal Legend of you. Just as you'd check the nutrition label of the food you're about to eat, make sure you're putting quality nutrition into your mind, heart and soul. The reality is that you are what you eat. If you spend your time with cruddy people and sub-par media, you won't grow into the best possible version of yourself, let alone achieve your Personal Legend level. But, if you put high-quality heathy food in, you cannot help but get high-quality output, in the form of your best possible future self, or your Personal Legend level as author Paulo Coelho would say.

Now, time for kinaesthetic learning.

Who is a mentor you would like to connect with?

Incidentally, Jay Munoz, Liam Ryan and the rest of the AFL Academy mentors and the AFL team are here to serve you.

How could you approach them to create a mentor relationship? Write a starting email below.

Jay.munoz@assetsforlife.co.uk & Liam.ryan@assetsforlife.co.uk

What are five blogs/articles/books you can read to gain perspective?

1....
2....

3. ...
4. ...
5. ...

E. Circumstances and the power of our own perception

You cannot control anything except for what you can control. Your circumstances are what they are. Worrying about them accomplishes nothing.

The trick is to use your circumstances to your advantage, no matter what they are.

For example, if you grew up with no money and no advantages — this can give you valuable lessons. Struggle is what defines you. The more adversity you must overcome, the better person you will be.

This is a wonderful quote by Marcus Aurelius that I have now learnt by heart and that may help you to truly embrace this concept.

'Impediment to action advances action. What stands on the way becomes the way.'

In order to turn obstacles into triumph, defeat into success, you'll need to follow a simple three step process:

1. Change how you perceive difficulties
2. Change how you act in the face of them
3. Learn to grow in defeat

We begin with how we perceive the world around us. It takes discipline and skill to control our emotions, but it is learnable quality.

And here I leave you with this other amazing quote:
'Objective judgment, now at this very moment.
Unselfish action, now at this very moment.
Willing acceptance—now at this very moment - of all external events.
That is all you need.' — Marcus Aurelius

Rubin 'Hurricane' Carter, a top boxing contender of the 1960s, was wrongly accused of homicide and sentenced to a lifetime behind bars. Though knowing his innocence, he refused to take his time inside as a negative. As an example, on his first day of being a inmate, he made the following comment to the prison guards:

'I'm willing to stay here until I get out. But I will not, under any circumstances, be treated like a prisoner - because I am not and never will be powerless.' - Rubin 'Hurricane' Carter.

He spent all his time reading and learning. After finally being released, after 19 years of captivity - he didn't even ask for an apology, because he refused to believe he had been negatively impacted. In fact, he left jail being wiser and smarter. What happened wasn't bad - it was just the circumstances.

The point here is that there is power in our perceptions. An event that others see as hopeless or frightening - you can see as an opportunity. The story we tell ourselves about an event necessarily defines that event, not the event itself.

Now time for some kinesthetic learning:

What is your biggest disadvantage in life?

Example: I have ADHD.

How is this actually an advantage? Most people do not have to constantly and consciously think about what they're focusing on. For me, though, the fact that I was aware of my own attention at a very young age, actually gave me an advantage. Now that I'm older, in my professional life, I'm often able to quickly notice when I'm not paying attention. This is extreme self-awareness, which is obviously valuable.

F. Discomfort

'The ups and downs of entrepreneurship will present failures but you must learn from and be grateful for these rather than run and curse them'
- Jay Munoz

In order for us to grow in the right direction we need to embrace discomfort. Make it your best friend. You need to consciously, almost obsessively even, attack discomfort as if it were your duty to do so. From discomfort comes the evolution and expansion of your comfort zone.

In fact, if you are not pushing your boundaries by viewing discomfort as a positive, as steroids for your growth, you will be left behind by your peers who are pushing themselves.

Find something that makes you uncomfortable — and do it. This is the way to mastery.

Now time for some kinesthetic learning:

What is something that you are scared of? What makes you uncomfortable?

Example: Public speaking. Asking for investment money for one of your great property deals? Writing a book.

Pick a place/time when you are going to attack this discomfort. How can you overcome it immediately by ripping off the bandage of your self-doubt?

G. Misogi

'Go where others won't go or will never think of going' - Jay Munoz

Hold on — what is a misogi? It is a Japanese practice of purification. We can now interpret it a bit differently. 'Put one big thing on the calendar at least once a year that scares you, that you never thought you could do, and go out and do it. If you can also raise money for charity then you will be more than welcome in the AFL family'.

Kyle Corver, an NBA basketball star, is famous for his misogis. Every six months or so, he does something that is very difficult, that has a larger chance of failure than success, in order to challenge himself. IS THIS VALUABLE?

Doing a misogi teaches you that you can do anything. Whenever you're faced with a difficult challenge, for the rest of your life, you'll be able to look back and say, 'If I did that — I can do this.'

It's a tool. Finishing the misogi is not the goal in of itself — it should instead be used as a stepping stone.

Examples of misogis are (my comments in brackets to amuse you):
- Run a marathon (did the London Marathon for charity in 2010)

- Swim for 24hrs in the winter in the UK (as I write we are aiming to do this with the AFL team soon for charity)
- Bike for 100 miles (not done yet but did 24hrs cycling for charity with rest of the team)
- Ask a stranger out on a date (good luck as I am married!)
- Ask 100 strangers out! (ditto)
- Go on a 50-mile day hike (on my bucket list)
- Camp out in the middle of nowhere for a weekend (done)
- Don't go online for an entire week (Good luck with this Liam Ryan!)
- Write another book

Now time for some kinaesthetic learning.

Application to life

What is a misogi that you can do this year that would prove to yourself that you can do anything? Remember: it should be difficult, but not impossible.

I've always wanted to start my own business in property.

H. When successful conflict equals progress

Inevitability conflict

> 'You're either going to have a good day or a damn good story — whichever it is you are going to learn' - Jay Munoz

The more successful you become, the more conflict will arise. This is a fundamental truth of success. The more you have, the more responsibility you have, the more people depend on you, the bigger challenges you will face — this all equals more conflict.

Therefore, just like discomfort, successful people need to change their perception of conflict. It should not be avoided, but relished and felt gratitude for.

Conflict = Progress

At the end of the day, it is how you react to conflict what makes who you really are.

Time to do some kinaesthetic learning.
Rate yourself on your conflict management skills:

1 2 3 4 5 6 7 8 9 10 (1 terrible to 10 incredible)

Do you avoid or move toward conflict?

1 2 3 4 5 6 7 8 9 10 (1 avoid to 10 run toward)

What's a big conflict you've been avoiding?
Why?

Now go confront it! Get it over with. Pull off the plaster. You'll feel much better, I promise.

I. Time is one of your biggest Assets for Life

'Your experiences, the people around you and the way you spend your time come together to create this particular moment' - Jay Munoz

I'm absolutely fascinated by this concept so I created a tool (*My AFL Journey*). My main driver to develop this tool was to empower you to plan and achieve your goals, be consistent, be grateful for each day by focusing your energy on your priorities.

If you get hold of it, you will learn how to harness the power of intention and cultivate new skills, achieving more by concentrating on the key habits that you might already have.

Learning to review your progress, even when it is slow, will teach you to stay motivated and inspired when adversity arises.

If you use this journey, you will learn how to develop techniques that will allow you to build the life you want.

Your habits are the bedrock of your life, and building good habits as a foundation make the difference between achieving your goals and falling short.

Without a way to successfully use new insights and track your progress, such as in this journey; it is easy to do nothing more than process information but never utilise it. If nothing is measured, and nothing managed, then nothing can change. Joining up the dotted lines of your own journey is critical to implementing new behaviours and getting the most out of what you learn.

By making small focused steps forward by using insights, you create a SUCCESS list, not a 'To-Do List'. What is the point of making a long list of a million tasks which feels impossible to complete? Instead, why not track your progress against set goals within a time frame which makes them achievable? In simple terms, every single human being has the same amount of time in a day — and yet somehow some people accomplish so much each day, week, month, year—in their lives. But how do we do make ourselves more like them?

The real key to this is prioritisation. There is more than enough time to have an awesome relationship with your family, your friends, work hard, invest money, play hard, have time for effective leisure, constant learning, fail, dust yourself off and persevere. But you have to make conscious decisions. You cannot let your life happen to you — you must be in control of your time day-in day-out and have goals and constantly plan ahead. There should be also an element of surprise now and again to spice things up but if you don't know where you are going how on this beautiful earth are you going to get there?

Now time to do some kinaesthetic learning.

Make a list of what is working for you and amplify those gains.

But also make a list of what is not working for you (AKA: what you need to cut out) and ruthlessly eliminate them from your life.

1.
2.
3.
4.
5.

Family, learning, writing, property investing, physical health...

For each, what can you do every single day to improve and maintain those priorities?

1.
2.
3.
4.
5.

Eat breakfast with my kids and husband/wife every morning, listen to podcasts on my way to work, write in *My AFL Journey* a gratitude list every morning and at night before bed, take ten minutes on my lunch break to search inward, and switch to a standing desk to promote movement.

What are the five things you need to cut out in order to have time for your true priorities?

1.
2.
3.
4.
5.

Random s**** television, obsessive social media scrolling, reading news articles in nonsense newspapers, going to the pub and getting drunk after work, eating junk food.

Finally have you bought a copy of *My AFL Journey* yet? If not what are you waiting for - take immediate action? We guarantee 100 per cent satisfaction - https://www.amazon.co.uk/My-AFL-Journey-Jay-Munoz/dp/1527234444

J. Generosity is the key to real happiness

'Life is about contribution and not acquisition — real happiness comes when you give back not when you take back' - Jay Munoz

I do hope that by taking consistent action on the previous nine mindset points you have created new powerful habits that as a result have led you to change your mindsets — but what is the real reason for this?

When the going gets tough (and it will), what will keep you going? What is your big WHY?

The best chance you have of keeping motivated is to frame your entire life as a chance to give to others.

As part of the AFL values and principles, we are very keen to help our local community. We support our local Colchester Emergency Shelter and have raised several thousand pounds to support such a great cause. I have spent time cooking for less fortunate people that one way or another don't have shelter and they have no option but to look for help at such organisations. Here is a photo of me and one of our team members Rebecca Wade volunteering.

At AFL we are also mega keen to help and support less fortunate families that work hard day-in day-out and don't get paid accordingly. As you may recall I was born in Colombia and the social differences are far higher than in most parts of Europe.

The middle class is a minority and the wages are a misery that doesn't give the opportunity to people to even have a decent shelter over their heads. Hence we decided to give to a family in need the chance to build their own home themselves. I was lucky enough to have met Professor Carlos Ariel Hurtado who was one of my lecturers at Cauca University during my BSc in Civil Engineering.

I was privileged enough to be his student and be influenced by his passion for education and helping others. I lost contact for a few years until a friend of mine told me that he was heavily involved in helping poor families building their own homes so, intrigued, I hunted him down one day when he was teaching at my old university. We got chatting and agreed we were going to work together helping one family per year. He then introduced me to Familia Yande who I had the privilege to meet. Here is a photo of us when we met....

Belen (mum), Andres (dad), Luisa (eldest child), Helen (second child), Andres Jr (youngest child)

Property Metamorphosis

If you follow me on Facebook (www.facebook.com/Jay.Munoz.AFL/) and Instagram (jaymunozafl), you can see a video I did around their house and I was so shocked by how they lived in such appalling conditions.

When I watch this video back now it constantly reminds me of how lucky I am to have what I have and feel even more grateful every single day of my life for having so many countless blessings.

When I came back from Colombia to the UK I had loads of ideas in my head on how to raise money for this which is now our new baby/charity.

One day I came up with the idea of doing a calendar and to call it Arses for Life. Which we proudly did and here is the proof…

Here is our team from left: Austin Behan, Liam Ryan, Alex Harvey, Jay Munoz, Paul Greig-Smith, Seb Brantigan.

Chapter One

Property Metamorphosis

I used to be chubby and ever since I was a teenager I always wanted to do a bodybuilding competition but I never had a big driver rather than myself. However this time around my big WHY was completely different and in my head every time I trained to achieve the best shape of my life I had this family in my head and it made me even more hungry for it at a level that I would have not been otherwise. At the beginning I was a bit cocky and thought that following what I knew about exercise and nutrition was enough to get me in the best shape! Well I didn't succeed and it got to the point that I panicked and decided again to get a mentor who was ahead of me on this. Then I contacted a friend of mine back in Colombia. Engenio Caicedo is an international bodybuilding champion. Even though he is in his early 50s he still looks like a teenager! He gave me all the knowledge and gave me clear and detailed instructions of what to eat, exercise and how much time I need for each single element of it. Twenty-two days before the calendar photo shoot I was looking like this (below).

But after sheer drive and determination and having a BIG WHY, I managed to look like this...

So 22 days later I achieved this shape (right) which I am now very proud of. Not only for me but for what it actually meant to familia Yande. How-

Chapter One

ever, the diet Engenio gave me was not pleasant as it meant zero carbs for several days which I had never experienced before. What happens is you get very cranky as you take away the fuel for your brain which reflects on your mood so my wife was not very happy about this.

On the positive side I am now more sympathetic with my dad who suffers from diabetes as I believe he feels the same way sometimes.

Once we finished the calendar the money was sent to build the house. We kept a close eye on the construction. It was so inspiring to see how the neighbours (who they were also sharing a toilet with, seven, yes, seven families share one toilet), were helping to bring materials to the site and even the kids took part. We received photos showing the daughters and son were mixing concrete and doing hardcore labour. They were so happy working in harmony with the rest of the family which was so inspiring to see. About one and a half years after the start of the project I went to visit the family. The house was almost ready here is a photo of it...

Unfortunately the kids had left to go to school even though we arrived with Professor Carlos Ariel at 6 a.m. The family were so grateful to us and could not believe that we helped them without expecting anything in return. In fact we said that the only thing that we were expecting back was that they help another family at some point as a way of paying it forward.

Andres told me that as he built the whole house with this own hands he was now able to find a better job in the city as a construction foreman and as a result his life and his family's was transformed. This was an effect we had not considered and were obviously extremely pleased with. In my view this has been the most rewarding project AFL has undertaken and will continue to be our legacy as a company.

I would like to take this opportunity to thank all the people that have contributed to this fantastic cause. I won't mention names but you know who you are and should be extremely proud!

Our next challenge was to build a second home for a family in need who lost their home in a fire. Seven children and mum and dad. I have not met the family yet but will do so in due course. For this I came up with the idea of doing a 24hrs static cycle challenge. At the beginning we wanted to be in the *Guinness Book of Records* and were aiming high to do more than 1,000km between us all. I started training for it and it was very tough but I was committed to it.

Later I realised that the kind hearts who were supporting our cause were pulling out as they were saying that they won't be able to be at that elite level and were going to leave.

Then we decided to scrap the Guinness record and focus on what was important which was to build the house for the poor family and decided to ask all the AFL team members to take part. This was a great day where everyone got involved including member of staff, AFL academy members, friends and family and here is the video of it if you would like to watch it...

https://assetsforlife.co.uk/community#charity

Here is almost all our AFL family working together as a team for such a great cause.

Above we have Michelle Lucas and Sacha Bamforth, two of our amazing students, now financially free through property. Incidentally the time is 1.43 a.m!

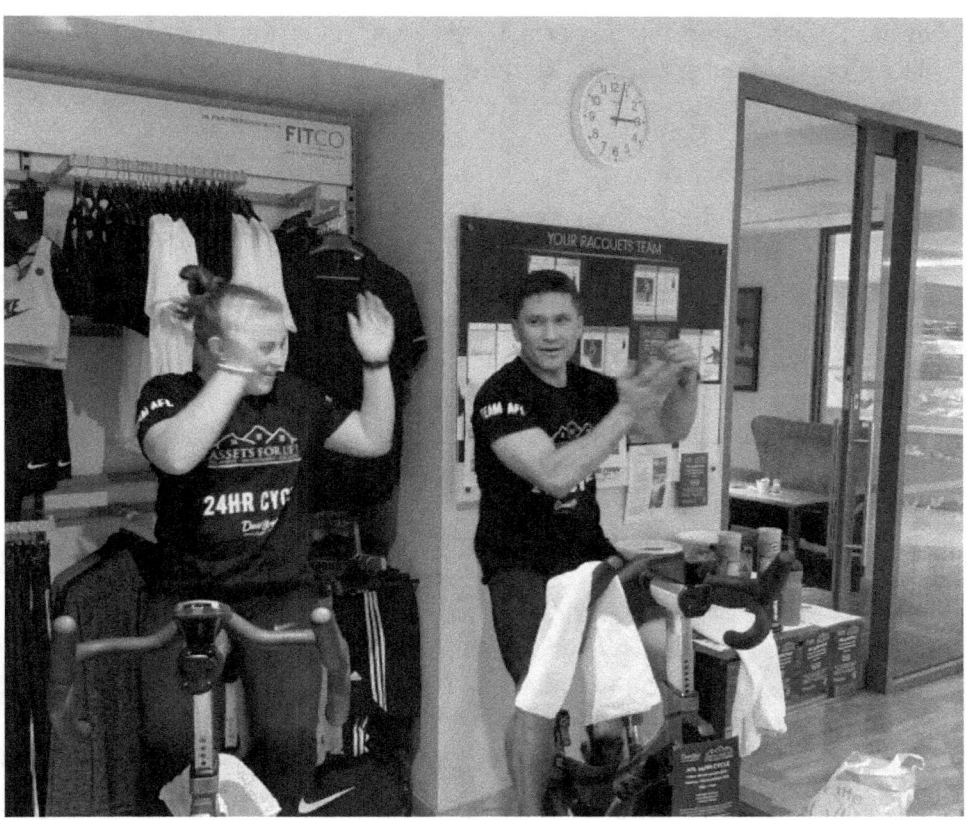

Above we have Gabriela Szarowicz, one of our of our amazing students, who is now financially free through property, and myself. And the time is 03.04 a.m!

At the time of writing we are trying to prepare for our next challenge set by one of our students, Katie Birkitt. She said let's swim across the English channel and I was like, what? But in the end we are trying to swim from Tarifa in Spain to Morocco and let me tell you it scares the hell out of me as I am definitely not a good swimmer!

Now some kinesthetic learning time.

What is your big WHY? Why are you on this planet? What do you want to impart? What is your legacy? Have you written your epitaph yet? If not get a copy of *My AFL Journey* and do it – make it happen!

My family. My entire goal in life is to take care of my three children and give them more opportunities and challenges than I was given...

How can you incorporate generosity and gratitude into your daily routine?

K. Call to Action & Contemplation

'In order to live your best life, tough decisions have to be made'
- Jay Munoz

Taking a career change leap is one of the most difficult decisions that I have ever made. The fact that you have a steady salary coming to your bank account every month, especially when you have dependents, scared the hell out of me when I made the decision. The little monkey over your shoulder is telling you that you are not good enough to make it happen, sometimes the people that you surround yourself with don't encourage you to make this pivotal decision. However if you want it bad enough and resilience, perseverance are your second and third names then anyone with this mindset can do this.

One of the key nuggets that I picked up from Napoleon Hill's book *Think and Grow Rich* says, 'understand that achievement begins with a burning DESIRE of something definite'. So what is your burning desire?

How much money do you want? Be specific. What are you going to give in return for the money? When will you receive it? When I read this I came up with this analogy. At the time of writing, I decided to go off grid a bit so I went and stayed in a hotel room in Mijas, Spain.

During this period I was also training for the swimming charity fundraising challenge.

Here it goes.

Imagine your are under water and your head is being pushed under by someone and you can't get up. You can't get up and you are struggling and you're gasping for air so badly but you can't breathe.

Are you picturing this? You would do or pay anything for air and you gasp for air even more and you really feel the need of it and you are close to dying for it. And then suddenly you're pulled up above the water and you are able to breeeaaaaath awww.....that is a BURNING desire. You have to want success and whatever you really desire so badly, the same as you would want air and you're under water and you are drowning. It has to be a passion, even an obsession, and you have to keep feeding that flame but the most important part of this desire is articulating what it is.

Sometimes passion is not good enough to make this leap, you have to be obsessed with it to really break though. In other words to really understand your ambition, you must get out of your head and into your heart and soul.

If you live too much in your feelings you won't be able to withstand the emotional whiplash - thus the stereotype of the callous capitalist. But stoically separating yourself from your emotions is not the solution.

However hard at first, you must get used to the ups, dips, turns, and twists of your entrepreneurial rollercoaster. Take time and reflect on those times of confusion and really feel the growing pains within yourself.

Rather than attempting to escape the depths of your personal lows, consider why you've come to this place, and embrace the learning experience.

Once you explore that moment — through contemplating powerful questions, journaling, and perhaps even expressing yourself through art or poetry — you will come out with a better understanding of how you got to that negative experience and how you can lift yourself out. It's those hard-won lessons that will fill you with confidence in your vivid vision and make you a more resilient leader.

Conversely, if you run from your feelings, they'll follow closely behind you with persistence. You cannot escape or logically deduce all your emotions.

By allowing for emotions — yes, even in business — and approaching them head on, you may be able to let go of the darkness once and for all. Sometimes the subconscious mind takes over so you may want to look at your previous experiences and past.

If you need professional help by all means invest in some as we can't always get over stuff like this without the input of professionals and the correct tools.

Once you do this you need to fight back and at the end I'm sure if you still have this burning desire you will be victorious and forever grateful and happy.

Now time for some kinaesthetic learning
Stop. Breathe. Reset. Refocus. You'll be stronger moving forward.......

L. Have you found and are you looking after the horses that propelled you forward?

> 'Don't waste time resuscitating dead horses. Keep feeding the good ones that propel you forward' - Jay Munoz

Who you surround yourself with and who you allow yourself to be influenced by will determine who you become.

One of the best life analogies that I have heard is this: Imagine that your life is a coach propelled by horses. They are the engine of your life, they are constantly helping you move forward in whatever direction you ask them to go. You still read the compass and provide direction but they are the ones that help you achieve your goals.

Napoleon Hill talks about building mastermind groups in his book *Think and Grow Rich*. The idea is to build your own network of support and accountability with friends, mentors, or peers.

Remember, the horses you spend the most time with significantly impact your reality, so you must be mindful about who you choose to have as part of your circle. Who will be in your group? Get together or connect with your mastermind AFL academy group each week or month to share what you've accomplished and what you're still struggling with. It helps keep group morale high to reward the person who has made the most progress that week.

This is your success family — you choose each other and use your collective insights and strengths to inspire and encourage everyone to keep pushing forward.

There are three types of people/horses you want on your team.

The Visionary horse: They magnify your ideas. They want to build it even bigger, expand on it, help it grow. You need these people to achieve your full potential and see the impact your projects can have on your life and the world.

The Realist horse: The editor. Finds the problems, finds the issues, finds the holes in your idea. You need their input and feedback to make sure your ideas and projects are tested and can actually hold water.

The Accountability horse: They don't find the problems, they don't build your ideas any bigger, they hold you accountable to your commitments. You need these people to stay on course and make real progress. If you spend all your time finding holes in your ideas and then expanding on your projects, you won't make consistent progress, and consistent progress is the secret to every big success.

Now time to do kinaesthetic learning:
Write down the name of your current three most influential horses and if you have not found them now is the time to find them!
1. The Visionary
Who?
Why?

2. The Realist
Who
Why?

3. The Accountability
Who?
Why?

I must stress that if you have people/horses in your life that are dead (i.e. negative people, pessimistic, positive energy suckers etc) the fact is you don't lose one horse but two, as you have to carry their weight as they are still part of your coach/life.

It is probable that you're the average of the people you spend most the time with — it's time to do some calculations please.

Have an informal chat with each influencer in your life and fill in the table below with their answers.

I've suggested some metrics to consider but make sure you ask about the information that's most relevant to you (but make sure it's measurable — if you can measure it, you can digest and manage it). The one below is most applicable to me personally.

Now time to do kinaesthetic learning:

Name
How many holidays do you have per year?
How many books do you read per year?

What is your current nutrition and diet?
How much exercise do you do per week?
What are your yearly savings? How much of this do you invest?
Other:

Hear me out here for a minute. Think about the person you want to be, the property developer you want to be, the social entrepreneur you want to be, the partner you want to be, the mom, dad, son, daughter etc you want to be — the influential person you want to be or become. Becoming the ideal version of you or acquiring your personal legend level requires firm solid intention. The more time you spend with the types of people you want to be influenced by, the more there will be people in your community that slowly fall away. The truth of the matter is, if you want to achieve your personal legend level, whatever that is for you, that requires change. You have to start hanging out with a different crowd, talking about stimulating ideas rather than same old things, and working toward different goals.

Let the individuals or dead horses who don't add positively to your precious life drift away from you — but be mindful not to let friendships slip away just because someone isn't meeting your new criteria of income, holidays, or fitness goals. Be the kind of friend and mentor you'd want to have — don't make perfection the price of your time and attention. Your team will make the difference to your success, and that includes having people there for you, who know you well when times get hard. This is why at AFL we created the academy. This amazing community is full of driving, propelling forward horses that would certainly magnify your ideas, constructively find the holes and keep you accountable.

Now time to do kinaesthetic learning:
How can you keep important people in your life while making space for new, positive influences?
Example: *I will join the AFL academy and mastermind groups, Facebook, Instagram communities, AFL Youtube channels....*
Here are our details:
www.assetsforlife.co.uk
Instagram: Jaymunozafl
Facebook: www.facebook.com/jay.munoz.AFL
YouTube channel: https://youtu.be/y566_40XNFE

Have you done it yet? If not what are you waiting for?

Jimmy Tomczak author of *Lakeside & Tide* believes that one of the most powerful, soul-searching, life-changing questions you can ask is one of the simplest: *'Who do you want to spend your time with?'*

Don't you agree? If you do and take action and apply the above concepts, you will soon become be the vivid testimony of how your precious life has been enriched by that question. So I will leave you this challenge.

Tomczak calls on the wisdom of his friends and family throughout his book. They live between the lines of his writing, in scenes where they discuss their hopes and fears, exchange supportive emails and advice, or share a walk on the beach at sunset. This is of course sometimes not applicable. I know for a fact there are plenty of people out there that don't get on with their families and soon they build relationships with friends that at the end become more than a family member.

For lots of people, including myself, you can read all the great authors and live by their quotes, but it's often a close friend — one who knows you and loves you unconditionally — who has just the wisdom and warmth you need to hear. I would like to take this opportunity to thank Dr Rosamond Kate Munoz, now my wife, Martin Munoz, Lorena Munoz, Mireya Munoz, Luis Munoz, Julieta Munoz, Dr Pablo Castro and Francisco Gallo who have been there for me during the thick and thin periods of my life. Tomczak reminds us that 'The best place in the world is inside the hug of someone who loves you.'

Tomczak also reflects that you will sometimes seek company for the wrong reason: external validation. When you are preoccupied by what

Property Metamorphosis

others think, you are no longer living in your own truth. To let go of that approval-seeking mindset, remind yourself that:

'My purpose is stronger than my need for validation. Let go of being liked; instead, give your time to those who you like'.

How can you surround yourself with people who support your happiness rather than deplete it? Keep company with those who appreciate humour, who live with meaning, who see value in their lives, and who spend their time purposefully.

Then, give all you can to them. When you rally together with those you love, you can conquer any problem — what money can't fix, the right people can.

Now time to do kinaesthetic learning:
Ask these powerful questions to your beautiful self:
'Who do I want to spend me time with?

And: *'How do I want to spend one of my most precious assets for life?'*

Answer these questions for yourself—but don't stop there.
You have a lot to learn from friends, family, and others you admire.
Who are your teachers?

Ask them the same two simple questions to get a deeper understanding of how they have navigated their own lives, hardships, and successes.

Chapter Two

Property investment concepts

My mission is that after reading this book you will learn a 'hands-off' approach to property development / real estate investing. I want you to sack the boss the same way that I did a few years back and avoid getting another job, otherwise you go back to where you started without even realising. I specifically want you to discover how to achieve the financial independence / freedom that only around 4 per cent of people around the globe have by learning how to passively or actively invest in property / real estate. I know this is a big thing but anyone can do this if you have the right mindset and tools. In this book I am trying to give you both so you have no excuses not to make it happen now!

The following concepts are applicable worldwide but as I personally invest mostly in the UK, I will focus on our tropical island for the time being. The reason for this note is to take into consideration your precious feedback received during several Facebook Lives and posts where one of my best friends Francisco Gallo asked me if the book could be written so all the concepts can be applied all around this amazing planet.

I'll start with a quote that needs to be learnt by heart:

> 'Every single postcode / road in every city of the world is a micro economy' - Jay Munoz

It does not matter whether you are in London, Washington or Popayan (my home town in Colombia). Every single big and small city in the world has its own micro economy. It has its own demography, politics, economics, employment levels, transport links etc. In essence every road has a totally different value from the road 25m away. Of course this is not applicable if you happen to have identical houses within the same foot print, view, amenities, orientation etc. Therefore it is your duty as a property developer / entrepreneur to find out what is the value of every single square meter / ft in your goldmine or chosen investment area.

This concept is fundamental and you cannot call yourself a property developer if you don't know the selling, buying and developing cost of your product in detail. And how do you find out this value /cost?

Now is the time to do kinaesthetic learning:

1. Go to Rightmove (UK readers) now and input your chosen postcode or use your home postcode if you don't have any other option.
2. Select the properties do you want to analyse i.e. 1 bed flats, 2 bed flats, 3 bed houses etc
3. Hit the sold properties section and pick up at least 10 properties in each of the above categories
4. Come up with a spreadsheet table where you have all the relevant info such as address, size in m^2 or ft^2, sold price and photos.
5. For the size, if the property hasn't got a layout or is incomplete then visit the *www.epcregister.com*, type in your postcode and you will find pretty much all houses areas written on the top right corner of the EPC form.
6. Once you have found those ten like-for-like flats or houses, then calculate the average (mean) of the ten or in some cases you should calculate the mean as in some frequent cases the sale price may depend on many factors such as:

Location and view

One day I was doing this exercise for a development and one of the 2 bed flats was well out of the average. I decided to have a more in-depth dig and soon I ascertained that the flat in question was overlooking a lake hence the huge difference in the sold price. In this case it was circa £100k. Similarly when you have properties that have been sold well below the average, I would also be curious and would not take this into consideration. In statistical terms the number that you find is called the median rather than the average which I recommend you use as this may come back and bite you if you are not careful.

7. This statistical tool needs to be kept updated on a regular basis and can be used for all your deal analysis which is the basis of your magic formula that I will be sharing with you in the next few chapters.

Chapter Three

Active vs passive property investment

I have undertaken both of the above strategies. When I started my journey in property I thought that there was only one - ignorance is very expensive! If only I knew back then. Nevertheless, I wanted to continue with my civil engineering career as back in 2006 when I started investing I had a goal of achieving chartered status which at the time was taking most of my spare time - writing reports, collecting information and fulling all nine attributes that a chartered civil engineer must have to be able to acquire this qualification. However if I went back in time I would have for sure begun with my property education journey even earlier and now I realise that if I had hired a mentor then I would have 10x what I managed to achieved in a decade of passive investment which was more than 10 units spread in UK, USA and Spain.

To understand my initial passive income strategy, let's first compare the differences between active and passive property / real estate investing:

Active — in this strategy, you are doing all the leg work. You are the one that finds the deal, appoints designers and contractors, manages the refurbishment/development of the property and at the end if you don't sell it you end up managing it or paying someone to manage it for you. This strategy typically involves a lot of mindset, knowledge, experience, skills, and capital either from you or someone else to be able to do it properly.

Passive — the priority in this strategy is finding rent-ready (or turn-key) properties that produce cash flow from day one. In general, this requires less experience and capital and fewer skills.

After trying both strategies over the years, I prefer the active property /development real estate investing. The reason why? It's more fun, more rewarding and you are positively impacting far more lives in the process. Hence in my view this strategy is by far more rewarding and fulfilling especially at the level when you are able to teach others and give back to the community. However, this could be more stressful if you for instance don't have the right mind set, skills, knowledge, mentoring and team in place to carefully implement it.

My view is that if you are in this full time you must be prepared to spin more plates and be able to learn and implement all the advice and guidance that your mentors or teachers are providing you with.

You need to be able to appoint and manage people successfully. As with any business, property development is a people business and if for an example you hire a main contractor who is a cowboy and leave the job half finished and then you realise that you have to demolish whatever he or she built and start all over again - it is not fun!

In AFL we have the best training where we can help you with the shortlisting and hiring the best designers and contractors out there. We can also show you how to create a valued creative relationship with all your power team, pass on their best discounted rates which in essence is the base of your active property development journey.

On the other hand, if you are almost reaching retirement and/or want to have a more armchair-type of investment approach - perhaps living in sunny Spain or in the Caribbean part of Colombia and want to be stress-free, then I suggest you choose the passive option so you can relax while someone else is managing your assets for life and collecting the rent for you.

Chapter Four

Property market types

After understanding the basic principles in chapters two and three the third step in passive or active real estate investing is selecting which market is the best for your needs. Before doing so, it's important to understand that not all markets are the same. While you may read that the 'UK real estate / property market is down' in the news, the reality is every market is different from another. As mentioned in chapter two, every single postcode in every single city whether it be small, medium or big is different. There are many factors influencing every market location; politics, economics, demography, environment and jobs. It's better to think of each market as its own micro system in its own right.

People may disagree with me on this but please hear my point. Even though the simplest and most effective way of investing and managing a property is so any asset / development you purchase must be within let's say one and-a-half hours maximum commutable radius. The reason being is that if anything goes wrong you can jump on it straight away and sort out the issues. The fact is that depending on the economical cycle that you are in you may miss out on relatively low risk investments such as the one I am going to share with you right now. In my personal situation back in 2008 when we had the property crash and the economic downturn I was educated enough then to spot loads of opportunities.

I went to visit friends in Tampa, Florida with my family back in 2010 and they had a realtor friend that had loads of condos well below market value. I could not believe my eyes when we went to see a very nice condominium for less than you would buy a second hand car in the UK and I am not talking Ferrari level here, in fact less than £13k. Yes believe your beautiful eyes and if you are hearing this on audio, that was correct - £13K for a ground bedroom condo, with one parking space, communal swimming pool, decent landscaping garden and basketball pitch and playground.

When I saw the title deeds it said the property was sold a few years back for $65k. Being in the construction industry at the time I knew that I was not able to build the foundations for that building with £13k so this was a no-brainer as the agent was also able to manage the property for me once I purchased it.

One year later after we experienced all the process we decided to purchase a second property for around double our initial investment in a more central location with better transport links into the centre of town. I had to strike a deal with the realtor that sold me the first unit as these types of condos were very difficult to get hold of so it took us a few months until the right one became available.

We have never seen the second property ourselves but we still see the money coming into our bank account every month when we have tenants in the property.

My wife and I still own these properties and they have more than quintupled in value in less than a decade and we are still benefiting from the positive net cash flow that they bring to our household.

The point that I want to make is that if you are in a situation where you are able to purchase an asset that has huge potential and is relatively stress free and you have the cash then do it!

This is something we will teach you if you are one of our students.

At AFL we are all about infinite return on our investments and creating a win-win for all parties involved. What I am trying to say here is that you can potentially strike a deal with whoever has the cash to purchase or has a good enough credit record to get a mortgage and you can manage the property and do the leg work. There are so many ways to come up with a win-win that you only need one single unit to create your own empire with none of your own money. I wish I'd known this concept before as I would have certainly bought dozens in Tampa if I were back in 2010.

Based on my personal experience, investing solely in local markets may not be the best way forward for you if you have the contacts. At the end of the day it's who do you surround yourself with? If I did not have my friend Alba in my file I would have probably never invested in Tampa. She was clearly a very good driven horse for me at the time and we are forever grateful for her and her husband for sharing with us their abundance mind set.

While it may be somewhat advantageous to be able to see the property, it's not necessary to be able to create a passive income. As I mentioned I have never seen the second condo we purchased, yet it continues to generate cash flow for us and I am sure there are loads of people out there that took advantage of this opportunity and are benefiting from such amazing cash machines, as I call them.

There are three types of markets you are able to get your hands on:

Cash-flow markets — these assets are smaller, generally stable markets that don't appreciate (increase in value), or depreciate (decrease in value), quickly. In cash-flow markets, rent prices are relatively high compared to the purchase price. This means you can start generating cash flow from month one. As we are based in the UK the areas for you to look at are north east and north west of the country where house prices are relatively low compared to the south of UK. Hence when you calculate the return of the investment based on the net rental income it will be much higher than the south as the formula denominator is much lower than if the property was located in the south.

Time to calculate the ROI of your own house or investments:
ROI = (Net rental income / total asset purchase value) * 100
If you come to one of our complimentary property events or one of our paid boot camps (which are incidentally amazing value for money) we can then explain the above formula in more detail and we can also teach you other formulas that are, in our opinion, more important and relevant to our line of business as our aim is to purchase, add value and refinance so you can recover your initial investment to buy more and more assets for life.

Growth markets — these assets have a tendency to appreciate more than others. You must understand that sometimes these types of markets can be speculative; however, growth markets can be a great addition to a portfolio when you have the cash flow available and can get in at the right time. The best thing to do in this scenario is to find out the asset's history. Go back ten or twenty years and look at the growth. Typically in the south east and west of UK the asset value doubles every 10 years despite economic downturns etc. The truth of the matter is that shelter is more or almost the same level as water for us human beings to be able to survive.

Hybrid markets — hybrid assets are the best of both worlds; we benefit from the cash flow AND appreciation at the same time. At the time of writing the UK is going through Brexit hence some areas of London cannot be used a hybrid markets.

However some good examples of hybrid markets are south east, some areas of London where houses are still affordable. ie. an average salary of a couple can afford them. Typically in London it's around £600k and outside London in the south west around £400k which happens to be under the 'help to buy' umbrella that we will discuss later in another chapter.

At AFL we ourselves invest and also encourage our students to invest in such hybrid markets. One example is buying relatively large houses (more than 3 bedrooms) and renting the rooms individually rather than the whole house. They are called houses of multiple occupation or HMO. This way you are benefiting from great capital appreciation as well an extra net rental income, which in simple terms a HMO is around 50 per cent more profitable than a single let asset.

Chapter Five

The AFL rules for market selection

A. How to determine how much you can borrow on a mortgage?

When I am considering a market, as anything else in life I don't feel comfortable taking unqualified and quantified risks and avoid speculation by all means possible. While there are good and bad times to enter a market, it's easy to get caught up in finding the perfect moment to enter and procrastinate as I did for a while waiting for that perfect moment that may not even happen!

The way to see it is that even though there are times where uncertainty hits and it is difficult to predict outcomes, like Britain leaving the EU that we are going through at the moment. Even in times like this we can safely invest in markets such as affordable units for first time buyers. This is very strong market as you may know. Right now in the UK there are millions of people trying to get their hands on their first home. For this I have come to the conclusion that providing a product for such buyers and calculating the maximum financing you can achieve based on the rental income as well is critically important to ensure you are in a very safe place to start investing.

Let me explain this concept with an example on how much you can borrow on a BTL mortgage. At the time of writing what a RICS valuers determines for the lender affordability calculation, is the market rent that the property can achieve from a tenant. This can be higher, lower or the same as the actual passing rent if the property is tenanted.

The valuer's determination of the market rent is what the lender uses to determine the maximum loan you can borrow using what is called a rental test assessment. Due to recent tax changes this varies if you own the property in personal name or a limited company. If it is a personal name then it can differ if you are a basic rate payer or a higher rate payer.

Example: for a purchase in a limited company or a basic rate tax payer. Let's say the valuer assesses the rent at £1,000 per month renting a flat in east London. Then they calculate the yearly income. In this case £12,000 per year. Then what the lender calculates is to deduct an amount for voids maintenance and reallocate the rental income. In this case it is now £9,600 per year. Then this figure gets divided by the current 5 year fixed rate which at the present is a typical is 3.50% per cent. So if we do the affordability calculation the maximum loan you can borrow will be approx. £274,286.

**Disclaimer: please do your own due diligence as this formula may vary from time to time and also depends on borrower's risk criteria, so can only be used under your own responsibility. I would like to thank David Tonks, our AFL power team member, for his input on Section A.

B. Rent to value ratio

Another universal rule is called a rent-to-value ratio, or R/V ratio. This is a litmus test you can use to determine the value of a property.

The formula for finding the R/V ratio is as follows:

Median Rental Price / Median Property Price

The ideal R/V target you want is around 1 per cent and the higher you get it, the better for you.

If we use the same sample above, we find that the R/V for the same rental income is around 0.44 per cent based on the rental asset value of the property.

You can calculate the same ratio for both the bricks and mortar and rental income and ideally these numbers should be similar.

If you do this for certain areas of London you can find out that the asset value based on rent is nowhere near the asset value based on bricks and mortar i.e. comparable so I would be very mindful of investing in areas where the difference from one value to the other is too big.

C. Further criteria

Potential to grow

Another rule is looking for stable economies with potential for growth, otherwise known as GDP. Information about GDP of markets can be found online for free. Ideally, you want to invest in a market where GDP and population are growing. Also, avoid markets that are 'one trick ponies'— that is, they are producing income from only one source (such as oil, gas, etc).

Another example of a one trick pony is big infrastructure projects. I had the privilege of working for EDF New Nuclear Division.

I was at the time in charge of enabling packages to build two new nuclear reactors to generate electricity for the whole of the UK. The project was worth well over £20bn and as you can imagine this would generate a temporary huge housing demand impact in the area.

Once the plant has been built and is in operation unless there is another infrastructure project to follow the 'temporary' accommodation used by the people that worked at the plant will be vacant. Hence the value of the asset will be much lower.

Finally, pick a country that's landlord friendly. The laws should favour landlords, not tenants. There are places where people abuse the laws and will stay in places without paying rent. And eviction will be very costly making a huge hole in the landlord budget.

At AFL our preference is to rent to young professionals working typically for blue chip corporations or small companies that are desperate for a nice modern friendly environment where they can share with other like-minded people.

Time to do some kinaesthetic learning. Identify areas with great potential to grow.

1. ....Why

2. ....Why

3. ....Why

Look for future infrastructure to be built and assess the potential growth impact in the area.

There is also plenty of information in council planing portals, where they hold a plan of development for each area, which will also give you a good idea of how the area is going to develop in the next few years.

The south east, London and the home counties have the most detailed plans and as a result they attract a lot of new investments to their areas.

Shortlist at least three areas and list them below
1......

Why...

2.....

Why....

3......

Why...

Neighbourhood selection

After selecting a market and doing your research on all the areas to a very high level of detail and having shortlisted at least three areas as above, the next key thing is the neighbourhood selection. The neighbourhood affects your property's performance more than the market itself. While the economic big picture (the market) is important, the neighbourhood you choose affects the day-to-day experiences of your tenants much more. If you put yourself in the tenant's shoes - would you live in an area that looks run down even though it was next to your place of work?

There are many factors that you need to consider when choosing a neighbourhood, these are the four main areas I will also look into before investing:

Demographics

This is the main factor of the three. As I always say to my students,

'As an entrepreneur if you want to serve yourself you have to forget about yourself and focus on your customers' - Jay Munoz

Hence knowing your customers inside out is paramount for any line of business. Things to consider when looking at demographics include age, gender, income level, and profession. As a property developer and real estate investor, your tenants and buyers are essentially your customers. Your tenants and buyers are your biggest asset for life. If you don't find good tenants to pay your rent then you have no business.

Particularly when renting a flat, landlords sometimes forget that the product that they are selling is actually huge. If you are selling a single let rental unit for instance of let's say £1,000 per month the product that they are selling is £12,000 if the tenancy agreement is signed for one year.

If you are selling a room in a HMO for let's say £550 per month with all bills included the product they are selling is £6,600 per year. This is actually more than the value of a brand new car nowadays. I have tenants in my units that have been there for over a decade so you do the maths!

The point that we want to make is that apart from the deal itself our first most precious asset for life is our tenants and they should be treated, looked after as celebrities as they are the ones that are the core base of our business. I'd like take this opportunity to thank all the customers that we have had the opportunity to serve during these wonderful years since I started my property business in 2007.

I feel forever grateful that they chose us as we provided them with a great product and in some cases exceeded their expectations and will continue to do whenever possible.

Growth Potential

Certain areas are more likely to grow than others. The amount of appreciation in an area is affected by things such as gentrification or local economies. The best example is east London in the UK. Before the London Olympics back in 2012 the area where the Olympic Park now sits was a rubbish dump full of old factories and as result the land was contaminated. The fact is that there is still loads of contamination in the ground in certain areas that have been either long-term treated or isolated to facilitate construction. The people that spotted this and kept and developed their land are now probably living in a private island somewhere in the Caribbean.

Saleability

Finally, the amount of real estate activity in the neighbourhood is worth looking into. You want to look at neighbourhoods where people are buying and selling. In other words, an active real estate market. One way to check if an area is active is going to Rightmove and inputting a particular postcode and hit the sold button and record this number. Then go back and now hit the Sold subject to Contract.

If there is a considerable difference between these two numbers it means that the property around this particular postcode is active and people are buying and selling in the area. However this also depends on factors such as tax changes, political changes, market conditions etc. The best example is Brexit in the UK. If you look at the average number of transactions in central London has almost reduced by 50 per cent since the Brexit process started.

Based on the factors above, at AFL we use a 1, 2, 3 class yardstick for a neighbourhood selection process.

The first class, a '1' neighbourhood, is higher priced. In the 11 market specific areas that AFL is in, these typically start at £250,000. The R/V ratio for an '1' neighbourhood is lower, typically around 0.8 per cent. If it is a HMO and 0.5 per cent if it is a single let, but that's okay because the neighbourhoods have a tendency to have greater appreciation.

One of the benefits of this type of neighbourhood is lower turnover; tenants stay longer, have fewer financing issues, and are overall, better quality tenants. For these areas such as west and north London, West Sussex and Surrey and south east are a perfect example where capital appreciation has steadily grown for the last decade. I personally bought at the pick of the market back in 2007 in areas where I saw potential such as Crawley, west and east and North London and they have now almost doubled in value.

Next, '2' neighbourhoods are the middle ground between '1' and '3'. These are more likely to follow the 1 per cent R/V ratio rule. Because '2' neighbourhoods tend to have a good balance of cash flow and appreciation, they're a great addition to your portfolio. In these areas however the capital appreciation is not as high.

Finally, '3' neighbourhoods require thicker skin. If you can manage them, the cash flow can be better than '1' or '2'.

But, while the cash flow is better, the appreciation is very low.

Unless there's something going on in the neighbourhood, the value of the property will generally stay the same over 5 years. At AFL we have no experience in this market as it is out of our risk profile but we know other developers take it and make it profitable.

15 simple rules to get steady passive income from property

As a bonus and way of summary, here are the main rules and principles of investing that we at AFL have used over the years and we are confident that if you do apply them to your life and the ones around you, you will change for the better.

Follow these, don't give up on the first obstacle and there should be nothing standing in your way on the road to generous passive income.

1. Educate yourself

As Robert Kiyosaki would say, 'Ignorance is very expensive'. This rule sits at the top of your journey and is the most important because (of course) the best investment you can make is in yourself. The things you don't know are costing you money.

Those who learn more and played the knowledge earn more.

It is a simple as that. Personally I started with mindset, once I was ready I started with technical knowledge when I was ready with both I started using my own money and when I was ready I started using someone else's money which has in essence exponentially grown my wealth and many others out there that are mentored by us.

Take further action and book one of our complimentary free events or enrol into a 3-day boot camp where you learn all our strategies.

2. Set investment goals

It's a proven well known fact, that people who write down their SMART goals, and read them often, check progress, are more likely to succeed in achieving them.

In fact the statistics demonstrate if you do write your goal down you are around 70 per cent more likely to achieve them.

When a goal isn't on a paper or written anywhere, it's only a dream. For this I have created an amazing tool called *My AFL Journey*.

Take action and buy a copy of the book now. It will change your life for the better.

You can also add personal goals into this or any kind of goals but the key is to write smart goals as we explained earlier in this book.

You can buy the book from www.amazon.co.uk/My-AFL-Journey-Jay-Munoz/dp/1527234444

3. Take calculated risks and never speculate

Let's take previous economic downturns such as the 2007/8 financial crisis as the lesson here — investing isn't gambling. Look at supply and demand and affordability of units. Humans needs decent shelter. If you get the market right and aim for hybrid or cash-flow investment, instead of a speculation you are buying an asset for life that can be passed on to your offspring.

4. Invest for cash flow

Cash is king in property investment real estate. You need to survive and without it you can't build a business. It also provides you with an immediate return you can measure and re-invest and get other people over the line to invest in your business.

5. Diversification pays off

There are as many micro economies in the UK as there are postcodes, so don't limit yourself to just one. Different things happen in each market during different periods. Invest in a market that makes the most sense at a given time. Once you are comfortable in an area then start investing in other areas. It is sometimes impossible to predict market trends so if you are spreading your wings in different areas then you are spreading the risk and rewards more efficiently.

6. First things first

In other words take a top-down approach. This means focusing on the big picture. Hence analyse the market first, instead of a particular property. You might fall in love with a nice house, but if there aren't any tenants looking to rent that nice house and the jobs and population in the area are not growing — even the most amazing house has the potential to bankrupt you.

7. Diversify across class categories

Think of real estate as an asset class category. Once you have built a steady income stream for a particular asset class such as HMOs or service accommodation you want to diversify into different asset classes such as single lets or commercial buildings.

I suggest investing in 3-5 properties in 3-5 different asset class categories.

8. Appoint professional managers

Once you have purchase the physical asset the money that this asset will generate over the years is based on how good your management team is. In other words your net cash flow will be strictly dependant on how good your team is at finding new tenants, keeping them happy and managing the property itself.

Though some people with tremendous experience and skill can manage properties themselves, we strongly suggest hiring professionals or JV in professionals.

Doing so takes the duties off your shoulders, so you can generate more passive income by focusing your attention elsewhere in income-generating actives such as finding new deals or investors (cash) rather than another job.

9. Focus on values and principles before investing and joint venturing

Stop for a minute and think of your five core values and principles as a person. Every time I make a difficult decision, I think about this as it helps me tremendously with my decision-making process. If I have five choices for instance, I always try to chose the one that aligns the most with my five core values and principles. The same applies in property. Always try to purchase a property that is part of your set criteria. The principle also applies when you are thinking of getting into a partnership with someone, first find out about their core values and principles as if they are not in line with yours at some point the relationship will crack and crumble.

10. Maintain control

When you joint venture or do business with people that you have not experience with try to maintain control for your first project. If the relationship turns bitter sweet and you end up in chaos you at least have control and are more likely to turn it around. Hence it's better that you try to keep yourself in control and have the power to make the last call that may save you from bankruptcy.

11. Leverage your capital

The power of real estate investing is in the leveragability of your capital. You can use OPM (Other People's Money) for 80 per cent of your investments, allowing you to create wealth faster.

12. Be part of a mastermind group

A mastermind group is the coordination of knowledge and effort, in the spirit of harmony, between two or more people, for the attainment of your definite purpose. Always surround yourself with intelligent creative people / horses that propel your coach forward. From experience, one of the reasons that we have been very successful as property developers is because I have chosen to hang out with big players in the game that were ahead of us.

For this initially we had to pay several thousand pounds for their input and time. For any normal human being a £25,000 bill to get only a few minutes of their time and blog to a club of other investors per month would be expensive. However now thinking back this has been one of the best investments that we have made and the ROI has been in many cases infinite as a result of what we learnt and experienced. For this reason we have decided to create a mastermind group where we all meet on a monthly basis to share experiences, ideas, successes and failures where everyone learns from each other and speak the same entrepreneurial language.

Having had the corporate mindset for years now I realise entrepreneurs also need to be surrounded with like-minded people to be able to flourish and prosper. If you surround yourself with losers and people that like playing darts in the pub and drinking eight pints of beer every day you are most likely to be doing the same. If you surround yourself with people that are constantly on the hunt for the next deal / opportunity or are able to raise money through the network the chances are that you will be doing the same or end up JV with one of them if your vision and values are aligned.

13. Always focus on your customers

'As an entrepreneur you need to forget about yourself and focus on your customers' - Jay Munoz

Whoever the customer is we always need to make sure that we are serving and solving as many of their problems as possible and our product or service fulfils or even exceeds their expectation so they can recommend your product or service to someone else.

In AFL we try to serve as many different customers as possible in the best possible way. Call them tenants, first time property buyers, students etc we are always thinking of how to make sure the get the best experience and achieve their goals or dreams. We are very grateful that we have an excellent reputation for services and products that we provide and people achieve their goals if they follow the steps and action that we give them as mentors.

14. Have fun

There is no point in doing something if you are not having fun. At AFL we try to combine business and pleasure whenever possible.

This year we have been skiing in France with other property developers; we have been in Dubai with our families meeting several investors; we have been to Vilnius, Lithuania where we wrote our vivid vision for the next three years; Serbia where we met a friend and now an investor and also Odessa in the Ukraine where we took several team members and did several masterminds.

At the time of writing I am travelling to Spain with the family where we are going to spend the next two weeks. To be honest, prior to my entrepreneurial life I used to plan my holidays around work and I was ever so looking forward to my holidays now I plan my work around my holidays and even better I try to combine the two whenever possible.

Here are some photos of our trips away.

At the Monaco Grand Prix

Chapter Five

Russian World Cup in 2018

A skiing trip in the French Alps

With friends in Cannes, France

Chapter Six

The only formula you need to know in property development

Before I became a full time property developer, I thought that I needed to get a civil engineering degree or equivalent to become one. The reality is that I was alienated by the environment. Back in Colombia if you don't go to university you are no one and the general cultural mindset is to go to university, get a degree and work for a big company.

I do not regret going to university. I met some wonderful people that inspired me such as Professor Carlos Ariel Hurtado who I now work with helping less privileged lives forever. I also met many good friends there and had wonderful memories of laughter, tears and hard work especially in the seventh semester when we had to revise all day and night for several days in a row. The maths, physics and so many other subjects that I learned then were in someway applicable to what I was doing a few years back as an engineer. In some cases it has now helped me to challenge others (contractors mostly) when they have asked for variations but the reality is that you do not need a degree nor be a chartered civil or hold any other degree to be able to understand and play this simple formula.

Asset purchase price = gross development value - all costs - profit margin

This formula is fundamental for your new journey and you should learn this by heart. I wish all estate agents and commercial agents knew this. I will expand on this more in the next few chapters.

Chapter Seven

Layout is King

This is one of my favourite chapters of the book after mindset and property cycles. Actually I can't decide which one I get more excited writing about as they are so mega important to get right from the start of your property journey. Please make sure you read the following information carefully (ideally after meditation and a nice Colombian coffee) and get this single nugget right as it will be vital to make money out of thin air - literally!

Every single area in any country in the world has a value both based on bricks and mortar sold, comparables and rental income (commercial and / or residential) valuation. Hence as an entrepreneur it's your duty to make sure that you know the answer to the following questions:

1. What is the value of each property in any given postcode? For this you can look at sold prices on Rightmove and make a list of the different types of properties.

If I were you I'd make a spreadsheet (you know I love them) and input different residential C3 categories such as: 1 bedroom flats, 2 bedroom flats, 3 bed flats, same with houses and bungalows. Now find at least 10 of each that have been sold in the last two years and for each find the median not the mean /average. The mean is the average you may be used to and which I have wrongly seen in most deal analysers out there outside our AFL family. The mean is where you add up all the numbers and then divide by the number of samples. This is not accurate enough as even in areas where you have the same postcode, view and other factors may influence this critical value. After doing thousands of deal analyses once I came across this flat in Sudbury, Essex that was well over priced above the mean. When I looked into the detail I realised this unit was overlooking a beautiful lake and as a result the cost per m^2 was over 25 per cent and as a result would have affected my calculation.

Hence from that moment onwards our AFL Deal Analyser calculates the median which is the middle value in the list of numbers and as a result will provide you with a more accurate and conservative number. For this the value also gets rid of the cheapest unit too as there are circumstances that in our view have been sold well below market value which will also affect the price of your comparables. It is your duty as a developer to make this call as your individual case may be different and may have other factors that will affect such a critical result.

Now that you have the median value of any given assets class on a specific area in £/m².

Write down here the answers please:

A. In XXX.....postcode, the median value of 1 bed flats are............£/m²
B. In XXX.....postcode, the median value of 2 bed flats are............£/m²
C. In XXX.....postcode, the median value of 3 bed flats are ....£/m²

At AFL we have a spreadsheet that helps you do this systematically. Please contact us if you need further explanation.

2. What is the construction cost for each given postcode? For this you can talk to local quantity surveyors (ideally chartered) that have carried out similar projects in the same postcode for the last two years and ask them a simple question:

A. How much does it cost to build traditionally on block work up to 2 stories high, 3 stories high, and 4 stories high based on a worst-case scenario - ground conditions i.e. piling needed and contamination and good ground conditions (strip foundations).

A.1 In XXX....postcode the construction cost up to 2 stories high poor ground conditions is.......£/m²
A.2 In XXX....postcode the construction cost up to 3 stories high poor ground conditions is..........£/m²
A.3 In XXX....postcode the construction cost up to 4 stories high poor ground conditions is..........£/m²

B. How much does it cost to build using timber frame structure? Up to 2 stories high, 3 stories high and 4 stories high based on a worse case scenario ground conditions, i.e. piling needed and contamination and good ground conditions (strip foundations).
B.1. In XXX....postcode the construction cost up to 2 stories high poor

ground conditions is........£/m²

B.2 In XXX....postcode the construction cost up to 3 stories high poor ground conditions is..........£/m²

B.3 In XXX....postcode the construction cost up to 4 stories high poor ground conditions is..........£/m²

C. How much does it cost to build using modular (CLT or similar) if applicable (only if you are building more than 10 units and they are all identical)? At the time of writing this type of construction will not be feasible for fewer than 5 units.

C.1. In XXX....postcode the construction cost up to 2 stories high poor ground conditions is........£/m²

C.2. In XXX....postcode the construction cost up to 3 stories high poor ground conditions is..........£/m²

C.3. In XXX....postcode the construction cost up to 4 stories high poor ground conditions is..........£/m²

Once you have this information then you have the £/m² of construction.

If you are doing a refurbishment project similarly you can get an estimate of £/m² from your quantity surveyor.

Apart from a local QS you can also get quotes from local builders. However I must stress that based on our experience you need to add at least another 20 per cent on top of what they quoted depending on your site specifics.

For our first new build development project we had quotes of around £1450 £/m² mark and we end up paying around £1750 £/m² in 2016 when we signed the JCT conditions of contracts.

My best advice is for you to work on the average £/m² for the area postcode and get a QS input or your business mentor to check your numbers as this could be deal breaker for your project / development.

If you do your costing based on an initial quote and you don't have a healthy profit margin this could mean that you won't be able to make money on your project and it's best to let it go and move to the next one.

At the beginning of the journey we allow our emotions to take over and the more time you spend doing something the more attached you get to it and I found it very difficult to let it go. However after many years of experience I decided to only do projects that meet our strict criteria and are protected from all kinds of risks rather than doing multiple projects that will make decent profit.

At the end of the day you must write down your criteria and stick to it. The numbers do not lie and your investors and JV partners will thank you for it rather than curse you if you went ahead and carried out the project just for the sake of being active in the industry.

My best advice to you is do not overstretch and only go for projects that you are making at least 25 per cent profit margin on GDV on an upwards curve or 30 per cent profit margin on GDV on a staggered or onwards curve. This way if the property market goes down you can at least sell all the units and pay your investors or you can also refinance each individual asset and pay all your investor backs and keep the asset for life.

3. Now that you have the value of a property to sell and have an idea of the construction cost you need to then add the value of the land, design, finance, legals and other fees. A rule of thumb (we do have an specific spreadsheet for this at AFL) is that you add around 15 per cent to 20 per cent of construction cost for **design** and project construction cost, 1 per cent to 2 per cent for legal cost, 1 per cent to 2 per cent for selling cost and between 6 per cent to 10 per cent for senior development funder cost per year.

Hence you end up adding another 27 per cent to 32 per cent on top of construction costs. If we used the same figure that means that £1750 goes up to £2,223 to £2,310 £/m^2 and this does not include the land value. This is also assuming a traditional method of construction with good access and good ground conditions. I must also stress that this is a back-of-the envelope calculation.

4. If there is an area where the current value of any particular asset is below £2,223 £/m^2 this means that it doesn't make financial sense to build as there is not enough profit margin on this particular area.

On the other hand if you find a specific area where the £/m^2 is above the £2,779 £/m^2 then it makes financial sense to build as there will be at least 25 per cent profit margin if your construction cost were around £2,223. To put this into an example:

Let's say that your average 1 bed flat in XYZ postcode is £2,780 that means that a 45m^2 flat will cost you £125,100 and to build this unit it will cost you £100,035.

Once again the above will be based on a bricks and mortar valuation and now if you decide to ascertain the value of the commercial residential valuation then you would need to find out how much each asset will rent for as follows:

At the time of writing if you are looking for a single let asset value or a commercial valuation based on rental income then look at chapter five.

Sometimes, not always, you find golden areas where the conversion from bricks and mortar to commercial makes perfect sense. However you need to be careful of the rental income and ascertain if the switch makes financial sense as there is not a straightforward rule of thumb once you complete the refurbishment / conversion as you need to tick several boxes on the commercial survey that assesses your asset. I have been told by a local commercial RICS valuer that loads of uneducated investors think that putting locks on every room only will automatically grant you commercial valuation and this is definitely not the case based on our experience.

Here are some typical examples of projects where we have successfully converted from a C3 dwelling house to C4 house of multiple occupation.

Case Study One

Property address: 25 Burlington Road, Ipswich, IP2
Layout: 3 Bed C3 dwelling house
Purchase price: £185,000
We bought the property initially with the following layout:

Ground floor prior conversion: living room and kitchen

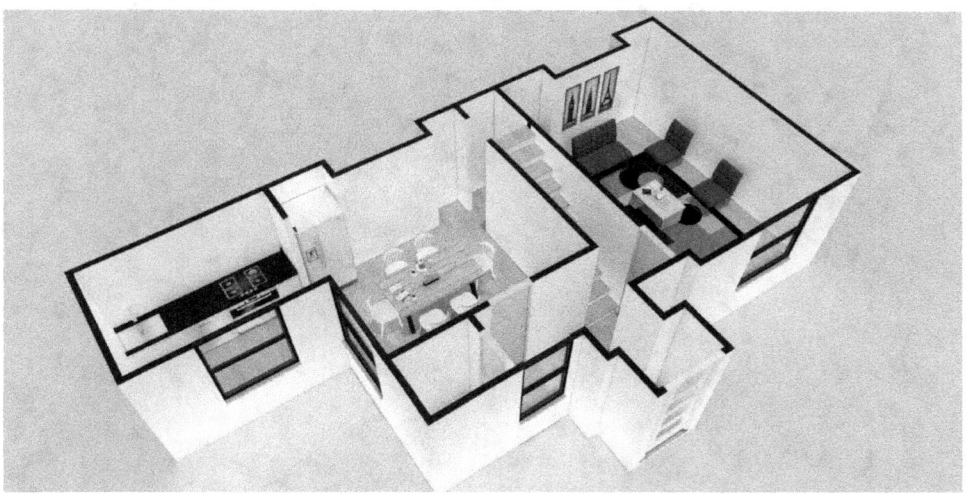

1st floor prior conversion: 3 bedrooms

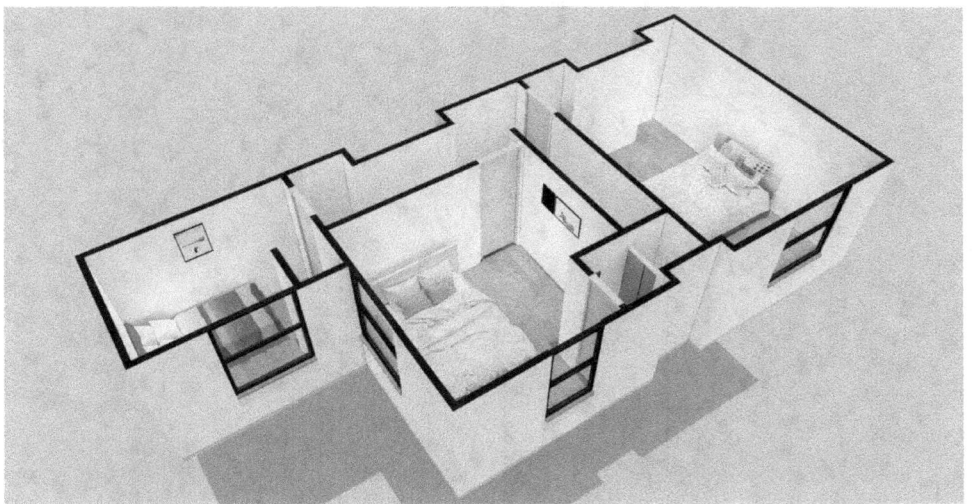

Ground floor after conversion: 2 ensuite rooms and communal kitchen

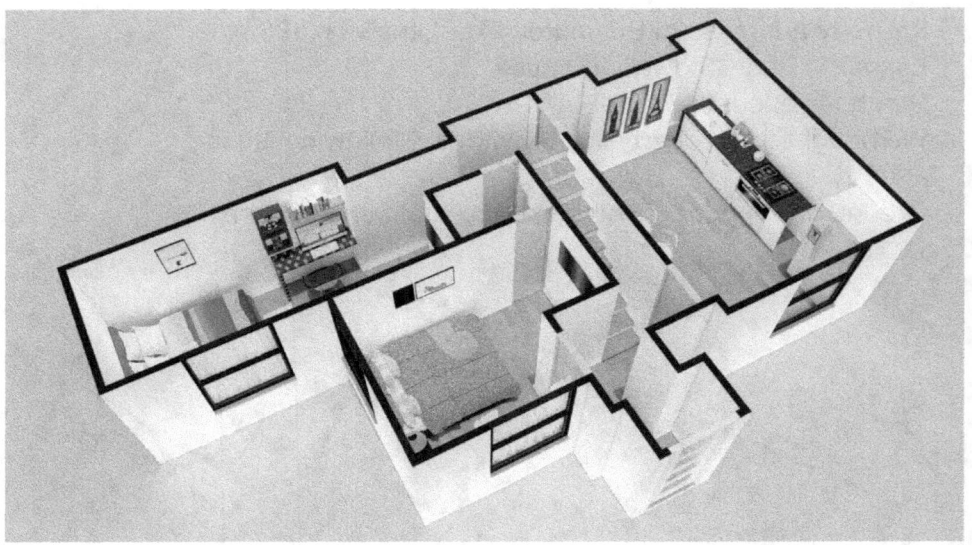

1st floor after conversion: 3 ensuite rooms

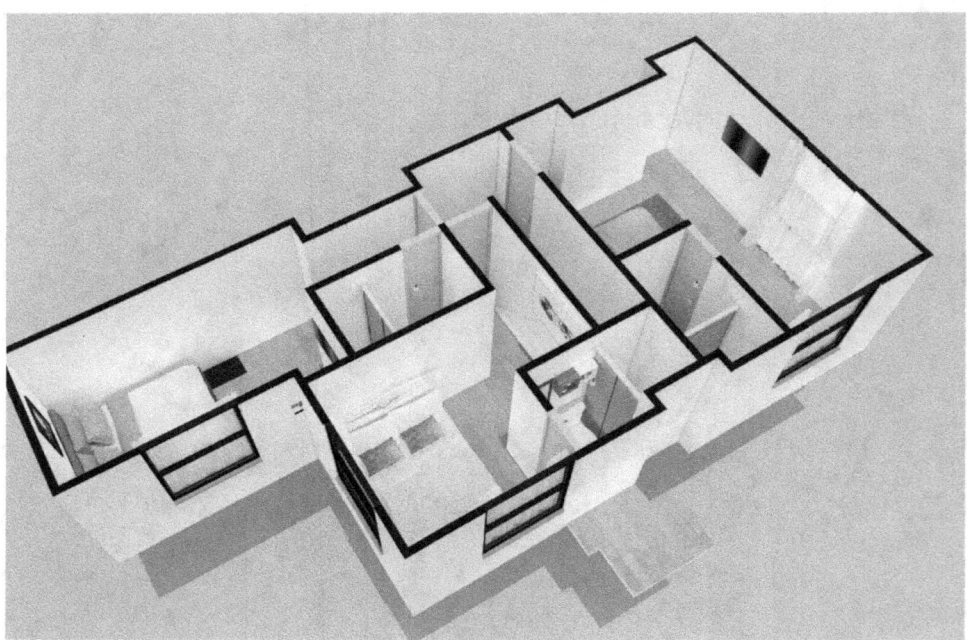

Bricks and mortar valuation before the development

The house layout was clearly not the best and there were plenty of rooms that were not maximised. The value of every 1m² according to our calculation was:
£138,500 / 96 m² = 1,432 £/m²
If we bought the property and rented it out as it was, it would be:
Gross rental income = £900. Net Rental income = £320

Now after doing all our research we ascertained that the area was perfect for conversion and carried out all the works.

Commercial valuations achieved after the development

£250,000 / 96m² = 2,604 £ / m² for each m² we increased the value to £1,172!
Total increase per m² = £1,172 and we also increased the gross rental income to 305 per cent
Gross rental income pm = £2,750 and the net rental income in 293 per cent
Net rental income pa = £936

Kinaesthetic learning time:

Now it's time for you to find a project that could change your life for the better in your chosen gold mine area.

Here is another example where we have maximised the layout of a much bigger asset for life.

Case Study Two

Oak House, Colchester

Before we move forward I would like to teach you a golden formula in property development. The story behind this property is the prime example of when layout is king again. This property was advertised as straightforward conversion from a B1(A) use which is office use into a C3 residential dwelling. When it was presented to us it had permitted development rights to be converted into 8x2 bedroom flats and once you have done the calculation you can clearly ascertain that the asset value is not as high. Hence after meditation and some nice Colombian coffee we came up with a much improved layout which meant each 2 bedroom flat was divided into two and now the whole scheme was converted into 16x1 bedroom flats instead.

Here is the layout of the B1A office that was offered to us with permitted development rights to be converted into 8x2 bed flats.

Ground floor 4x2 bed flats

First floor 4x2 bed flats

Now after all our magic here is the new layout worth almost £1,000,000 more with exactly the same footprint.

Ground Floor 8x1 bed flats

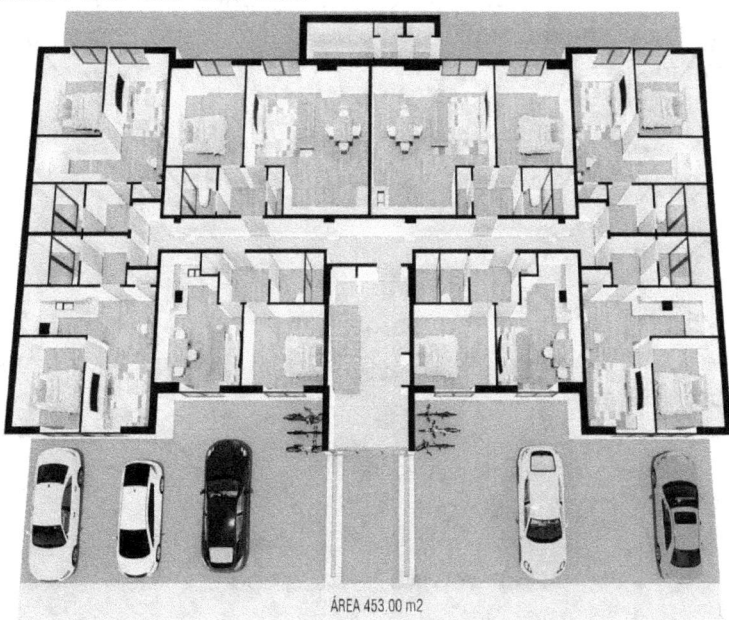

First floor 8x1 bed flats

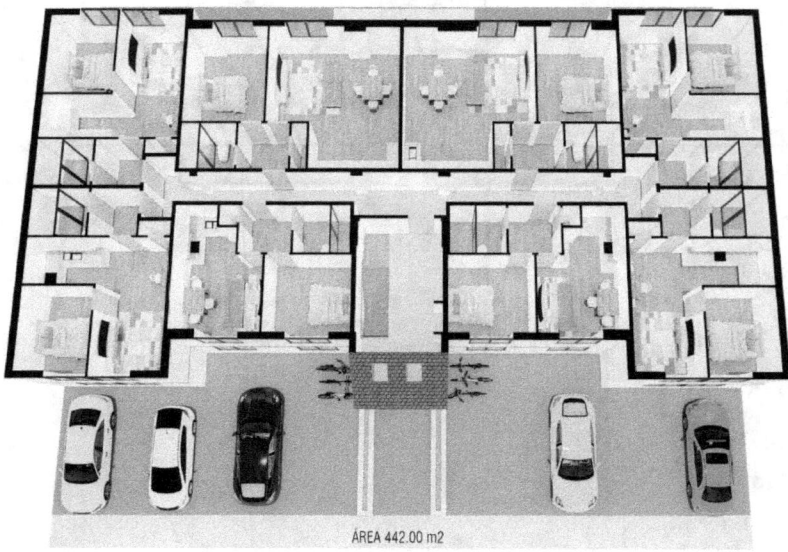

Bricks and mortar valuation before the development

The house layout was clearly not the best and there were plenty of rooms that were not maximised. The value of every 1m² according to our calculation was:

£900,000 / 895 m² = 1,006 £/m²

If we converted the property and sold off the units with only 8 flats the GDV would have been approximately £1,760,000. Hence:

£1,760,000 /895 m² = 1,966 £/m²

Following the formula that you learnt in the previous chapter the purchase price would have been only £201,250 assuming a 25 per cent profit margin on cost. Hence:

P = GDV - all cost - profit margin
P = £1,760,000 - £1,118,750 - £440,000
P = £201,250

Now after doing all our research we ascertained that the same area was

not maximised and that we were able to convert it into 16 flats instead. Now the figure looks like this.
Total GDV £2,700,000 / 895 m2= 3017 £/m2

Now that we have increased the GDV the purchase price is as much as the vendor wanted, making it a win-win for all. The numbers looks like this now:

P = £2,700,000 - 1,200,000 - 600,000
P = £900,000

If you thought you've had enough great examples we have even more life-changing projects that our students achieved after doing our training and joining our academy. These projects are our testament that property development is life changing if you learn and apply all the knowledge that we teach you at our Assets for Life familia. Hence I do strongly advise you not to procrastinate to get a mentor just like Liam and I did and start copying and pasting everything they do and start your own property metamorphosis now.

Case Study Three

Let me introduce to you to one of our action couples, Julie (French born) and Alex Camisan (Ecuador born - one of my homeland neighbours)

Here is a bit about them.

Julie Buffandeau and Alex Camisan, husband and wife and co-founders of Pride in Property Development.

'We joined the academy in September 2018. We have enjoyed being part of the academy as we were able to connect with many property investors following different strategies as well as getting access to very knowledgeable mentors who provided us with clear direction and guidance when we faced many challenges. We have also learned to analyse deals in much more detail, which made us target deals that really stack!'

'As a result of the training provided we bought the flat overleaf for £274,000 in late 2018 and the new value achieved after modifying the layout was £425,000 six months later.

'Furthermore the rent we managed to achieve was about 15 per cent higher than other flats around the area due to the finish and size of the property at £1,650ppm for a single let at time of writing.

'The total area has not increased dramatically but the 'King' layout (as per the 3D models below) gave us the opportunity to almost double the asset value.'

Here is the link to original property:
https://www.zoopla.co.uk/property-history/23-darlington-road/london/se27-0ud/49265379

Here is the layout prior to the development

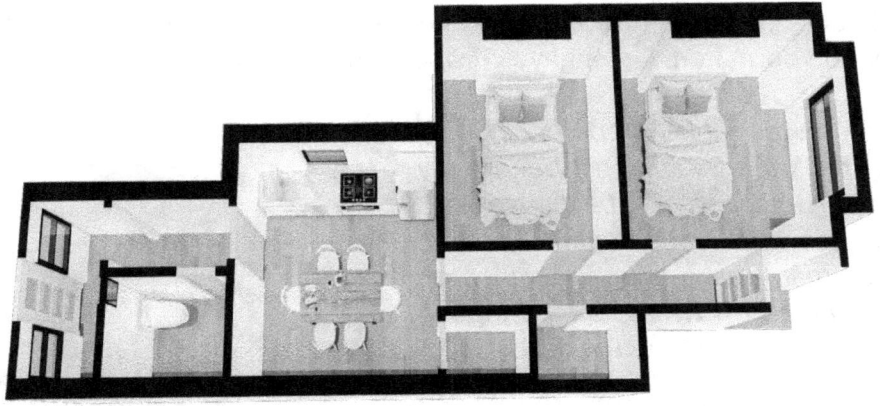

AREA 57.95 m2

Here is the layout after the development

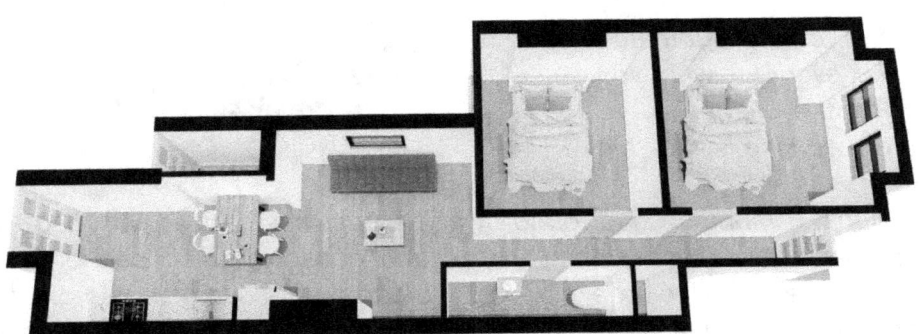

AREA 78.00 m2

Case Study Four

Let me introduce to you to one of our amazing mentees Mark Richards (London born) from Greenhayes Property Investments Ltd.

'I started this property journey way back in 2000 when I bought my first BTL property – the house next door to where I was living in London. Since then I have bought another, on average, every two years relying on capital growth to fund the next.

'As soon as I joined Assets for Life it gave me a huge burst of enthusiasm knowing that I was now working in conjunction with a team that 'knew their stuff'. I realised that to make things happen I must implement everything that I am being told;

"Put yourself out there"
"Tell everyone what you do"
"Positive Mindset"
"Networking is Key" etc.

'Within 3 months I had found myself a business partner who had the same desire as me and we had our first offer accepted on a 3 bed terraced property we hoped to redevelop into a 5 bed all en-suite high end professional HMO. Fortunately we were able to fund the purchase ourselves and funding for the refurb was loaned to us on a fixed rate return by a wealthy friend of ours who had heard about our plans and became very interested.

'During my one-to-ones with Jay I soon realised that layout was key to maximising the return. With clever use of space and extending outwards we finished the project on time and filled all 5 rooms within 3 weeks.

'Immediately on completion we were able to refinance the property, pay back the investor and leave £21,000 in the deal.

'We have consistently made £1,650 per month profit on this project since completing the refurb and all money left in the deal paid back within

12 months. Without working with Assets for Life I would have plodded along on my single BTL journey not knowing about the huge cash flow generated by clever thinking and clever layouts.'

Mark Richards, Greenhayes Property Investments Ltd.

Some case study specifics:

1.A. Purchase price and valuation of asset bricks and mortar
£138,000 paid cash (approx. £20k below market value. Property was unmortgageable)
B. Area of the property in m² or ft²
103 m² .
C. Type of Mortgage commercial or residential bricks and mortar?
Paid cash.
2. Refurb cost
£96,000 incl all fees and stamp duty.
3. Area of property after refurb.
120 m²
4. Valuation of asset after refinancing and type of mortgage - was it commercial or bricks and mortar?
Bricks & Mortar valuation of £285,000
Mortgage of £213,750 @ 75 per cent LTV
Rental income £2,600 pcm for life

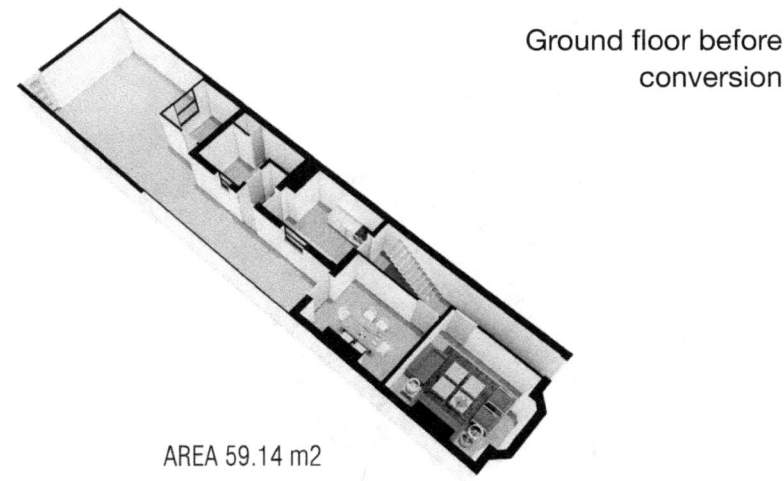

Ground floor before conversion

AREA 59.14 m2

Property Metamorphosis

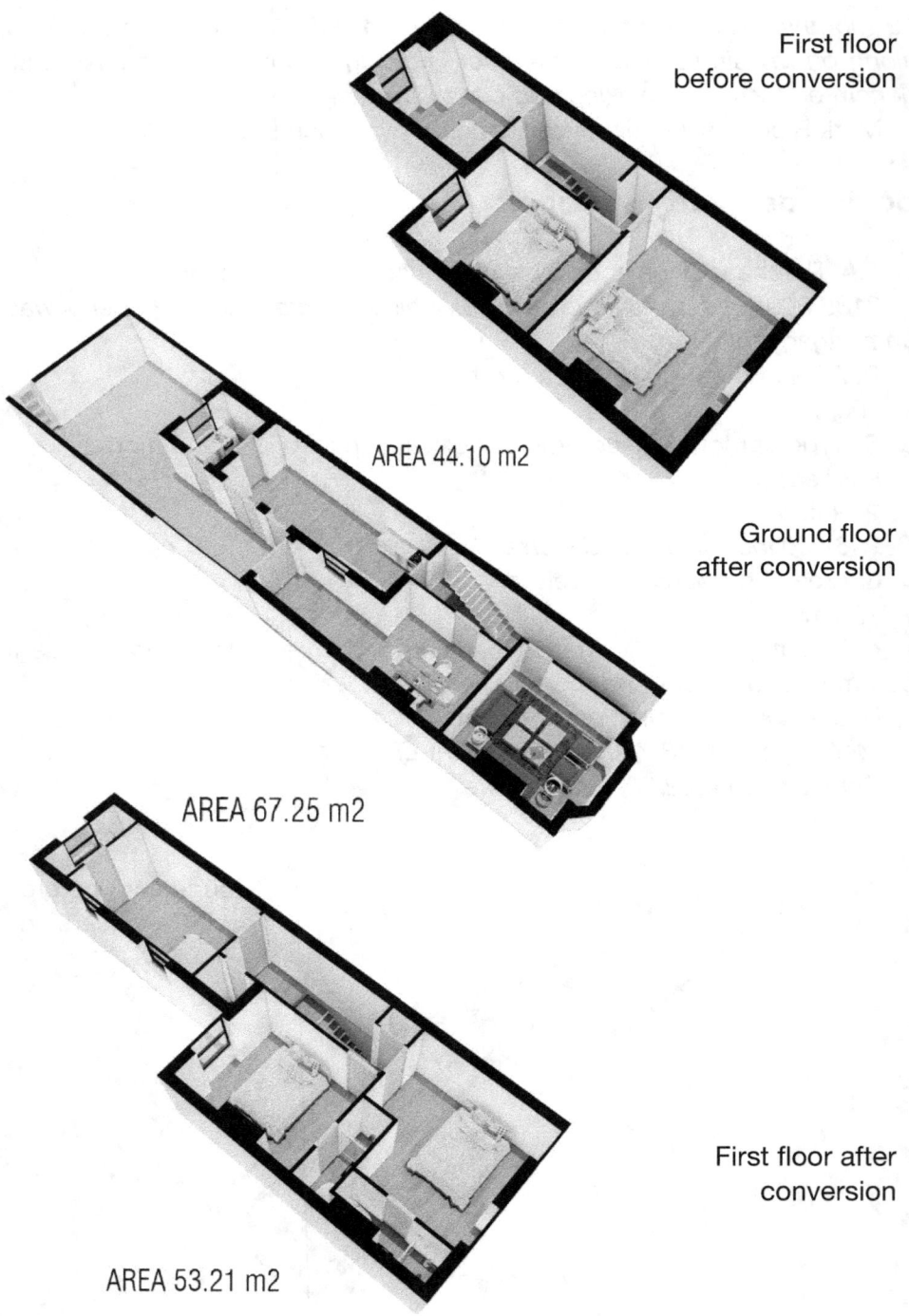

First floor before conversion

AREA 44.10 m2

Ground floor after conversion

AREA 67.25 m2

First floor after conversion

AREA 53.21 m2

Case Study Five

Let me introduce to you one of our amazing mentees Krishna Gurung.
www.krishnagurung.com

Krishna Gurung is from a rural village in Nepal.

'I was a part time trekking guide and while studying in college in Nepal, came to UK 1998 and worked hard for 72 hours as a waiter for £140 a week and later opened my own restaurant.

'I'm always looking forward to learn new things with 'never give up' mindset, lots of failures and challenges. Started as a property investor since 2014, however biggest breakthrough happened since joined Assets for Life.

It was slow start but one private mentoring session with Jay and Liam of Assets for Life inspired me to make a big difference in my development.'

Here are the details:
Bought for £325,000 at auction
None of my money as investor put in the deposit and I arranged Lloyds Loan.

Property description:
Mix - commercial - shop downstairs, office in first floor and 3 other apartments but in bad condition. Whole property in long 20 years lease for £14400 (that was the main thing which gave us great potential).

Strategy:
Planning gain for office to 2 bed flat
Planning gain for top floor large flat to 2 two bedroom flat
New lease for shop and negotiated old lease to surrender with £60k fee

Total costs:
Conversion Development of 5 two bedroom flat funded by Lloyds = £120,000

My investor partner - £60,000
Lease fee - £60,000
Utilities - £16,500
S106 - £12,650
Architect plus planning consultant - £9,700

Total cost - £278,850
PP - £325,000
Total - £603,850

Income now:
Shop - £1,100 pm with 20 year lease
Flats - £4,500 pm (£900 per flat) to SA company

Total Income - £5,600

While building we still had income from shop and 1 flat
Total - £2,000 pm

Now going through valuation dealing by David Tonks of Advocate Finance Recommendation of AFL.
Market Value - £1,250,000
With 75 per cent loan to value £937,000 of which we pay off Lloyds Bank and Investor loan, balance £333,650 cash still available to invest. Monthly interest only payment of £3,850 which means net cash flow of £1,750 pm.

I will shortly get all the survey report with exact figure of loan and repayment above is now sent by David Tonks.

Address of the property:
65-67 Lynchford Road
Farnborough
GU14 6EJ

In a nutshell:
'When you have a mentor and strong desire to take action you can make it happen. I was bit nervous at first on this deal and I was planning for 4

apartments but with Jay and Liam's insight now the profit margin is great, not only this but my investor partner is also very happy. Now all complete with sign off by building regs. And fully tenanted. Now time to move to the next project.

'Thank you Assets for Life, thank you my mentors Jay Munoz and Liam Ryan for the inspiration and insight.'

Here is the layout before the development:

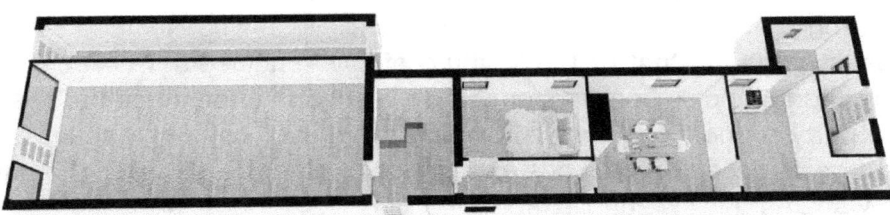

AREA 128.76 m2

Here is the layout after the development.

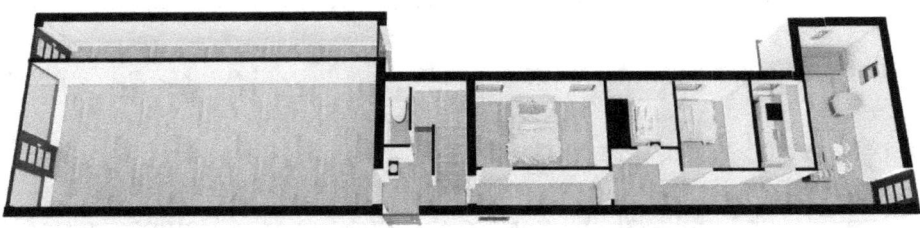

ÁREA 128.76 m2

Chapter Eight

Property economics

As you know, building an asset-for-life based business is a great vehicle to create wealth and truly change people's lives for the better. The reality is that anyone can do this with the right education, tools, environment and commitment.

The following chapters will dig into more detail - numbers and property 'lingo' with which we property developers should be familiar. I decided to go on a research mission to get the most up-to-date information for you based on previous data. For this, I went to several websites and several libraries, including that of the Institute of Civil Engineers. I collected as much information as possible for you, so we can all understand the basics of property economics, as well providing information on how to assess different deals based on previous experience of other developers who have kindly shared this invaluable information.

Please remember that we don't have to fully understand all the detailed concepts that I am about to share. These are only given so you can understand some of the calculations and simple formulas that other people, cleverer than me, have come up with so we can then take calculated risks and have a more detailed picture of what level of risk and reward you are going to embark on.

As before, every chapter should be read with a nice cup of Colombian cafe or tea, ideally after a few minutes of mediation or first thing in the morning – you have been made aware. Enjoy.

8.1 The Property Investment Market

The particular aspects of the property investment market currently are:

8.1.1 Legal estates in land

The English legal system, which originated from the Domesday Book of 1086, was updated by the property statutes of the 1920s. Therefore, there are now only two legal estates in land: freehold and leasehold.

Freehold

In common law jurisdictions such England and Wales, the freehold is the common ownership of an asset (property or land) and all static structures attached to such asset. The freeholder in practice acquires a bundle of property rights, rather than the property itself; but in practice, the difference is not significant. Should a freeholder die intestate and without next of kin, the property reverts to the Crown. The 'charge simple absolute in possession' is nominally held of the Crown, but in practice it confers ownership. This means that the owner may do whatever he or she wishes, though it is subject to the rights of others, as well as the other laws enforced at the time. The subsoil may also be reserved from any sale, allowing the transferor to exploit mineral deposits. In England and Wales, the Crown owns gold and silver below the land, with the exception of the small coal mines, the right to mine for coal belongs to the state.

Leasehold

The property reverts to the owner of the land after the lease period has expired. The lease sets out the terms of the tenancy, which includes the duration, the rent, the responsibilities, and any other matters over which the landlord may wish to exercise control. This means that the tenant is entitled to exclusive occupation. The planning laws are likely to set out the use, after which the landlord could further restrict any element of that use. Subject to any limitations in the lease, the leaseholder may create subleases, but only of a timeframe that is less than the remaining term. A lease of seven years or more must be granted by deed; otherwise, it will be deemed as an equitable interest only. With the exception of very limited cases, there is no restriction on the length of a lease.

In some cases, properties built on land were granted leases of up to 999 years, though many are for shorter periods. For residential properties, there are provisions whereby a leaseholder can apply to enlarge the interest to a freehold, despite any wish of the freeholder, and are therefore subjected to compensation computed, as set out in the relevant legislation.

The Land Registry keep records of all transactions, which maintains a register of ownership, and collects and stamps duty land tax on any transaction. Limited information with respect to ownership is available, now, by payment of a fee. Some of the information is publicised in statistical form. Most developed countries will possess some form of land registration and planning control, although the details may vary.

In circumstances where a leasehold interest is to be valued, it is essential for the valuer to obtain a copy of the lease, and with regards to matters of interpretation, it should be referred to a lawyer for advice.

8.1.2 Team players

A range of team players determine the outcome of the property market.

There are asset owners, who may also use their asset as either a living accommodation or business premises; and then there are tenants, who agree on specific terms with the owner in regards to using the premises, for a period that is subjected to a number of terms, all of which are contained in the contract which is referred to as a lease.

Many properties that are acquired, are then altered, extended, or redeveloped by us property developers. By property developer, I mean any person or special purchase vehicle that creates or converts a building, for which they may provide the funds, either directly or by borrowing (I will expand on this in the next chapter). For this, we also appoint specialists as part of our team, who manage these activities; such persons are inclusive, but not limited to, lawyers, valuers, building surveyors, architects, and chartered, civil and M&E engineers.

When a landlord leases the property to a tenant, it is an investment. But when a property is purchased with the intention to occupy, it is a consumption of goods. For generations, houses have been purchased for use as living accommodation, with the additional benefit of selling at some future date, and making a profit. In this way, many people have moved up the property ladder, aided by some, or all, of the profit made on the earlier house. In many places, including our tropical UK, there is a growing practice of buying and letting residential accommodation which is within the reach of investors with limited funds, or even using Others People's Money (OPM) as we teach in our AFL academy.

Land to build on

The reality is that the land is a permanent factor, whilst the assets built on it can be altered, added to, demolished, or have their use changed, in response to the demands of us, humans. There are various reasons why a business would prefer to lease rather than buy a property; in the case of retail units, the all-important feature is its location within a specific area, or the owner of the suitable premises' desire not to sell. In many cases, business owners prefer to regard an asset as another cost of production, and may find it cheaper to lease rather than to buy, using a substantial loan. Leasing also gives the occupier flexibility, should the business grow and require larger premises.

The overall supply of land is either limited, especially in the tropical parts of the UK, or is highly inelastic, often referred to as 'fixed'; although through planning permissions, redevelopment, alterations and adaptations, the supply may be varied to a limited extent.

Whilst land is described as one of the factors of production, it may also be defined as natural capital, because of the fact that any activity to alter it has taken place, particularly where it has been 'improved' in some way. Therefore, it is mainly respected for its ability to enable a person to achieve a particular objective.

Virgin land can either be available where planning permissions exist, or obtained from a particular development. Purchasing of such land, without first exploring the possibilities within any planning framework, would be a risk that I wouldn't be prepared to take unless I have a plan or some certainty that I will be able to develop it. In many countries, including the UK, a planning system has provided a broad framework, from which it is difficult to depart to any great extent. Therefore, the availability and nature of any planning permission has a considerable effect on the land value. Authorities can intervene to achieve any particular objectives, either nationally or regionally, by offering the following: grants; speeding up the planning process; limiting certain payments, such as property tax; or providing infrastructure. Most of these incentives are time-limited, and used to stimulate the market, where it would otherwise remain dormant. Government and state interest in the control of the planning process may be extended to embrace energy efficiency, actions to lessen global climate change, and creation of employment. In other circumstances, the government could continuously restrict activity by various means; including an increase in transaction taxes, such as stamp duty, which at the present moment, with Brexit, has resulted in fewer transactions after the increase.

Economics affecting the property market

Similar to any other type of economy, there is a state of equilibrium when there is a balance of supply and demand for goods and services. It is similar to an auction, where the auctioneer accepts increasing bids from buyers who continue to require the goods or services being presented. In due course, the bids will find an equilibrium between the demand of prices and the supplied amounts. It also envisages the situation where a different and preferable combination occurs.

Perfect competition supposes that:

- There is an unlimited number of buyers and sellers.
- Buyers and sellers are aware of each other's intentions.
- Factors of production are available without delay, and each unit is homogeneous.

None of above apply to the property market. Specific factors are applied to land and buildings, for a number of reasons:

- Property can be used for personal residential use, or as an investment, or both.

- Land is fixed in place and quantity.
- There is no physical market place.
- Confidence in the market is essential.
- Buildings are sometimes valued for their lifespan.
- Quality of tenant is paramount for commercial use.
- High transfer purchase and costs accompany the sale.

In these terms, the demand for, and value of, the property is extremely difficult to calculate. For example, any number of individuals may be seeking to buy or sell, but on a 'one-off' basis, and not all of them will eventually go through with a transaction. The market, such as it is, is extremely secretive and poorly informed. Typically, when a particular demand is identified, but there are no suitable premises that are available at that time, satisfaction of that demand through the building process is likely to be slow whilst the various steps to meet that demand are being taken.

Therefore, by the time the new building is finished, the market may have already changed. Finally, each property unit is heterogeneous, and whilst more than one of the available buildings or sites may serve the purpose, there may be problems identifying suitable buildings and locations that meet all the unique prerequisites.

The market is divided into property that is available for sale, and that which is offered on a rental basis. As outlined above, a lease is the contract through which an owner provides a property to an occupier for a period of time, although some transactions are dealt with on the basis of licences. The latter are usually for short terms, and these are rarely used as a means to create investments; owners and investors tend to prefer using leases. Some specialist providers concentrate on one sector of the market, while others are prepared to range across the spectrum, which, in the case of long-term holdings, may be a useful approach to offsetting risk.

The property market is not transparent, though in recent times, in the UK, it has become more so due to the availability of transaction information through the Land Registry, together with online price comparisons and projections, plus research data from the major firms of surveyors and estate agents. However, much of this information is still incomplete, and thereby requires assumptions in order to make its use viable. It is important to remember that a valuer is responsible for the valuation submitted, and there is no substitute for personal knowledge and reasoned interpolation. A well-informed valuer operating in a specific market or location may have access to formal, and informal, sources of intelligence, and the ability to cross-check data to some extent. It is important to note that any information which is not capable of verification should be treated with caution.

Theory of prices

I cannot stress enough that every single road in the UK is a micro economy of a dynamic macro economy, and can react to events in the market. At the time of writing, Brexit and stamp duty changes have had an enormous impact on the volume of transactions. Additionally, when supply exceeds demand, there is a downward pressure on price; conversely, when the demand exceeds the supply, prices rise to restore the status quo, or to a state of rest. The ultimate goal would be to find a balance, but that goal is very elusive.

By its very nature, property investment has its own peculiarities, and from that consequences can occur. It is heterogeneous, durable, has high transaction costs, and experiences long delays in response to demand and price hikes, pending resolution of shortages.

Economists point to the inelasticity of the supply of property, brought about by the extended timescale needed to respond to a perceived increase in demand. Any decision to respond to the additional demand is an act of faith, given that any increase in the stock will be delayed by many months, if not years. Also, apart from information on recent planning applications and decisions, there is little indication as to what other investors are doing in response to the new demand. Provision is uncoordinated and fragmented, and may lead to an oversupply of building stock at the expense of the developer. The planning process and its control mechanisms are not primarily concerned with matching supply and demand in individual cases, although it attempts to anticipate future needs in a locality.

The universal laws of supply and demand are fundamental aspects of our economic theory, and the price of any economic good is determined by the interaction of these two components. Therefore, changes in either most certainly affects the price, although other factors may intrude that subsequently modify the effect.

The laws of supply and demand are subject to the concept of elasticity. In the case of demand, it would be expected that a higher price would result in lower demand. But this may not be the case if , for example, the indications are that the price will continue to rise.

The two terms are defined in detail, below.

The fundamental law of demand

The fundamental law of demand is that the price of a product will inversely influence the demand for that product, other things being equal. Where the supply is not sufficient enough to meet the demand, the price will rise until a balance is found. This general law, however, is not absolute: a household's requirements for, say, bread or milk are fairly fixed, so halving or doubling the price is unlikely to make any discernible difference. Where consumption falls as income rises, those goods affected are referred to as inferior goods; in general, they are being displaced by other goods, more to the liking of the household, which can now be afforded. Demand for certain goods can also be affected by changes in the prices of other goods – in other words, they are substitutes. Market demand sums all the individual household demands; it ranges from repetitive purchases, to the requirement for accommodation, transport, holidays, and the like. The sum total of demand, for a product in a particular time period, requires not only a desire for a product, but the ability and willingness to pay for it – that is an effective demand.

The basis on which decisions are made is set by the buyers and the sellers in the market. In general, state interference in real estate is limited to ensuring some order in the public interest, such as planning and employment policies, which in turn may be designed to direct development or redevelopment to specific areas. In some cases, development is promoted through the offer of support, such as grants, civil infrastructure and so on.

Demand for accommodation varies with the price of the asset, the price of alternatives, and the impact of future events, such as changes taste. These are referred to as determinants of demand. As previously stated, it would be expected that a higher price would result in lower demand, but this may not be the case where the indications are, for example, that the price will continue to rise. On some occasions, the demand for a product increases as the price increases, breaking the normal relationship between the two strands. This is referred to as perverse demand behaviour. It is most often due to speculation, in which a price rise is seen as an indication that there may be further price rises to follow, so a purchase in advance makes sense. Alternatively, a price rise may be seen as an indication that the quality of the product has improved, to the extent that it is regarded as having a different market.

A specific form of demand targeted at resources is known as collateral demand. For example, demand for a building will subsequently create demands for mortar, bricks, plasterboard, etc. In a free market economy, the price of most goods is governed by demand and availability. And the price of property, both commercial and residential, is no different. Whether for occupation or investment, the vendor will take advice on the best price obtainable, whilst the intending purchaser will seek advice on the value and look into the feasibility of pursuing the purchase to completion. The prospective purchaser of a property investment will seek to compare the current and potential income with other forms of investment. A prime consideration will relate to the Return On the Investment (ROI), but other factors such Return On Cash Employed (RCE) and Return on Cash Left In the Deal (RCLD) are also important, depending on the level of investment.

Further factors include: the size of the investment and the extent, if any, to which external funding is necessary; the burden of management; the ease of resale; the physical condition of the buildings; and future prospects of maintaining or improving cash flow, including the possibility of redevelopment. When residential accommodation is being acquired for occupation, the considerations are somewhat different, with primary focus being given to the location, and its accessibility in relation to the individual's current priorities, such as schools, public transport, civil infrastructure, closeness to work, etc. The house purchaser will have a price range, most likely related to their level of savings available as a deposit, as well as a sufficient income which can be used to fund the concurrent loan payments. These personal requirements will vary from one purchaser to another and carry different weightings.

The fundamental law of supply

The fundamental law of supply defines the amount of the good or asset that will be offered for sale, at a particular time and at a particular price. As the price varies, so will the supply. Where supply is greater than demand, there is a subsequent downward pressure on prices; similarly, where demand is greater than supply, the prices are forced upwards. Where the amount offered is similar to the amount required, the normal, or equilibrium, price pertains.

When supply increases, it is likely due to a response to demand, whereby the producer identifies the possibility of increasing profits from more sales. But such a reaction will depend upon the practicality of increasing supply; including the availability of the factors required for the production, which is necessary because of the increase in activity. Should the decision to increase supply be dependent on the acquisition of expensive machinery, or the employment of experienced staff, such a decision is unlikely to be taken without some level of confidence that the increased supply has some level of permanence.

When supply and demand are balanced, the price will remain the same, but any substantial change in demand or supply would inherently affect the price and therefore upset the balance.

The situation may be defined as 'a state of balance produced by the counteraction of two or more factors', which provides an indication of the application of the term to the economic theory of supply and demand. It is the concept used for determining price, given the conditions of supply and demand.

When the amount of any good or service is at the equilibrium price (meaning that the amount available is equal to the amount demanded), supply and demand are in balance and both parties are satisfied. The market may change following a substitution or restriction on the part of the consumer, and/or additional facilities, and marketing by the producer. This statement assumes:

- The amount supplied is equal to the amount demanded.
- The demand is based on maximisation of the utility, based on the market price.
- The rational approach of commercial and residential agents, who are not incentivised to affect the balance.
- The supply is determined by the maximisation of profits.

When any of these factors above are compromised, there is an imbalance which can cause chaos. With excess supply, there is downward pressure on price, whilst a shortage of supply results in an increase of the price. in both cases, equilibrium will eventually be restored.

These relationships are particularly important in the property metamorphosis, where the time lag between identifying a demand and meeting that demand is significant. For example, a company wishing to acquire a new office would experience a lead time of one year or more, particularly if there were locational limitations. Additionally, the building supply would involve some detailed enquiries and action. There is also the process of identification of site, negotiating its acquisition, obtaining permission for the proposed development, inviting tenders, and arranging finance, before the physical provision can commence. This procedure tends to take some time, with a consequent delay in gaining possession. The search may be stopped at any of these stages by either party, or by unfavourable information regarding the viability of the plans, or of gaining planning permission. The company can limit these inconveniences and delays by seeking an existing building, given that it meets the requirements without any major alterations or additions that will cause delay.

The supply of land is limited and fixed, and most buildings are designed and built to last for several decades. There is some mitigation, although additions to the stock tend to be modest in relation to the existing supply. Any delay may be sufficient to have a marginal effect on prices, when the premises are required urgently.

There is the risk that the market may change by the time the new building is available, and these changed circumstances can affect the decision to go ahead. At the same time, there may be particular attractions of a new building, which cannot be offered by an existing one.

Balance

The theory of balance provides an explanation of pricing in a free market economy. It states that balance is achieved when the price and quantity of goods respond to the demand.

It assumes that producers and consumers behave rationally; and that the producer will do whatever is necessary to maximize profits, whilst the consumer will seek out the best price.

Where goods contain substitutes, the rise in the price of one will produce excess demand for the others.

Both statements are subject to qualification; for example, if a producer could sell more goods but only after increasing production by further investment, then the initial costs of enabling that additional production may not justify the adjustment.

Similarly, the consumer may devote all, or part, of the budget for those particular goods to an alternative and therefore reduce consumption of the previous goods.

Their respective actions may vary between what is practicable in the short term, and what is subject to a longer timescale. Where supply and demand are equal, it is said that the market is in a state of balance. It is the concept of determining the price, given the conditions of supply and demand. Where supply is fixed in the short term, as is the case with property, the price would be governed by demand; meaning that any change in demand would trigger a rise in price. This imbalance is referred to as disequilibrium.

Price

Now let's have a look at factors affecting the price, which is directly related to supply and demand. Some of the main factors include:

1. Affordability

Higher salaries mean that people can afford to spend more on a roof

Source www.economicshelp.org / Nationwide

over their heads. During periods of economic growth, the demand for houses tends to rise.

As per the graph, affordability index is associated with housing cost. Points above 100 indicate that a typical family may struggle to qualify for a mortgage on a home in a specific area, while a value of 100 indicates that the typical family has more than enough money to qualify.

This graph also shows that house prices (and therefore demand for housing) can rise much faster than earnings, suggesting there are many other factors influencing demand – at least in the short run.

At the time of writing, the government has implemented a Help to Buy scheme that has contributed tremendously to the affordability of housing for first time buyers and helped developers (including us) to sell the units at a faster rate.

2. Confidence

Demand for houses depends on consumer confidence. In particular, it depends on people's confidence about the future of the economy and housing market. If people expect prices to rise, demand will rise so people can gain from rising wealth. In a boom, demand for houses rises faster than incomes, as seen in the graph above.

3. Interest Rates

One of the biggest factors in determining the cost of mortgage interest repayments is the Bank of England's interest base rates. The majority of UK homeowners still prefer to take out variable mortgage rates (unlike the rest of Europe where fixed-rate mortgage deals are more common). Hence, any change in the base rate will immediately affect the mortgage interest payments. This is a major factor in determining the affordability of houses. Mortgage payments take a high percentage of people's personal disposable income (average is between 19 to 48 per cent, but for some

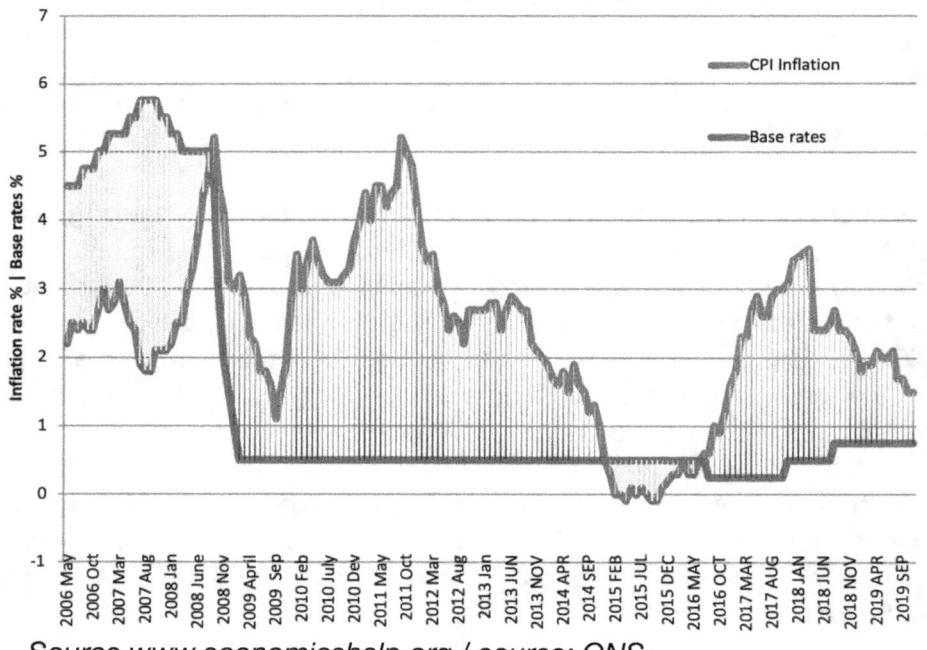

Source www.economicshelp.org / source: ONS

homeowners, especially in London or Cambridge, it is higher). If you have a £300,000 mortgage, a 0.5 per cent change in base rates will change your monthly payments by about £120 a month. Therefore, even small changes in interest rates can deter people from buying an asset for life.

Back in 1992, when interest rates reached 15 per cent in England, demand for housing collapsed, causing a large fall in demand. The relatively low interest rates of the later 1990s and 2000s encouraged more people to buy a house. However, in 2008-09, when interest rates were cut to just 0.5 per cent, demand remained low. This was because other factors were reducing demand for housing, like the recession and the prospect of rising unemployment.

To help the economy, the government created a Help to Buy scheme that has helped greatly with the increase of the demand and the economy in general.

4. Population

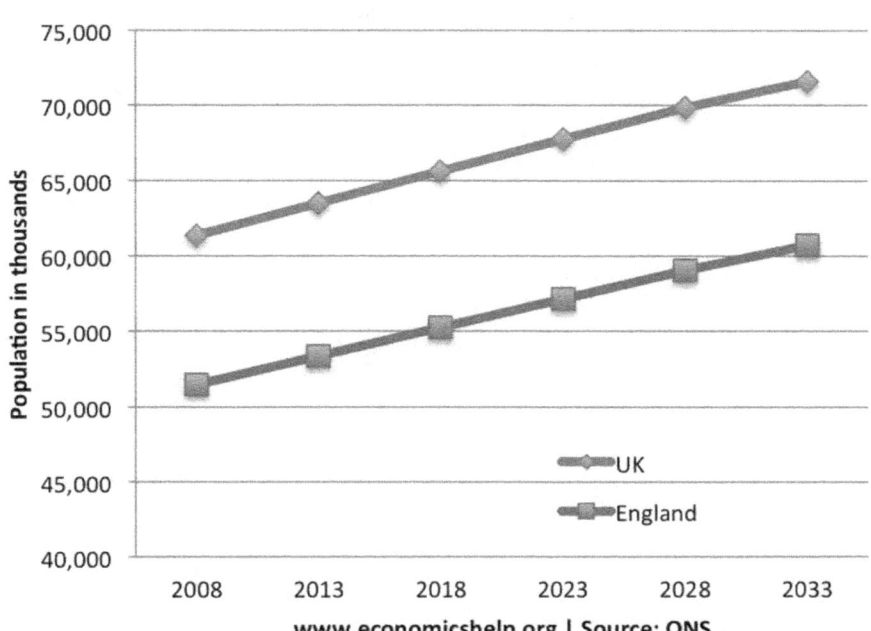

Source www.economicshelp.org / ONS

This is a very important factor. It is not just the number of people, but demographic changes. For example, the growing number of single people living alone has led to increased demand for flats and small houses. The demand for housing doesn't just depend on all the inhabitants in a particular place, but also the average size of a household. Some social and demographic factors are causing a rise in the number of households (faster than the population increase). These demographic changes include:
- People are living with their parents for longer.
- Increased life expectancy, leading to more single old people.
- Divorce rates, increasing the number of single-parent families.
- Immigration, leading to more people from other countries.

5. Mortgage availability

One key factor that determines the effective demand for houses is the willingness of banks to lend mortgages. If the banks are willing to lend money with bigger income multiples, then the effective demand for houses is greater. The willingness of banks to lend mortgage finance can vary, depending on the strength of the interbank lending sector.

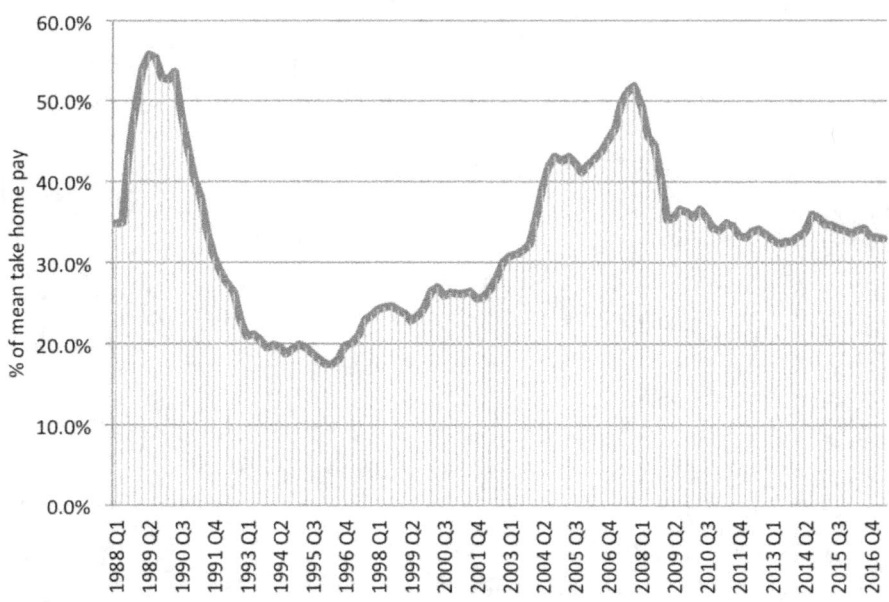

Source www.economicshelp.org / Nationwide

The credit crisis of 2008 led to a sharp rise in the cost of interbank lending and a fall in availability of mortgage finance. Many mortgage products have been withdrawn, making it more difficult for would-be homeowners to get on the property ladder. For example, 125 per cent and 100 per cent mortgages, available until 2007, were withdrawn.

I benefitted from this luxury myself and I honestly wish I bought more units then as I bought them in the right areas then. Now, banks are increasingly demanding a higher deposit before lending mortgages.

Currently, the average is a 25 per cent deposit for a buy-to-let; while, with the Help to Buy scheme, first-time buyers and other buyers only need five per cent.

6. Economic growth and real incomes

Rising household incomes enable people to afford bigger houses/ mortgages and encourage demand for housing. In affluent periods, demand for housing grows rapidly, suggesting it is income-elastic.

7. Cost of renting

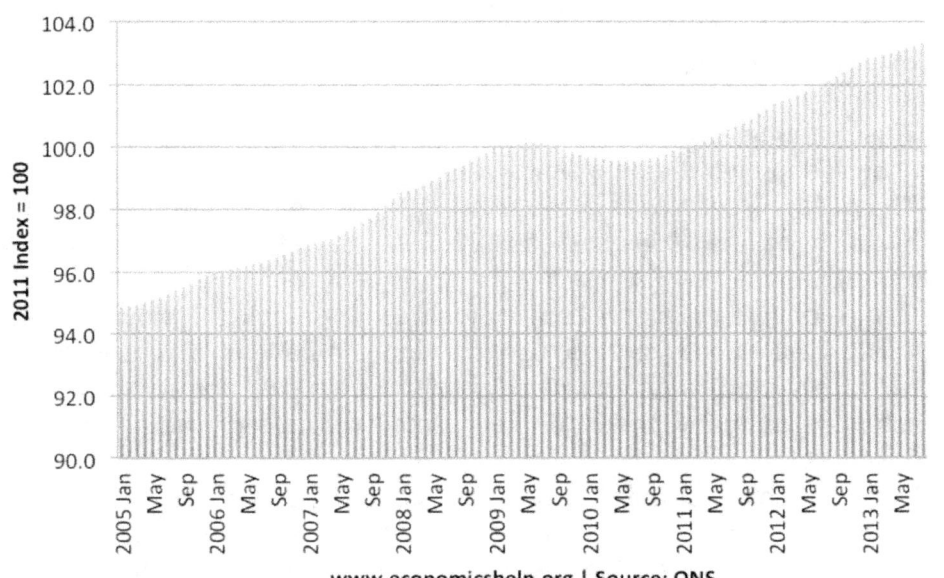

The graph overleaf shows the constant increase in the cost of renting, despite the financial crisis and housing 'crash'. This helped to cause UK house prices to continue rising.

If the cost of renting rises, then households will make greater efforts to buy properties through mortgages, which become relatively cheap when compared to rental costs.

Factors affecting supply

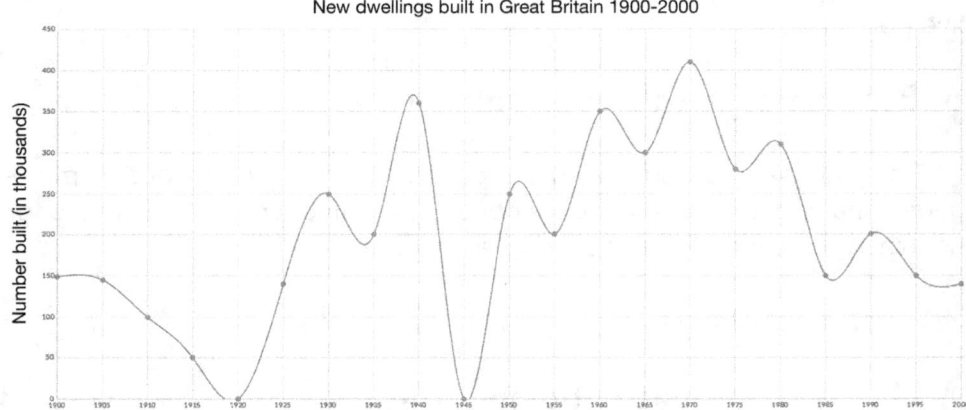

Source www.ons.gov.uk

This graph (above) shows how the number of new houses built in the UK has varied over the past century.

The peak, as seen, was in the late 1960s, with more than 400,000 built per year, In the late 1990s and early 2000s, that fell to 150,000 (fewer than required).

Some of the biggest contributors to the lack of housing are: planning restrictions on the use of land; limitations on building on Green Belt land; and local opposition to new homes, which is widespread as many prefer to live in smaller villages without increased congestion.

The profitability of building new houses is dependent on the demand for houses and their prices. In a boom, builders are usually keener to build more and falling house prices can lead to a restriction in supply.

UK house prices

A fundamental problem in the UK housing market is the persistent shortage of housing. The number of households is forecast to grow by 232,000 a year until 2033, and yet the current rate of home construction is struggling to increase above 150,000 to 200,000 a year.

Source www.economicshelp.org / Nationwide

According to Crisis report (Nov 2018) by Professor Glen Bramley, the widespread perception is that housing needs have increased and current levels of housing supply are inadequate in scale and scope.

There is currently a backlog of housing need of 4.75 million households across Great Britain (4 million in England). Around 3.66 million households are in housing need; they are either in concealed and overcrowded households, have serious affordability or physical health problems, or are living in unsuitable accommodation.

In 2007, the government set a target of increasing the supply of housing to 240,000 additional homes per year by 2016.

Within this overall target was a commitment to deliver at least 70,000 affordable homes per year by 2010-11, of which 45,000 were to be new social-rented homes. However, since the credit crunch of 2008, this target has severely fallen behind as housing construction has slumped.

Policies to deal with expensive house prices in the UK have sometimes focused on demand, such as 'help to buy' which offers credit to groups of young homebuyers. But increasing the availability of credit doesn't directly address this problem. Housing completions have fallen close to 100,000 a year – well below the level needed to meet the growth in the number of households. (*Source: https://opendatacommunities.org/def/concept/folders/themes/house-building – Live tables on new housing*)

There is hope that improved mortgage availability will increase private sector construction. However, that doesn't resolve other issues, such as planning regulations and local opposition to building homes on a large scale.

New housing

The graph below and as per information previously shared above is showing that demand for housing stock has been growing faster than net additions to the housing stock, pushing up house prices.

(Source: Understanding supply constraints in UK housing market, Shelter)

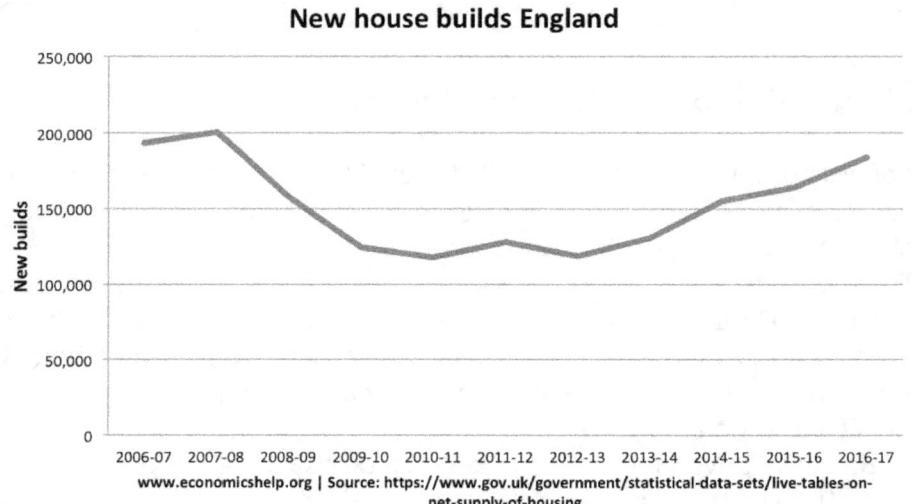

Chapter Eight

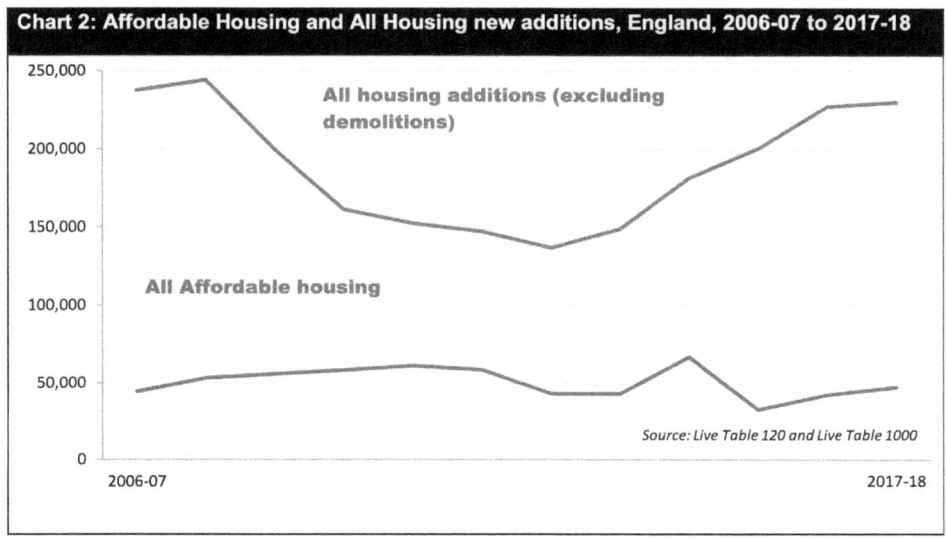

Forecasts for future number of households

Despite a lack of housing supply, the number of households in England is projected to grow to 27.5 million in 2033, an increase of 5.8 million (27 per cent) since 2008, or 232,000 households per year.
(Source: https://www.gov.uk/government/statistics/household-projections-2008-to-2033-in-england)

Implications of housing shortages

1. House prices will continue to rise in the long term

Despite two housing crashes, real house prices show a remorseless upward trend. The limited supply also tends to make house prices more volatile. Because supply is relatively inelastic, a small change in demand can cause a significant change in price. This is a major factor behind the UK housing market's tendency to boom and bust.

2. Housing will become more expensive as a percentage of income

The ratio of house prices to earnings for first-time buyers is already higher than in the mid-1980s – despite the housing correction of 2008/09.

If the long-term trend of rising population is combined with limited supply, this is likely to squeeze prices higher. See more details on the UK housing affordability section on page 103.

3. Switch to the private rented sector will continue

If house prices continue to rise, more people will be looking for private rented accommodation.

4. Growth in wealth inequality

Rising house prices benefit homeowners (typically older people). However, it reduces living standards of those without a home.

The UK will increasingly become divided between those who own a home and those who don't.

5. Upward pressure on rental prices

The shortage of housing will put upward pressure on the price of rented accommodation. Housing costs will take a bigger share of people's incomes, leaving them with less disposable income.

Chapter Eight

Housing stock in England

There were 24.4 million dwellings in England on 31 March, 2019, an increase of 241,000 dwellings (1 per cent) on the previous year. Figures for all years since 2012 are provisional and subject to revision following the 2021 Census

(source:https://assets.publishing.service.gov.uk/government/uploads/ system/uploads/attachment_data/file/886251/Dwelling_Stock_Estimates_31_March_2019_England.pdf)

Housing statistical release

The figure below shows the estimates of total dwelling stock from 2001 to 2018.

Table 1: Annual estimates of total dwelling stock for England and annual change, as at 31 March 2001–2018			
	Thousands of dwellings		Percentages
31 March	Total stock	Net change	Net change as percentage of existing stock
2001	21,207	..	..
2002	21,354	147	0.69%
2003	21,513	160	0.75%
2004	21,684	171	0.79%
2005	21,870	186	0.86%
2006	22,073	203	0.93%
2007	22,288	215	0.97%
2008	22,511	224	1.00%
2009	22,694	183	0.81%
2010	22,839	145	0.64%
2011	22,976	137	0.60%
2012 ᵖ	23,111	135	0.59%
2013 ᵖ	23,236	125	0.54%
2014 ᵖ	23,372	137	0.59%
2015 ᵖ	23,543	171	0.73%
2016 ᵖ	23,733	190	0.81%
2017 ᵖ	23,950	217	0.92%
2018 ᵖ	24,172	222	0.93%
ᵖ Figures for all years since 2012 are provisional and subject to revision following 2021 Census (see the 'Revision Policy' section for further information).			

(Source: https://assets.publishing.service.gov.uk/government/uploads/ system/uploads/attachment_data/file/803958/Dwelling_Stock_Estimates_31_March_2018__England.pdf)

Property cycles and how to profit from them

Introduction

This section includes material from a blog written by Andrew Schulhof, a real estate investor and licensed investment real estate advisor for more than 25 years, combined with thoughts based on my own knowledge and experience.

(Source: Look before you Leap. An Insider's Guide to Profitable Real Estate Investing).

Some text has been amended to reflect UK market trends and conditions. It is meant to be used a general guide; as a developer, it is your duty to identify the specific, localised cycle conditions of your area of interest.

If you understand how to capitalise on property cycles, you will be able to harvest the fruits of property development and investing by avoiding and/ or mitigating all risks. Learning about the phases of the property cycle is fundamental to successfully investing in real estate. The property cycle is usually a long-term phenomenon; based on previous data, it lasts for ap-proximately 18 to 20 years.

While it's difficult to predict precisely in the short term, it's important to remember that it is a cycle with definite phases. Once you understand this basic concept, you can then set your strategy based on the phases and take full advantage of it.

Currently in the UK at the time of writing (going through the Covid-19 virus), recent actions taken by government at a national level are impacting real estate markets and causing phase changes within the property cycles.

Fortunately, these actions are currently impacting positively on the economy and hence improving confidence of all investors.

However, these actions can sometimes work in a localised manner and there could be areas where these actions may not even work.

This means that it's even more critical to understand the markets in which you have investment properties and plan accordingly, in keeping with the phase of the localised real estate cycle (remember from the previous chapter that property is a micro economy by road/postcode within a wider macro economy by the whole country).

Don't assume that there's one consistent UK real estate market.

The reality is that some strategies are in positive phases of the real estate cycle, while others are in more negative phases.

Influencers on property cycle

Banks

Banks have traditionally been the main source of finance for the property sector, both in terms of development and providing long-term financing with regards to ownership.

They tend to be at the heart of expansion for the development market; indeed, they have been criticised for fuelling development booms. Figures from different sources show us that the increase of developmental activity in the early 1970s, late 1980s, and from the late 1990s until 2006, coincided with a great increase in bank lending.

This may be a function of the behaviour of banks in lending to the property industry. The property market tends to run in cycles, something which is common in the general economy; indeed, the contemporary thinking among government macro-economists is to dampen the swings in the general economy. Cycles in the real estate market tend to be bigger in amplitude, and this is partly due to how the banks lend to the property sector. They tend to lend when the property market is already healthy, with rises in rental and asset values well established.

When compared to other ventures which pose a higher risk, property lending is an attractive option for banks. The rates at which banks lend are relatively high, giving a good return with the added security of the underlying worth of the property asset to fall back on.

This latter factor is not really available in lending to businesses. With businesses, the bulk of the value is usually in the ability to earn cash flow in the future; this can evaporate very quickly. Banks operate in a very competitive environment, and are therefore keen to lend within sectors that will give them a good return. The tendency to lend when values rise is understandable, but the rise in values is often a function of previous low levels of lending in the immediate past, when the property market is poor and when development supply is low.

Shortages in supply tend to fuel price rises, hence enabling both development and developmental lending.

The result of this self-generating cycle is a series of chain reactions that is very difficult to stop. Where the amplitude of the up-cycle is large, the consequent downturn is usually much larger.

This occurred in the late 1980s, early 1990s, and mid 2000s, resulting in banks becoming large-scale property owners, following the collapse in the commercial property markets where previous years of excessive supply coincided with a downturn in the general economy.

The banking sector is therefore mega influential for us, as property developers, as it is the primary source of finance for small to medium-sized enterprise (SME) developers, like us at Assets for Life.

They are not as dominant overall, however, as the outsider may believe. Developers are also able to use other sources of funds, such as a small self-administered scheme (SSAS) and private equity, of which we are currently taking advantage, and teaching to all of our students.

Other factors that alter the cycles

- Buyers' emotional cycle, from optimism to euphoria to despondency and back to optimism.
- Confidence (sometimes based on gut feeling).
- Government policies.
- Employment/unemployment rates.
- The collective mindset.
- The media (TV, radio, social media).
- Supply/demand and scarcity.
- Liquidity.
- State of the economy.
- Social issues (pandemic, wars).
- Big infrastructure projects.

Property cycle

Each real estate market follows a long-term cycle consisting of four phases that follow a predictable pattern.

What isn't so predictable is the duration of each phase within the cycle, and therein lies the challenge of understanding the cycle and appreciating that when you understand what phase a particular real estate market is in, you can utilize the most appropriate investment tactics for that phase.

Chapter Eight

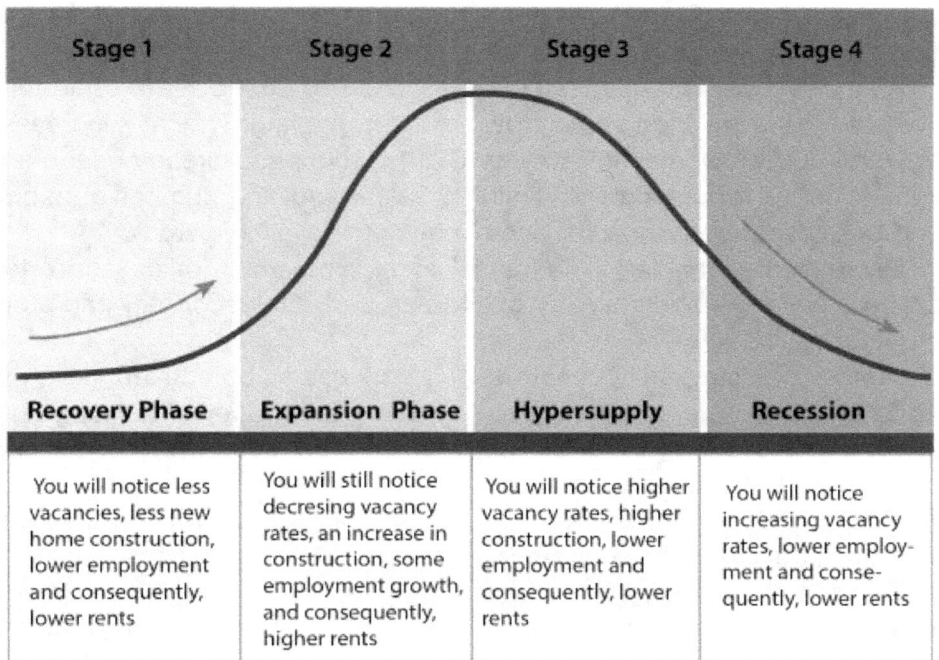

© 2020 Andrew Schulhof do not reproduce without written permission

The four physical phases are:
1. Recovery
2. Expansion
3. Hyper-supply (this can be regionalised only)
4. Contraction/recession

There is also a corresponding emotional cycle with the real estate cycle.

As a real estate market moves from a recovery stage through the expansion phase, the emotions move in synchronisation i.e., from hope to relief to optimism, excitement and so on through all the corresponding phases.

Recovery

This phase represents a property market's recovery, from a contraction or recession; meaning that the market is recovering from factors such as higher unemployment, higher vacancy, decreased consumption, decreased investment/development, oversupply of housing (if applicable as this could be regionalised), and lower property prices.

As the recovery proceeds, there are increased employment opportunities, and the population starts growing and improving. Typically, increased growth in Gross Domestic Product (GDP) would have already begun and vacancy rates would start to diminish, as the growing number of people and businesses in the market begin renting the available stock.

Decreased vacancies in industrial and commercial (office and retail) space is another good indicator of a turnaround in the economy and property market.

Typically, single family construction continues to be active through all phases of the cycle, but suffice to say that there are fewer building construction sites during the latter parts of the contraction phase, and the earlier part of the recovery phase.

What are our opportunities here?

During the recovery phase of the property market cycle, a strategic investor holding the Asset for Life should be seriously investigating the opportunities in the market and identifying investment properties that may be ripe for acquisition. However, one really should look at the areas within the market that are going to have the highest potential for growth.

We should be able to answer the following questions:
1. What major announcements have been made recently?
2. Is there new infrastructure or transport links to be built? If so, where and when?
3. Is there gentrification going on in specific areas?

I personally invested in a flat in Woolwich, east London prior to the Crossrail project being announced. Every time I have refinanced this flat, something improbable has always happened: the valuer comes to the property and provides us with a higher valuation than we predicted, which is real music to the ears of a property developer/investor. This also happened to many investors prior to the Olympic Park being built. Once the announcement was made that the location of the Olympic Park was going to be in east London, property prices almost doubled overnight in some areas.

The early stages of this phase are not always a vendor's market. However, as it gains momentum, it can shift that way. A key really knowing whether it's a vendor's, neutral, or buyer's market, is to understand the trends indicated by the quantity of housing inventory supply, the days on the market, the pricing trends, and the sales-to-listing ratios.

The human emotions associated with this recovery phase are cautious optimism and a sense of potential and hope.

Expansion

The transition from the recovery phase to the expansion phase occurs when the existing stock is increasingly being bought up and/or rented. When factors such as GDP, jobs availability, and population continue to grow, vacancy rates continue to decline and landlords start to raise rents as the demand begins to exceed the supply.

During the early part of this phase, there is typically minimal new construction and usually no new, large housing schemes being built, because the property values are usually below replacement cost. Once developers see that there is a realistic opportunity to make a profit, they usually start investing, in land first and then building, in anticipation of launching successful projects. Single family dwelling construction typically increases in this phase and housing starts to grow.

Nevertheless, there is a short dead period within the expansion phase, as it takes time to put together new development and investment projects, get them built, and then sold or rented out.

Large housing schemes, like semi-detached homes and blocks of flats, can take two to five years, from conception to finish.

As the expansion phase continues, the real estate market becomes very active as everyone looks to take advantage of the recovery.

What are our opportunities here?

During this phase of the property market cycle, a strategic investor holding the Asset for Life should consider the following:

• Investing in assets that generate heathy cash flow, or if they are in the early stages of expansion, ensure that there is a high probability for positive cash flow within this phase.

• The construction cost, including finance, at the beginning of the cycle may be below replacement cost, which allows for equity gain appreciation once the asset is built. This is also the phase that enables maximum return, with the least amount of risk. Be mindful that the further this phase of the cycle advances, the more competition you will encounter and it will become more of a vendor's market. Therefore, ensure healthy cash flow so that you are not relying entirely on asset appreciation.

• As the asset value increases, there will be more stock being built. This is when we have to be careful due to the probability of over-development and getting into the winner's curse part of cycle as per noted in the 18 year cycle graph on page 123. If you were going to sell for whatever reason, this is the best phase in which to do so, as there is still an upward trend.

During the expansion phase, us investors/developers should also create a capital back-up (rainy day lump sum to cover a year of overheads if there is not money coming in) for the inevitable next phases of hyper-supply and contraction/recession. This would also be the phase in which the strategic investor should be stress-testing their real estate portfolio for increased interest rates to ensure that they can survive the eventual downturn.

During the expansion phase, the associated emotional phase is characterised by optimism, anticipation and positive possibilities.

Hyper-supply

When a hyper-supply of stock takes place, in layman's terms, a turning point is achieved and the available stock starts to exceed the demand. After which, the market changes from a vendor's market to a buyer's market, as more properties are available for sale, and the vacancy rate increases sharply. This is due to the inherent lag in large developments/construction projects; stocks will continue to come on to the market, even though the demand is decreasing. Investors continue to put new deals together and the speculation continues; therefore, the super-active real estate market continues. But this is a very dangerous phase.

Initially, landlords can continue to charge top rental rates, but as vacancy rates increase, the landlords will get nervous and the first thing they usually do is lower rental rates to try and fill their voids. During the latter part of the expansion phase, and definitely during this hyper-supply phase, GDP, jobs and population will have already typically levelled out, and even begun going down.

Hyper-supply (an increase in empty rental units and unsold stock) is the first sign that the real estate cycle is changing and heading towards a downward trend. The billion dollar question is: how deep will the market travel, and for how long will the next phase last?

What are our opportunities here?

During this phase of the real estate market cycle, the strategic in-vestor holding the Asset for Life (long term) should be seriously considering 'battening down the hatches' and investing in tenant retention, whether that is physical or systems improvements, or lowering costs wherever possible.

If necessary, convert your assets from single-let units to multi-let houses of multiple occupation (HMO) or serviced accommodation to increase the cash flow/rental income to mitigate potential risks.

On the emotional front, people still experience thrill and euphoria until the phase begins its transition to contraction/recession as the economy changes and money becomes tight; then the emotions tend to shift to anxiety and denial.

Contraction/recession

During the transition from hyper-supply to recession, vacancy rates will increase above the long-term average. Surplus single dwellings and large housing developments continue to come on to the market, as projects that were started during the expansion and hyper-supply phases come to completion. This leads to even more surplus supply, which then results in higher vacancy rates, lower rents, and reduced purchase prices for real estate. The GDP continues to fall as the economy moves further into its recessionary phase, fewer jobs are available, and the market's population decreases.

The next detrimental factor that will hamper the recovery is the potential increases in interest rates, which further slows the real estate market and the economy. However, once the real estate cycle is firmly in the recession phase, it marks the beginning of an opportunity for us to get great bargains, and also help people that are suffering from financial issues. And so, the cycle continues back towards the recovery phase.

What are our opportunities here?

During the contraction/recession phase of the property market cycle, the strategic investor holding the Asset for Life (long term) should be maintaining the highest possible occupancy rate and continuing to work with their tenants to ensure as much positive cash flow as possible. In the case of negative cash flow, using the cash reserves you have accumulated will help you weather the downturn.

If necessary, convert your assets from single-let units to multi-let houses of multiple occupation (HMO) or serviced accommodation to increase the cash flow/rental income to mitigate potential risks.

On a positive note, if your property business strategy is long term i.e. keeping the asset for long periods and experiencing a net loss during this period, we still have the tax benefits to offset some of the losses. This is why carrying out a sensitivity analysis to your portfolio is so key during the expansion phase. Also, this is why we strongly recommend diversifying your portfolio. Asset class, i.e. a combination of commercial and residential as well as geographic diversification, can greatly reduce the risk of net losses throughout your real estate portfolio.

Having a rental income-based business, both commercial and residential, as well as capital appreciation units, can be a nice balance during this particular time. The emotions associated with this phase are fear, pessimism, depression and even panic, especially if the investor is either a neophyte or overextended.

Length of real estate cycle
This is the billion-dollar question. The reality is that there isn't a specific, predictable length of time for a property cycle, but historically full real estate cycles typically take from seven to 18 years to move through all four phases, depending on what factors affect and influence a specific market.

As these factors vary from region to region (remember that each road in the UK and around the world is a micro economy), there is an aggregate of real estate cycles: individual, regional and road-to-road cycles, and a collective, national real estate cycle.

This provides opportunity for the savy property investor, as usually there is always a market that will be in the upward phases (recovery and expansion) of the real estate cycle.

The graph on the right summarises the last 65 years of the national property cycle for you.

What to look for and how to take strategic advantage
For us developers, understanding the property cycle and its phases, is fundamental to knowing what to look out for when making strategic

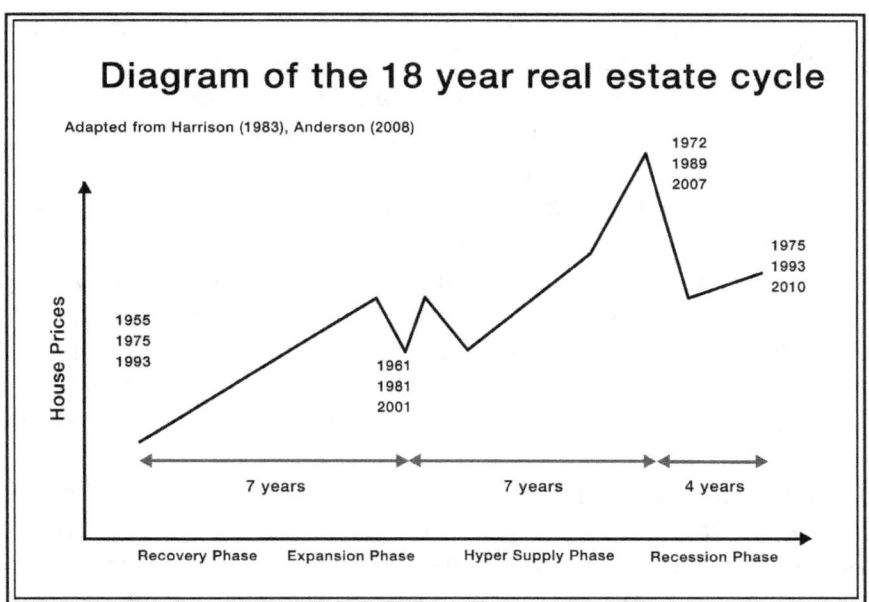

property investment decisions.

As a big tip for you, when considering investment opportunities, gather all the facts in order to identify in which phase of the property cycle that market is in. Additionally, focus on what's happening with the GDP in this specific area; this type of information can be easily located in bank reports and various government sources.

Check the UK mortgage data information on the market, and with city/regional planning for the area.

Ask questions about the job market, population and economic outlook; ideally there should be growth in all these areas.

Finally, find out what's happening with the market's vacancy rates and new construction/projects that are under development, but don't forget about the lag in these factors in the recovery, expansion, and especially the hyper-supply phases.

Conclusion

I have heard people saying "buy below market value, wait for a while and sell high", but that is easier said than done. It is almost impossible to ascertain the exact location of where we are in the cycle. The key to our decision-making process should be specific localised data (every road is a is a micro economy) and previous localised property cycles. Understanding the direction in which the cycle is heading, based upon the key factors we have discussed previously, could be life changing.

If you want to take a big nugget from us, please make sure that you fully understand the real estate cycle and its phases (I'd read this chapter again and again if I were you). This will enable you to make an informed (backed up by data), strategic decision about your property investment journey. We are all sick of hearing 'location, location, location' as the key to successful property development and investing. I'd now like to challenge this with the strong belief, backed up by data, that when to buy is most critical; knowing the current phase of the real estate cycle for the market in which you are interested. The reality is that location is secondary.

Ideally, what we should all be aiming for is buying assets or investing in developments that are about to start, or already in, the expansion phase, to minimise risk if you are thinking of selling at the end of the cycle. However, as I am a very risk-averse person who invests for the long term (hence why Assets for Life is the name of one of my companies), '' I try to hold the asset for as long as I can. Therefore, the cycle typically does not affect my long-term strategy. However, for a more opportunistic, risk-seeking investor, such as one specialising in flips, buying and selling between the contraction and the recovery phase can have its rewards. Flipping properties can be quite lucrative in the latter stages of the expansion phase, but it is the part of phase that can carry the highest risk if your only exit is a sale.

Carrying out some deep, localised research, and being aware of the key factors influencing the market, in which you are interested, as well as the characteristics of the upward phases of the real estate cycle, will enable you to make informed, and very lucrative, decisions about your property development and investment journey. If you don't do this, you can easily go bankrupt.

Kinaesthetic learning

Based on the above life-changing information, you now need to research a specific property cycle for your chosen gold mine area.

It is up to you if you want to do this for a specific road, postcode or city.

Once you have done this, compare it with the national cycle and see how it differs, where the opportunities are, and start applying all the knowledge.

Remember that only applied knowledge is power! Make it happen!

Help to Buy

Help to Buy is designed help purchasers struggling to buy a new-build home. At the time of writing, it offers a maximum 20 per cent (40 per cent in London) equity loan (minimum 10 per cent) on new-build properties up to a maximum purchase price of £600,000.

Launched in April 2013, with an initial budget of £3.7bn, the programme aspired to support 74,000-plus homebuyers in the first three years. The government's 2015 spending review confirmed £8.6bn of funding and extended the programme to 2021 to assist an anticipated 145,000 purchases. In October 2017, the government announced it will invest a further £10 billion in the Help to Buy Equity Loan programme.

More than 130,000 completions have already taken place by people using the equity loan, which helps people buy a new-build home with only a five per cent deposit.

The new funding means that the Help to Buy Equity Loan could help around 135,000 more people to buy homes by 2021. This would bring the total number of households across England that would be supported through the scheme since it began in 2013 to around 360,000.

Gearing

Gearing is the term that we developers use when we borrow from someone else to pay for a development or an investment. A mortgage is the most usual type, where a buyer arranges to acquire a property by paying part of the purchase price (deposit), raising the remainder by means of a loan from a building society or bank, which is then repaid with interest, usually at regular intervals over an agreed term.

The lender's terms will specify the duration of the loan and the rate of interest, almost certainly subject to adjustment according to the cost of money in the market. In this way, the borrower has found a way to acquire a property, the value of which is greater than the resources that are currently available, whilst the lender has identified a reasonably safe investment with regular payments of interest and capital, backed up by the security of the building.

Developers of commercial property may wish to borrow a large proportion of the development costs, secured on the land and the proposed development. This creates a much greater risk because the development is no more than an intention; there may be no lettings on completion, tenants will need to be found and a rent will need to be set, all of which are all uncertain because the conditions at some future date cannot be guaranteed. To that extent, there are significant risks in funding any development, and the lender will expect to be rewarded. The reward may be in the form of a higher interest rate; or, in return for favourable terms, a share of the investment on completion; and very often personal guarantees in case the project goes pear-shaped.

Where the lender provides a long-term loan for the completion of the development, the developer is committed to making the agreed upon, regular payments, regardless of the income produced from the development. Should there be delay letting or selling some of the units, the borrower will remain liable to make the payments under the agreement. It is essential that the borrower is still able to make the payments in these circumstances, so the finance arrangement should be examined carefully, to ensure that no undue risks are undertaken.

External intervention

In principle, as far as a free market economy is concerned, the government refrain from controlling the market, thereby leaving them free to act according to any event. However, government intervention may be needed to make sure the economy reactivates or bounces back.

This general rule is tempered by the need for government to set the framework of the economy, by determining the level of taxation and the way in which it is levied, and to allocate the funds as it sees fit.

In the UK, apart from income and capital gains taxation, central government oversees the collection of excise duty, value added tax (VAT), and stamp duty. It delegates other tasks to local government, in particular the collection of business rates and council tax. In a few cases, the local authorities have discretion as to whether to collect a particular charge or to fix the level of the charge, as is the case with the community infrastructure levy charge and section 106. In the UK, the detailed application of planning policy is within the remit of local authorities; planning charges are levied on applications for planning permission, change of use, and other aspects of planning. Charities and some other bodies do not incur tax on their fundamental work, and may qualify for recovery of tax at a fixed level, on donations received in money or kind from supporters.

At the time of writing, we are in the middle of a section 24 that was introduced in April 2017 and is being phased in over for four years. It means that you will no longer be able to claim mortgage interest, or any other property finance, as tax deductible. Instead, rental profit will be taxed with a maximum deduction for finance costs of 20 per cent, the basic tax rate, by 2021. The full name of the legislation is section 24 of the Finance (no. 2) Act 2015, also known as the 'tenant tax' because of the legal case launched to challenge it.

The property owner is free to own and manage the asset in whatever way is most advantageous, subject to the law of respect for the rights of others and any relevant statutory provisions. Most of the restrictions imposed by central and local government both affect and protect the property owner, and it is not difficult to imagine the problems that would result if there were no central oversight.

The principle, but not always the detail, of planning law is accepted, as it confers benefits as well as duties. However, the investor does not expect to have restrictions unless they are necessary. Further, it could be expected that landlords and tenants are able to negotiate their own relationships.

Chapter Nine

Introduction

This chapter starts by looking at the different types of property development and concentrates initially on the evaluation/appraisals which developers need to carry out to assess the bid they should submit for purchasing a piece of land.

Rather than just illustrate the calculation, the approach followed is to take a detailed analysis of the appraisal, illustrating how a developer needs to build a set of assumptions about the development envisaged. The type of assumptions required, and the way values are ascribed to them, are considered in detail.

Once all the assumptions have been made, the calculation can then be carried out. This is examined in detail.

This approach means that this chapter is rather long and, on the surface, complex.

In justification, it is intended to provide a comprehensive introduction to appraisal. Developers should have a good grasp of appraisal in order to be able to make sound decisions in the development process.

This book also accepts that appraisals are increasingly being carried out using specialist software. At AFL, we have created a simple spreadsheet version.

As a way of kinaesthetic learning, I have provided a live case study where we are building 14 flats and two offices in Loughton, Essex, UK.

The step-by-step process

There are a variety of points of view on, and descriptions of, the property metamorphosis process. At its most simple, property development can be likened to any industrial production process that involves the combination of various team players in order to achieve an output or product.

In the case of property development, the product is a pure metamorphosis of land use and/or a new or altered building that then becomes a beautiful asset to serve several purposes. This process combines time, land, labour, materials, and money. However, property development is complex, often taking place over a considerable timeframe depending on is the level of complexity. And the end product is unique, either in terms of its physical appearance and/or its geographical location. This could be a nice, warm home for a family, which is our primary focus at AFL, or any other civil infrastructure. It is also important to highlight that not many other processes operate under such constant public scrutiny.

The property development process may be divided into the following main stages:

1. Types of property development
2. Initiation
3. Evaluation
4. Acquisition
5. Design and costing
6. Permissions
7. Commitment
8. Implementation
9. Let/manage/dispose

However, property development is not an entirely sequential activity and the stages in the process often overlap or repeat. The sequence is typical of a speculative development where an occupier is not sought until the building has been completed. For example, if the development is pre-sold to an occupier, then stage eight precedes stages two to seven.

1. Types of property development

Some of the diversity covered by the catch-all phrase 'property development' can be appreciated when the different types of development are reviewed. These can be classified by the type of change in the property considered, as detailed below:

• New build: development on a previously undeveloped site, such as virgin land
• New build – brownfield: development on a previously-used site, such as one with factories
• Redevelopment – demolition: clearance and new build of a functional

and similar building
- Redevelopment – partial demolition: partial new build of horizontal and vertical extensions
- Refurbishment: retention of existing structure which is renewed or rebuilt, such as dwelling houses to houses of multiple occupation
- Conversion/change of use: existing structure substantially retained but for different use (eg. from office to residential use)

It is important to point that these divisions are not absolutes. It is easy to get combinations of these classifications in the same development, but they are useful sub-divisions.

2. Initiation

In addition to the types of property development, classified above, it is important to consider the motives of the body initiating the development which, again, can severely affect the outcome and the whole process. The common theme is that all development releases some kind of 'net cash' profit. This profit may be in the 'normal' mode of money return, but it might also be in the form of 'social profit' in terms of additional value to the community.

Some of the purposes for private sector development can be broken down as follows:

Initiator	Purpose	Motives
Private sector property developer	Develop property for sale or letting to third parties	Development profit Return on capital invested
Investor	Develop property for letting to third parties and for selling on to other investors in the long term	Development profit Return on capital invested
Corporate sector	Develop property for own occupation and use	1. Enhance profit-making potential of business operations 2. Acquire valuable tangible asset

In addition to the above, there are also public sector developments created for profit, non-profit, and combinations or hybrids; such examples are Private Finance Initiative (PFI)/Public Private Partnership (PPP) projects, where the government or some other public body is the initiator while the private sector is the executor. Before my current property development journey, I was proudly involved in several civil infrastructure transport schemes.

A property metamorphosis is initiated when either a parcel of land, or site, is considered suitable for a different, or more, dense use; or if demand for a particular use leads to a search for a suitable site. In this book, we will focus attention on residential, shops (or retail), and office uses.

Often, residential, office or industrial uses are combined; an example of a building suitable for such uses is described in the next chapter.

The desire to develop may come from any party or stakeholder in the development process seeking an appropriate site in anticipation of the demand or need for any of the above uses.

Alternatively, the initiative may stem from stakeholders anticipating a potentially higher value in the use of an existing site, due to perpetual changes such as population growth, economic, political, physical, or other circumstances. In this case, in order to identify the most appropriate use, the initiator will seek to research the market and define the potential to obtain the necessary statutory planning consent for the change of use.

The roles of the various different stakeholders in initiating the process are examined under 'team players' later in this chapter. The initiator may not necessarily be involved in the rest of the developmental process, depending on their motive or objective.

A key factor affecting the property metamorphosis of the past century in the UK has been the never-ending increase of parties eager to take part in this transformation. By the beginning of the 21st century, a wider variety of institutions are, or have been, key players in the development market. A full list of team players in the market would be almost never-ending. However, below are some the bodies that have a consistently significant influence on the market and the process:
- Property developers
- Banks
- Utility companies
- Pension funds
- Landowners

- Other financial institutions
- Local authorities
- Central government
- Property consultants and agents
- Pressure groups

End users

It is vital to identify the team players and their roles within the development process. This book is intended as a guide and concentrates on the philosophies and motives of the developers more than any other team players.

Landowners

There are a number of different categories of landowner, although ultimately it is the Crown from which the roots of land ownership arise. This section attempts to summarise the key players. The landowner is stated first, followed by examples, nature of holdings and comments.

The Crown Estates

Examples:
- Royal palaces e.g. Buckingham Palace
- Royal estates e.g. Balmoral estate

Traditional estates exist in many parts of England, Wales and Scotland. Landowners tend not to release land for major-scale development. The role of these estates is largely for the preservation of the status quo. Exceptions do exist, such as Poundbury, Prince Charles's experiment in sustainable development.

Traditional landed estates

Examples:
- Grosvenor estates
- Howard de Walden estates

Traditional estates had significant rural and urban landholdings.

With the development of urban centres, many of these landholdings are now located in high-value locations close to city centres.

This is particularly true in the centre of London, where significant parts of the West End are owned by the landed estates.

Some of the landed estates have little or no involvement in development, or the land and property markets.

Others, including the two listed above, are significant players and have used their landowning as a springboard for the establishment of major property companies. In the case of Grosvenor, this has extended far beyond the original estate boundaries.

Central government

Some examples are:
- Land owned by agencies of central government
- Direct government-owned land, e.g. Ministry of Defence estate

These large landowners own substantial areas of the country, particularly as part of the defence estate; including army bases, ports, air bases, and associated housing for the staff.

They also own major areas of rural land, such as Salisbury Plain, for testing, training and exercises, and live firing.

The secret arms of government (MI5 and MI6, defence research, etc) also are under this umbrella.

Agencies of central government include: air traffic control, the civil service commission, offices of government agencies like job centres, and parts of the NHS.

In recent years, the UK government has become less directly involved in property development.

This trend has increased with the development of the Private Finance Initiative and Public Private Partnerships.

The extent of their landholdings, however, still makes them highly influential in the development market.

This has been notable in recent years, with the release of significant parts of the defence estate, in particular old army bases that have since been converted into new neighbourhoods.

Ex-public sector utilities

Examples:
- Network Rail
- Transport for London
- British Waterways
- Electricity generation companies
- Former coal board sites

Many of the old publicly-owned corporations that were set up in the post-1945 nationalised environment had acquired substantial land ownership through the widespread application of their compulsory purchase powers. Landholdings include rail lines and adjacent land, canals and tow paths, with the addition of large tracts of land adjacent to water plus significant amounts of land formerly held by other bodies.

A lot of the land held by these bodies is still used for its original purpose; however, much is now surplus to requirement. This situation has existed for years and was exploited by many of these organisations while they were still in public ownership. British Rail had an active property arm that developed much of the valuable land adjacent to, and sometimes over, the station sites in major cities, particularly in central London and Cambridge. British Waterways acted in a similar way. The many private sector companies that took over these bodies also have the potential to develop their assets. This may increase in future years as many of the traditional factory-based industries in the UK continue to decline.

Institutional investors

Examples:
- Life assurance companies (e.g. Prudential, Scottish Widows, etc)
- Pension funds (e.g. National Farmers' Union, PosTel, etc)

Institutional investors hold land as an investment, i.e. to receive income or to obtain growth in capital values, or both. Landholdings include large tracts of agricultural and forestry land.

Institutional investors are active players in the development market, as described below. The large-scale landholdings that are owned outside the major urban cities are, however, rarely bought for development purposes.

Chapter Nine

3. Evaluation and financial appraisal

One of the key stages of the property development metamorphosis is evaluation, as it influences the decision-making of the developer throughout. Evaluation comprises customer feedback, deep market research, both in general and road-specific terms, and the financial appraisal of the proposal. The process of financial evaluation needs to ensure that the cost of the development is reasonable and feasible. For private sector developments, the evaluation establishes the potential for profit in relation to the specific project risks incurred, while for the public sector and non-profit making organisations, it will attempt to ensure that the costs are recovered if applicable. An additional objective of the financial appraisal is to establish the value of the land/site.

This stage of the process should be undertaken prior to any financial commitment, and while the developer retains the option to opt out or continue with the land purchase. Though the evaluation involves the combined advice of the developer's professional team, particularly the quantity surveyor (QS) or cost consultant, the decision to proceed and bear all the risk rests ultimately with the property developer. It is a continuous process with constant monitoring, relating directly to all the other stages.

The initial motivation for having a savings pot is to have a safety net available, should unexpected costs arise. In addition, there is a general concern that the future is better provided for where there are savings, the return on which will be available to augment; for example, a SSAS, SIP or normal pension, or even to provide one. When an individual has a level of income sufficient to go beyond just a required standard of living, there are three broad choices: increase spending, donate some of it to charitable causes, or reserve some or all of the surplus for wealth accumulation and as a foil to the uncertainties of the future. It is important to note that any savings accumulated in this way should be invested effectively; otherwise, the value of the capital is reduced by the effect of inflation. At the present time in the UK, the interest rates are low and a level of inflation exists, so it is possible for the total amount saved to have a lower.purchasing power. Hence, you are getting poorer. Savings may be intended to act as an insurance against a future expenditure, such as health issues, school fees, a major purchase, to repay a mortgage, or retirement income.

There is an unlimited type and range of investments available, although the modest saver would wish to avoid the more volatile ones which, while capable of providing substantial gains, may put capital at undue risk.

The choice that we all have is between spending it or wisely investing; the last one is more likely to take place where a reasonable Return On Investment (ROI) may be accurately predicted, usually based on past experience. That return may be from regular interest payments, in capital gains or a combination of the two. The ROI tends to vary depending on factors such as risk and opportunity. There is a hierarchy of investment opportunities where, in general, a high return implies a higher risk level. It is important that investment decisions are made after a detailed feasibility study and full risk register allocation, like the one we perform for all of our property development metamorphoses.

Property investors have a range of opportunities open to them. They will look for trust, first in the person behind the investment and then in a satisfactory ROI which reflects the level of risk inherent in any particular circumstance.

Development appraisal is vital

A feasibility study, also called a financial appraisal, is one of the most important aspects of assessing the viability of a development project. Deal analysis, as we call it at AFL, is used throughout the development process to fulfil a number of key objectives.

First, development appraisals are used to determine the price that should be paid for a piece of land or a site to be converted. Land for development has no intrinsic, or set, value. Development land has a value derived from the use to which it can be put. Each scheme proposed for any plot of land will generate a different land value. A landowner will generally sell to the developer who submits the highest viable bid. The appraisal process, when used to determine land value, determines the highest bid that a potential developer can make and still meet their target return.

Secondly, they are essential to determine the predicted profit, or otherwise loss, that any particular project will make. This is vitally important, not only to show the developer whether the scheme is viable, but also as a tool to obtain senior or junior finance. Potential financial backers, be it commercial lenders or potential purchasers, of the final development are not primarily interested in the aesthetics of the scheme, or the cleverness of its technical solution. They are mostly only concerned about their financial viability and if they are going to get the predicted ROI.

Chapter Nine

The reality is that both senior and private equity lenders will scrutinise each specific deal analysis carefully before shelling any cash at it. They will essentially be looking at the following:

1. If all the assumptions made and the programme of works for each specific development are sound. For this, they will ask several key questions, such as: are the assumptions made about the Gross Development Value (GDV) of the scheme sound? Is the development going to take as long to build based on the specific risks? Is the selling or leasing programme realistic? Are the construction costs a true reflection of the market? Us developers will have to prove that the components of the appraisal are soundly based.
2. If all the above questions are answered correctly, then the financier will look closely at the level profit margin predicted by the developer. Financiers must be satisfied that the developer will achieve a sufficient profit margin, ideally around 25 per cent on cost for residential **(See table on next page)**. This is because the profit level also represents a risk for each specific development. In very simple terms, the larger the profit margin , the less the risk that the borrower will default because there is less chance that the scheme will go into deficit if things go pear-shaped. There are no set criteria as to the expected margin that all lenders require. Nevertheless, the deal analysis must be carried out early in the lifespan of the project, essentially at the feasibility stage. Later in the project lifespan, other uses of appraisals are common.
3. The effects of planning gains i.e. adding saleable volume to the scheme, altering layout as per my chapter 'Layout is king', reworking, or re-timing a project. Projects often require rethinking during their lives. The appraisal is used to see the outcome of these proposed changes. In my next chapter, I will explain using a live project during which we got planning permission for an extra two penthouses after we started the construction period.
4. The deal analysis can be either a sophisticated or very simple monitoring tool used during the course of development. At AFL, we have created one tool for small, single units and another for multiple units.

This section will cover all of these potential uses of the deal analysis, in turn.

Approximation of what lenders have historically looked for

Type of scheme	Normal return on cost required by lenders (per cent)
Speculative commercial	20
Commercial with pre-lettings	10-20
Residential	15-25

Development Appraisals

Deal analyses are paramount. However, it is important to be aware of all the input data that is required for these appraisals. The outcome is often extraordinarily sensitive to change in some of the key factors and variables, and the appraiser is required to make assumptions about uncertain factors when building the appraisal model. This is inevitable, as the appraisal is a prediction into an uncertain future, and deals with constantly-changing factors. Therefore, the developer must make assumptions about: rental demands levels in the future; Join Venture partners' emotions; occupier requirements; interest rate levels; the timing of several factors, such as how long the scheme will take to get through extra planning, to build, to let, to sell. The list is almost never-ending! It is also inevitable that some of the assumptions made in the model will be wrong, and that developers will allow themselves to be too optimistic about the end result when they get attached to a scheme (I have been there several times myself). We, as developers, are optimistic people; risk-takers who need to see the up side to actually take the risk. Development appraisals can, with very minor differences in assumptions, be made to show just about anything from a given set of facts, and can therefore be easily manipulated and easy to mislead, either deliberately or unconsciously.

Here is a personal anecdote that may illustrate this important point. As a chartered civil engineer, I worked for big construction companies in central London. Part of the job involved bidding for new projects and coming up with value engineering options.

Part of my main role in the firm was preparing formal valuations and valuation reports, a role which required a degree of conservatism to produce a realistic valuation figure on which the user could rely. When I carried out development appraisals on projects submitted, almost all of my appraisals suggested that the projects would make a loss, or that the sale figure for the contract could not be supported.

My senior team members (finance directors) were, however, keen to proceed with the project. Their own appraisals clearly told them a different story, even though they dealt with the same proposed scheme, as the same sites, and in the same market as my own appraisal.

So, who was making the right call? The answer is that we were probably both WRONG! And both RIGHT! Only time would tell how wrong, or right, we both were. It is too easy to look at the downside; or to be too optimistic.

The former could lead to never carrying out a development, the latter to financial ruin. Clearly, one must find the middle ground, but this area is never clearly labelled.

The only sensible course of action is to become aware of the frailties and failures of both deal analysis and human emotions. We humans are creatures of emotion. It is essential that the characteristics of each financial appraisal are fully explored, checked, and rechecked by different,competent people. In particular, it is extremely important that a risk assessment is undertaken along with a development appraisal. This is also referred to as 'sensitivity analysis' and 'project specific risk register' within the development world, although, strictly speaking, sensitivity analysis is just one of a family of risk appraisal techniques that can be applied.

Development appraisals can be carried out by answering two 'what' and two 'how' basic questions. They are:

1. What is the real value of the land/site?
2. What net profit margin will be made from the development?
3. How much is the total construction budget for the proposed development?
4. How long is it going to take to complete the development?

The answer to these four questions represents the factor that is unknown at the time of the appraisal. This can be illustrated by looking at the basic components of a development appraisal to assess land value:

Gross development value/value of scheme on completion
minus
costs of development
minus
developer's profit
equals
value of land (the unknown part of the equation)

Here, the developer/appraiser knows the top four items. The balancing sum, the unknown, the residual, is the land value for the purpose proposed by the developer. Compare this with the developer wanting to know what profit can be made on a development. Is it sufficient to go ahead with this scheme, or to purchase a piece of land at the asking price?

In this case, the developer must know the price of the land and must form a judgement about the other items. The one piece that is left, the residual in this case, is the profit (or loss) figure to balance the equation:

gross development value/value of scheme on completion
minus
costs of development
minus
price of land
equals
developer's profit (the unknown part of the equation)

By a process of elimination, the third alternative considered is where both the profit figure and the price of the land are known. This may occur when the land, or the building being redeveloped, is already owned; but it can also occur in other circumstances, such joint venturing with the owner. Here, the unknown is the total construction budget. Hence:

value of scheme on completion
minus
value of land
minus
developer's profit
equals
budget for development (the unknown part of the equation)

Although there are many different ways to ascertain the level of risk for any specific development, the fundamental steps above underlie them all. The two most common across the UK, and worldwide, are the ones that we have mentioned here; and it is these that we will concentrate on from now onwards.

The basic development appraisal model

There is a traditional model where many of the assumptions made are implicit; but there are also more explicit and complex cash flow models which, in my view, are too complicated to use and explain to investors.

Across the UK, property market Discounted Cash Flow (DCF) is most widely applied during deal analysis. In fact, as in other areas of valuation, the truth about the two models is that they are essentially two versions of the same outcome. Both the traditional and DCF approaches are, in fact, discounted cash flow approaches. The former is, however, a greatly simplified DCF. This simplification has both disadvantages and advantages; a disadvantage being that simplification leads to inaccuracies that can be expensive. The advantages include saving time and ease of interpretation by all parties.

Rather than one being more accurate than the other in all circumstances, each has their particular use and a developer needs to be familiar with both types of approach. As a rule of thumb, the traditional approach is best applied in the early stages of a project, such as the initial feasibility, where the details of the proposed scheme are not finalised; while the time and effort required to construct a DCF are best rewarded when the scheme's details are at more of an advanced stage, eg having construction drawings and accurate quotes from designer and contractors.

The reality is that much of these calculations are artificial; reflecting a historical fact that, before the advent of personal computers, appraisal was restricted by calculation difficulties. Some calculations were too problematical or too time-consuming for accurate estimation; as a result, the traditional residual appraisal approach contains substantial simplifications. These simplifications may lead to costly inaccuracies if risks have not been eliminated or mitigated as a last resort.

Other approaches are superior, especially with the commercial development software available; although often presenting results in a traditional format, one must carry out the calculations in a sophisticated way (usually using a cash flow). The traditional presentation has advantages in terms of the clarity of the presentation, which simplifies the whole process.

We will first examine the traditional AFL approach. The starting point will be the reverse-engineered calculation of a bid price for the site/land. In order to do this, we need a site to analyse. This could be a small single unit or multiple units.

Base site for appraisal

The base scenario we will use for the appraisals is a medium-sized residential development; a commercial conversion office to residential of seven flats and two houses (my first medium-sized development in the UK).These are real numbers, based on 2018 market conditions.

The site under consideration is 650 m2, close to the city centre in the established business area. There was obsolete 50-year-old stone masonry and the site was both derelict and vacant. Here are some photos of the area when we bought it:

The peat ground meant poor bearing capacity and there was also contamination on the site. The title had a ransom strip around it, hence legal encumbrances. The site was partially serviced with electricity and a combined sewer runs to one side of the site. It is not in a conservation area. There was a detailed planning consent for the site to be developed for seven flats and two houses, up to a total built area of 590m2. It was envisaged that a modern, block work and precast beams-framed building would be constructed on the site. The specification was typical of a medium-specification building in such a location.

The residential market had been good over the past decade, with indications that there was sufficient demand for a development of this size. The development was speculative, i.e. the building was marketed as it nears completion and was not to be built for any specific client, and we developers intended to sell all the units.

Once the building was sold, we also sold the freehold with the benefit of the lease, to an investor.

Some of the assumptions in this scenario give an indication of the areas where complexity can creep into the development appraisal and process.

A development value is derived from a combination of physical factors, the legal and planning environment, and market conditions. Although property development is not rocket science, as an experienced developer once remarked, "the context in which it takes place is often amazingly complex, and the appraiser must be aware of this and consider all these factors".

This list of assumptions, or the facts that the appraiser must gather in real life, must be specifically related to each development. This stage is effectively an accounting exercise, with all the key factors being considered. It is common to whichever appraisal method is applied.

Before we started the development, the specific areas where assumptions were made were broken down into four broad areas:

- The building dimensions
- The timing of the development and its stages
- The costs related to the development
- The factors related to its value

Each of these broad categories will be considered in turn. It should be noted that our AFL in-house deal analyser was used in the construction of this appraisal.

The specific assumptions

In summary, the specific assumptions which were fed into the financial appraisal pertinent to this site are listed below. How each was derived will be considered in turn.

Building dimensions

One of the key factors that will influence the value of the site is clearly what can be built on the site. A number of factors will affect this:

1. The physical and volumetric/spatial characteristics of the site
2. The planning and legal situation
3. What your customers want and need

Each of these will now be explained below.

1. The volumetric characteristics of the site

Clearly, this is a very important factor with a number of interrelated issues which affect individual sites. The dimensions are obviously important, but the shape is also very influential in terms of the number and size of buildings that can be built. Narrow sites, or those which are irregularly shaped, can lead to problems with access and spacing of individual buildings. In city centre locations, where 100 per cent site coverage is to be expected, these factors can lead to challenges with layout, access and uneconomic remnants of sites.

Other factors to consider include the bearing capacity of the ground and topography, i.e. the shape of the ground surface (slopes, etc). These can be negated by the design or engineering of the building. An example is poor ground-bearing capacity which can be corrected by piled foundations. The main impact of these factors is cost and reducing the profitability of development; and only indirectly on the quantum of built area that can be constructed.

In this case, as noted, the city centre location implies 100 per cent coverage. The site is regularly shaped, so there is no loss of space. The building-on plan will maximise the site area, and so will therefore be around 650 m2 on plan.

2. The planning and legal situation

The planning system is a major bone of contention in the UK and has a major influence on the quantum of buildings produced, as well as the type of development allowed in particular areas.

Planning authorities can impose density regulations on sites, allowing only a certain number of dwellings per hectare or a certain percentage of site coverage or, as in this case, a restriction on total built area. They can also have requirements for certain types of development to be included on sites, such as low-cost housing or starter industrial units where the developer, if unrestricted, would develop a higher proportion of the most valuable use. Other ways that the quantum developed can be restricted is by height restrictions, requirements for setbacks (allowing a gap between the building and the street) and building lines.

For decades, car parking has been a major concern for the planning authorities, particularly within big, congested and polluted cities around the world. Urban authorities have been preoccupied with the increase in transport congestion, limited parking, and the pollution caused by a never-ending increase in non-electric vehicles. In an attempt to counter this, they have tended to impose maximum limits on the number of car spaces that can be provided.

This has not restricted built area but has, of course, influenced it greatly. An alternative approach is for planning authorities to impose a car parking requirement per unit of built floor area, for example one space per 200m2. This happens when the authorities want developers to provide spaces so that public or on-street spaces in the locality are not placed under pressure, or when the authorities are trying to restrict the amount of useable space developed.

Planning authorities work within the framework of the Town and Country Planning Acts and within the rules laid down by legal precedents. Their ability to impose restrictions on development is not, therefore, infinite and there are some things that they cannot do legally, even if they want to. One way in which planning authorities can get around this is by entering development agreements under section 106 the Town and Country Planning Act 1990 (now covered under the revised Planning and Compulsory Purchase Act 2004), which can influence the shape and form of development. For example, a development site within an established retail park area which was suffering from excess traffic problems. The purchasers of the site were required to enter into a section 106 agreement which:
- restricted the site to non-retail development; and
- allowed for a development that would accommodate no more than 100 employees in the buildings.

This naturally has a direct effect on the built area.

Development sites can be either freehold or long (in excess of 50 years) leasehold tenure. In the latter case, the detail of the lease contract can determine what is built on the site; indeed, that is often the reason that bodies such as local authorities retain the freehold ownership of a site while granting a long lease to an occupier or developer.

The lease allows control, either specifically in the construction of clauses, or simply by requiring the landlord's permission to carry out developments or make alterations. This extra element of control is one of the key reasons why the value of sites held on leasehold tenure is always lower than that of sites held freehold.

Freehold sites are not, however, unrestricted. It is quite common for owners to place covenants on the title that will run with the land and bind future owners to abide by their requirements.

These restrictive covenants are often related to future development by the type, size or, in some cases, the materials to be used. Other covenants include giving certain rights to third parties, such as the right to extract particular minerals, or to graze animals or hold markets. Some of these restrictions on the title of land can have a major influence on the building that may be constructed on the site.

Historic or unreasonable covenants can be altered or extinguished by application to the Lands Tribunal in England and Wales, or by agreement with the relevant beneficiary of the covenant; but the process can be time-consuming and is by no means certain.

Other legal issues that can affect the form and size of the development include easements, wayleaves, rights of way and rights of light. Easements and wayleaves give rights over land to things such as pipes, cables and electrical transmission lines. Rights of way allow access over the land.

Rights of light are enjoyed by neighbours to the site. All these issues need to be fully investigated because they can often have a major influence on what can be built on a site and where. In a historical and densely developed country such as the UK, it is very rare indeed for a site to be unaffected by some of these legal factors.

3. What your customers want and need
I strongly believe that as an entrepreneur/property developer, you have to forget about yourself and focus on your customers.

In most for-profit developments, the requirements of the market listed below are paramount in determining the built form:
- Dwelling houses have requirements for certain features in residential developments;
- Retailers from particular sectors will only occupy units of a certain size, shape and layout;
- Industrial and warehouse users need units of specific sizes, heights

and with sufficient service areas to meet their needs;
- Office users require buildings of particular specifications and size, not only in terms of volume but also in particulars – such as sizes and shapes of floor patterns, lights, etc.

All these factors must be taken into account when the size and form of the building being developed is considered.

The four listed above have been considered in the dimensions of the building, as laid down in the assumptions. Questions may be raised regarding the net floor area of the building. This is a requirement related to the valuation of commercial buildings, particularly shops and offices. Occupiers of these types of buildings will only pay for the space they can actually use for their business. In an office, for example, space lost to columns, lifts, staircases, circulation space, internal walls, toilets and kitchens is, in most cases, excluded for the purposes of calculating rent. How a building should be measured is laid down in the Code of Measurement Practice produced by the Royal Institution of Chartered Surveyors (RICS). Whatever the case, just as we need to calculate the built area in order to determine the cost of construction, so we need to ascertain the net area of the building in order to assess its value.

Time is your biggest asset

Time is always critical to the success of a development. It is very important in the appraisal, and it is related closely to money – the longer a development takes, the more interest is charged, or the greater the costs incurred through giving up the right to use the money. The longer a development takes to complete, the longer the developer has to wait to recoup the capital expenditure. Money receivable in the future is worth less than money receivable now.

The time value of money needs to be carefully taken into account in the appraisal.

A development can usually be broken down into four broad phases. The first is referred to as the deal finding; this is period where lots of time is spent trying to find a deal that is commercially viable.

It can take months, even years, to find a deal that meets all the criteria for any given developer. At the present time, this is the criteria for our systems and procedures at AFL:

Document – 001
Decision to Bid Criteria

Sl. No.	Category	Description
1	Location	----------
2	Transportation	Close Proximity - 5 miles max
3	Size of site	up to £----mn GDV
4	Number of units	5- 35 Units
5	Local Amenities	Walking distance to schools, shops, restaurants etc
6	Flood Risk	check the area for proximity to streams, sea, lakes etc- http://www.checkmyfloodrisk.co.uk/
7	Ground Checks	contamination checks for the groundworks and area
8	Area Checks	criminal/ social area
9	Affordability	within London under £600k, out of London under £400k
10	Listings	check if the building has any listings against it
11	Planning	check any existing/ prior planning/ article 4 planning
12	Access	how is the site accessed- need for new roads etc?
13	Rental Stress Test	perform the rental stress test**

Rental Stress Test
1. Yearly Revenue = Total Rent (pcm) x 12
2. Net Revenue = Yearly Revenue / 125%
3. Asset Valuation = Net Revenue / Five-Yr Interest Rate
4. Re-Finance = Asset Valuation x 75%
5. Total Cash-in/out = Re-finance – Project Cost

Positive value in *Item 5* passes the Rental Stress Test

The second is the planning phase. This is the period that may start with the initial expenditure on the development, such as the purchase of land. Nevertheless, it is more accurate to consider it as commencing from the point where the decision is made to begin development, or the actual time of the initial appraisal. It is during this period that the development is designed, or the detailed design is finalised. All necessary consents are obtained in this period – planning, listed building, fire and safety and building regulation consents are just some of the things that need to be put into place. The contract documentation for the construction works is prepared and any title problems can also be resolved during this time.

There is no easy formula for determining the length of this period. Obviously, the rule of thumb is that it will be shortest in simple developments and will lengthen as complex issues increase; but beyond this, it is hard to generalise. If there are major planning issues, such as the development proposal being in conflict with the local authority development plan, or where consent has been refused, the planning phase may be lengthy. This is a situation where there is no substitute for experience, particularly within the development team. Some guidance can be obtained by looking at what has happened in the past with similar schemes. In our example, the planning period has been assessed as being 12 months long.

The timing of the second phase of development is easier to assess in most cases, although there can still be major problems. The construction phase is the period that commences with the start of site works and usually ends at practical completion, when the building is handed over from the contractor to the developer or building owner. In a traditional development, the developer employs a single building contractor to complete the project in an agreed time period and at an agreed cost.

The timing of this phase can be assessed in a number of ways. The most reliable way is to consult a construction professional who has experience of the type of scheme planned, such as a project manager (PM) and/or quantity surveyor (QS). They can also assess the cost implications. In larger schemes, it will be the PM or QS in tandem with the other professional team members (particularly the architect, structural engineer, service engineer and construction manager) who will assess the timing issues. On smaller scale projects, direct discussions with contractors may assist the assessment. Some guidance may also be found in building price books, but these are only approximate guides.

A number of issues can affect the timing of the construction phase and the ease of its assessment. Where a greenfield site is being developed and a straightforward type of building is planned, the timing is relatively easy to assess and the estimate is likely to be accurate. The process becomes more difficult, and the accuracy of the prediction less certain, when the site is in an existing urban centre; where there is substantial excavation in unknown ground; where demolition is involved or, particularly, where the work involves the alteration of an existing structure. The difficulties arise where there are unknown, or unusual, aspects to consider and about which assumptions need to be made.

Consider a developer working on the redevelopment of a nondescript 1950s shop in the centre of London (I have done this).

Many of the buildings are historic, with substantial archaeology under the ground surface. There are considerable potential problems with getting access to the site due to the presence of tourists and shoppers. In this case, assessing how long the construction will take once work has commenced on site is not straightforward. It is not easy for the appraiser to find the balance between being too cautious and being overly optimistic. It is here that the importance of sensitivity analysis and risk assessment, becomes apparent in our example; we are assuming that there are few of these challenges. Twelve months has been allowed for the development, which is about par for the course for a city centre office scheme of this size and specification.

The timing of the four broad phases is more problematical. It is the time required for the development to be sold (residential) and/or leased, and to start producing income. This is highly dependent on the state of the market. It is a very sensitive part of the development process, as it is the time when interest charges are accumulating on the full total of the amounts physically expended on the project and the total rolled-up interest to date. The debt charge can rapidly accumulate at this stage.

The letting period is, therefore, an opportunity for the appraiser to be realistic about when the scheme will be let, or be in a position to be sold. It is also a very important risk allowance. The longer the letting period allowed, the more the risk is being offset, i.e. the more cautious the developer is being.

Cost assumptions

There are 12 cost items to consider in our particular appraisal, but this list could be longer if items such as sourcing fees, planning fees, a planning consultant and an environmental consultant were to be included. As noted above, an appraisal consists partly of an accounting exercise.

For the purposes of our example, these items will suffice, particularly as they are the most typical of the cost items involved in a development. Each will be considered in turn.

Chapter Nine

Building costs

Construction costs are micro-economics by postcodes, or even roads by linear metre; building costs are dependent on many factors.

These include the specification of the building, its size and shape, the method of construction used, the nature of the site and its surroundings, its location within the country and the time period required to construct it.

An example of how costs can vary can be seen from the gross cost per square metre of residential construction in the UK, which can vary from £800 to £3,500 per square metre (or even more, spec depending).

Building costs in an appraisal can be determined in a number of ways and the cost data derived from a number of sources.

The methods of estimating building costs break down into three main categories:
- Superficial area
- Elemental cost
- Quantity surveyor's approach.

The superficial area approach simply involves calculating an approximate total cost of the development of all components of the building. For example, if we know that a 1,000m2 building costs £1million to construct, then we can say that the construction cost was £1,000/m2. This figure can then be used to calculate the construction costs of similar buildings.

For example, if we are appraising the development of a similar specification building of 800m2 in the same city, which is going to be built in a year's time, this figure may give us a good guide. Our estimate of building costs may be as follows:

built area (800m2)
multiplied by
construction cost (£2,150/m2 + 5 per cent inflation allowance)
equals
estimated construction costs
£1,806,000

Nothing could be simpler; indeed, this is the method that is used in the vast majority of initial appraisals and is usually perfectly adequate.

However, there are considerable problems with the approach of which the appraiser should be aware.

The fundamental problem is one of comparability that this simplistic approach requires.

Every construction project is different; buildings are not mass-produced, they are hand-built and tailored to meet the differing requirements of the procurer and the differing conditions and characteristics of the site. This is particularly true of commercial properties, each of which tends to be unique.

Two ostensibly similar properties can have quite different construction costs because of differences in ground conditions; or problems with access during normal working hours that forces weekend or evening working; or work that has to be carried out by hand instead of machine, the former being highly expensive.

One particular source of variance is market conditions: at times when there is little work available, firms may build at cost price or below simply to maintain cash flow and keep head office staff employed.

At other times, when there is a glut of work, firms may work with very high profit margins which greatly inflate construction costs.

All these factors can be incorporated in the superficial area approach by adjusting the rate upwards or downwards as they are taken into account. It is, however, always going to be an approximation and is likely to be an inaccurate predictor of actual costs, particularly in complex situations.

The challenges with this approach do not bar its use. It is still, and will continue to be, the most widely used of methods at the initial appraisal stage. However, it is best to be aware of the method's shortcomings so as to avoid being misled into making an incorrect decision based on the costs indicated.

The source of cost data used in this model will be considered below.

The elemental cost approach

The elemental cost approach to the estimation of building cost is not one approach, but a family of approaches that attempts to provide more detail regarding the development, thus achieving greater accuracy. The approach requires the built elements of the building to be divided into elemental components for more accurate cost estimation. These components can be technical, for example substructure, structural frame, structural walls, etc; or else functional, such as parking, office space, etc. This allows a more accurate estimation of cost to be made than with the superficial area method.

The Building Cost Information Service (BCIS) cost element breakdown is as follows:

Element

1 – Substructure (foundations)
2 – Superstructure
    2A Frame
    2B Upper floors
    2C Roof 2D Stairs
    2D External walls
    2E Windows and external doors
    2F Internal walls and partitions
    2G Internal doors
3 – Internal finishes
    3A Wall finishes
    3B Floor finishes
    3C Ceiling finishes
4 – Fittings and furnishings
5 – Services
    5A Sanitary appliances
    5B Services equipment
    5C Disposal installations
    5D Water installations
    5E Heat source
    5F Space heating and air treatment
    5G Ventilating system
    5H Electrical installations
    5I Gas installations
    5J Lift and conveyor installations
    5K Protective installations
    5L Communication installations
    5M Special installations
    5N Builder's work in connection with services
    5O Builder's profit and attendance on services

Building sub-total (excluding external works, preliminaries and contingencies)

6 – External works
    6A Site works
    6B Drainage
    6C External services
    6D Minor building works
7 – Preliminaries
8 – Contingencies

Source and acknowledgement: BCIS Publications

The Quantity Surveyor's (QS) approach

The final approach used in cost estimating is the QS's method. This is the most accurate, but also the most detailed and time-consuming to produce. It requires the building to be broken down into its components, each being accurately measured or estimated, with accurate costs per unit attached to each.

For example; the quantity of concrete used in the foundations would be calculated and a price to supply and fix that component per cubic metre would be assessed. This would be done for each component of the building, the sum of the total costs being the total construction costs less overheads and (usually) profit.

Although this is the most accurate method of cost estimation, it is often not practical in the early stages of a development project's financial appraisal. It requires access to detailed information about the project to justify its use, but this information is often simply not available in the early stages of a development.

Sources of cost information

There are several sources of cost information, which can be used with the models discussed above. This ultimately depends on a number of factors, including which model is used, the type of the development scheme, the exact property cycle point at which the appraisal is being carried out and the speed with which the cost information is required or, more accu-

Chapter Nine

rately, a combination of all of the above factors.

The sources of the data can vary in terms of speed, ease of use, accessibility, and, more importantly, accuracy. Those which are the quickest, cheapest, and easiest to access are also more likely to be the least accurate. There is a trade-off between these factors of which the person constructing the appraisal should be aware.

Some of the basic sources of data that may be available are detailed below.

Building price books

These include those books published by Spon's Architects' and Builders' Price Book 2020. They are commercially available and are compiled from information furnished by contractors and quantity surveyors.

The books contain pricing data suitable for use in all three basic methods of price estimation detailed above.

They also include information useful for calculating the regional variation in construction costs, and for assessing other items related to building cost, such as professional fees.

This source of data is relatively cheap, highly accessible, comparatively easy to use and provides a swift estimation of construction cost.

However, it loses out in terms of accuracy as it provides general, non-site-specific information, which may not reflect the circumstances of the development being addressed.

Quite often, a reasonably accurate estimate of building costs may be made using this method; but there is also a danger that the assessment may be inaccurate, and even misleading, in certain circumstances.

Computerised databases and estimation systems

There are several sources whereby information can be obtained. One of the main ones is produced by the Building Cost Information Service (BCIS). This organisation monitors construction contracts of all types, throughout the UK.

Here is their website: https://calculator.bcis.co.uk

They collate and analyse all the data submitted by their members, and incorporate material from other sources. The information is then made available through several publications and an online service. BCIS is a subsidiary company of the Royal Institute of Chartered Surveyors, and was established in 1962.

Subscribers are provided with data in an accessible form on the current, historic, and probable costs of building maintenance and property occupancy, and they can also access cost information for a wide range of commercial, industrial, residential, and public sector buildings. BCIS provides capital cost information, while the Building Maintenance Index (BMI) covers maintenance management information and building maintenance, property occupancy, and refurbishment costs.

Quantity surveyors

Quantity surveyors are the cost experts of the development team. If a QS is part of the team, she or he should be the normal source of cost information. If a previous relationship exists with a QS, this might still be a viable source of the requisite information.

Main Contractors and subcontractors

Contractors are themselves often valuable sources of cost information. Not only do they have hard information on project costs, they also employ professional estimators to price the construction work prior to bidding. If the developer has worked closely with contractors on previous projects, it may be wise to consult them in order to obtain current market cost information.

Previous development/construction projects

The final source of information on construction cost may come from the developer's own experience of costs on previous projects. Experienced developers hold a valuable well of information from previous schemes.

Risk register and contingency

At AFL, we carry out a risk register for each individual project, which becomes a live document through the project. Here we qualify, score and quantify each individual risk and, if there is a residual risk after mitigation, then we allocate a comfortable portion of money or time for such risk.

It is normal to allow for some degree of contingency in the calculation of design and construction costs. Contingency is effectively an allowance for risk in the design and construction phase. There will always be some items that will be difficult to assess prior to the commencement of work in a construction project. Similarly, when work is underway things can occur which cause construction costs to rise, including unforeseen ground conditions, the effects of adverse weather and the impact of design changes during the construction programme. The contingency is a realistic acceptance that this will occur. This is one area where a degree of pessimism in anticipating future problems allows a realistic appraisal to be made, rather than one that paints a misleading picture of future profits. It may be that the contingency is not used. In this case, a higher level of profit will be made on the completion of the development. This is always more welcome than the reduction in profit that will result from failing to allow for uncertainty.

The level of contingency allowance will vary from development to development. As a rule of thumb, lower levels of contingency allowance will be appropriate in simple developments of conventional buildings on greenfield sites, i.e. situations where the risk levels are low.

A higher contingency level is appropriate where the development is complex.

Particular caution should be taken where the development involves the conversion of an older structure and/or where there is a potential risk of contamination on site.

In this case, a contingency allowance of five to ten per cent is applied to the construction costs only. Some appraisers apply the contingency percentage to all costs of development, including professional design fees. The rules are not set in stone concerning this; it is down to the personal preference of the appraiser (or sometimes to the way that the software package used by the appraiser is constructed).

Professional design fees

Most of the normal cost estimation approaches and sources of cost information reviewed above do not include the cost of employing the professional team.

At AFL, we call it the power team. These costs are not fixed and are open to negotiation. The relative levels of fees will vary according to the size and complexity of the work involved and, often, the length of the developer's previous relationship with the team. The fees can be a fixed amount agreed between the parties, but it is more usual for the team to work for a fee calculated as a percentage of the construction costs. The total fee percentage depends on the number of different professional disciplines required for the project, which naturally depends on the underlying project's complexity. Here, the total percentage is around 10 per cent, which is relatively low.

A range of between 10 and 18 per cent of construction costs should be expected.

This is the situation with a traditionally procured project where the design and production phases of the project are separated. In alternative procurement regimes, such as 'design and build', the design costs are integrated into the construction costs and the total fees will probably, although not certainly, be lower.

It should be noted that recent lending practices of financial institutions have increased the percentage of professional fees that need to be allowed for in the initial appraisal. Banks, in particular, have increasingly insisted on having their own professional team within the project to monitor progress and safeguard the financial outlay.

The cost of this 'shadow' team is borne by the developer. This is, strictly, a cost of arranging finance and may, more appropriately, be included in the finance section of the appraisal, but it may be allowed for within the 'professional fees' section in some appraisals, depending on the preference of the person constructing it.

Marketing

For what we called at AFL 'flips', where you are not building to rent or keep the building , an allowance for marketing the end product will have to be incorporated. This sum covers all advertising, web page generation, renders, aerial photos by drones etc. It is a separate sum from the allowance for selling or leasing the property, which is covered below. As with most things, the sum allowed for marketing depends very much on the nature of the development. The larger and more unusual the development, the larger the budget needs to be. Residential developments often require an on-site presence during the period in which the units are being sold. It is normal to allow for this in the marketing sum.

The marketing allowance built into the appraisal is normally an appropriate lump sum budget that also depends on the product that is being sold.

Letting and sale fees

These are the fees that are paid to the agent who finds, and negotiates with, tenants and/or owner occupiers or Buy To Let (BTL) landlords for each asset that you built. Sale fees apply where owner occupation or

BTL investors are the result of the development, as in many residential schemes. With commercial schemes, it is likely that the occupier will lease space in the development. Agents are paid their fee once the leases have been signed; this fee is typically calculated by agreeing a fixed percentage of the annual rental value of the space which is let, although minimum charges may apply or the agent may work to a lump sum fee. However, this is rarer as it removes the agent's incentive to achieve the best possible rent for the client.

If the investment is to be sold on letting, and this is a common way for developers to recoup the development costs of a project and crystallise the profit, then a second tranche of fees is usually payable. This is for the agreement of the asset sale of the project to an group of investors (possibly pension fund) with a requirement for this type of investment. This sale fee is usually calculated as a percentage of the sale price of the property, typically between 0.5 and 1.5 per cent of this price. Nevertheless, once again a lump sum fee can be agreed. It is possible that two different firms may be appointed to deal with the letting and sale respectively of the property. However, if you have more than one agent at any given time, you may look desperate so need to consider perhaps initially choosing only one agent. In contrast, the investment market tends to be dominated by national organisations, usually through a limited number of London-based consultancy firms. These firms have greater access to the investment customers for the product and, thus, it is usually sensible to appoint one of these agents, even though the overall fee may be higher. For this, there are pros and cons. However, I would personally go for companies that more than anything have enough staff to first attract customers, and then to chase solicitors to complete the sales.

Developer's profit

Our developer's profit is a cost which must be added in separately for appraisals. Just as contractors will not carry out construction work without being paid, professional fees accrue to the advisors of the development, and interest is paid to the banks for the loan of funds, we developers need a 'payment' in recompense for our time, effort and risk exposure. Banks look very closely at this figure, as it is an important measure of the security of their investment. They will expect a developer to receive between 15 per cent (experienced developers) and 20 per cent (neophyte developers) on cost, and usually more in the appraisal given to them. These funds represent extra security if things go wrong. If a building is not let quickly enough, interest charges will rise and start to eat into the developer's profit.

A relatively high profit will ensure that this erosion can be covered for a fairly long time before the developer goes into the red on the project and, thus, potentially into bankruptcy.

Developer's profit is usually calculated as a percentage of the development cost, or as a percentage of development value. Each has its advantages and disadvantages, which will be discussed in the section covering development appraisal for profit estimation, below.

Finance and value factor assumptions

Finance and value factors:
1. Rental value
2. Investment yield
3. Rental incentive
4. Interest rate
5. Car spaces

These are the factors that determine the value of the development and the cost of financing the development (or the opportunity cost of the developer's own money invested in the project – see below).

Introduction principles on property values

The aim of this section is to give you an introduction into the way commercial property values are determined. It will not enable you to value your own commercial property, but it should give you a good idea of the principles.

The first thing to understand is that there is no magical formula for working out property values. Property does not have an inherent value like most marketable goods; it is worth what somebody will pay for it in the open market, i.e. in competition with everybody else.

If you commission a valuation of your property, this is essentially how the valuer will work out the figure to report to you: they will look at what similar properties have been sold for, or the rent at which they have been let, and use this evidence to value your property.

Valuers work to a set of rules when carrying out a valuation to ensure that the figure they produce is reliable and would hopefully be reproduced if a property were offered on the open market.

These rules are laid down by the professional body dealing with valuation, the Royal Institution of Chartered Surveyors, in a publication popularly known as the Red Book.

Among other things, the Red Book lays down the basis of valuations to be adopted under certain circumstances; clear assumptions that must be made by the valuer in preparing the valuation. There are several valuation bases, the most commonly used of which is market value (MV). The definition of MV in the Red Book is as follows:

"The estimated amount for which a property should ex-change on the date of valuation between a willing buyer and a willing seller in an arm's-length transaction after proper marketing wherein the parties had each acted knowledgeably, prudently and without compulsion."

Conceptual Framework, as published in Intl Valuation Standard 1.

The Red Book explains at length that all valuations for a certain purpose are produced using common assumptions and are thus not widely at variance with other valuations.

If this is the technical rule that a valuer follows when preparing a valuation, what influences the value of the actual property holding?

Most people have heard the old adage of 'location, location, location' being the three most important factors in determining the value of property. This is, of course, essentially true, but the detail of what makes up the value of a property is more complex. You must be tired of me saying that every single postcode is a macro-economy and here more so!

With business premises, usually two components or types of value are involved: rental value; and investment, or capital, value.

Rental value is essentially determined by how useful the premises are to the tenant. How good is the property for the tenant's business? What is the competition offering? At what point, or at what level of rent, would the tenant choose to take an alternative set of premises? The answers to these questions depend, of course, on the nature of the tenant's business and the nature of the property.

At a less fundamental level, rent (or, in actual fact, the usefulness of the property to the business) is determined by a combination of the physical make-up of the building, its size, location, quality, etc, and the nature of the legal contract under which it is occupied. These issues are explained briefly below.

At the end of the day, once the asset is built the real income is provided by the tenant who rents the asset. The capital value of income-producing properties is determined by finding the current value of the future expected income to be earned (or potentially earned in the case of an owner-occupied property). This is done by applying a discount factor to the future expected cash flow. This discount factor is referred to as a yield in property, and is a reflection of the investors' desired return for that type of investment given its specific risk, quantity, quality, and growth potential when compared with other investments in the market. This may sound complex but, in practice, both the choice of yield and the mechanics of valuation are relatively simple.

For a start, there is generally no need to try to explicitly forecast the future cash flows from the property if it is a freehold. Freeholds are perpetual interests, so it is assumed that the ability to earn income from the property will also continue perpetually. The effect of this is to make the valuation formula for freeholds:

INCOME × $1/i$

where i is the required yield. The mathematical formula $1/i$ calculates the present value of a perpetual income. For example, if a property produced a rent of £10,000 p.a, which represented the current market rent for this type of property, and investors were seeking a return of nine per cent, the value of this investment would be:

£10,000 × 1/9 per cent
= £10,000 × 11.111 = £111,111

Where does this magic number called 'yield' come from? Essentially, it comes from the supply and demand of any specific market. Valuers look at the yields achieved on like-for-like comparable assets and/or transactions and apply them to the subject, with alterations for any differences between the property being valued and that on which the transaction took place.

One point to note is the lower the yield, the higher the value. This may seem illogical, but it is not. Investors accepting lower income yields are paying more for a higher quality investment, either in terms of the quality of the existing income flow, or in terms of higher growth potential, or usually both.

In simple terms, this is how the RICS values market-rented freehold income-producing properties. The challenge that we face sometimes is when the property is let below or above the current market rent, and with leasehold properties. I am not covering this scenario in this book, but in principle the value is ascertained using adaptations of the above model to reflect the variable income flows of the former, and the terminable nature of the latter.

Rental value

Rental income value is the price per unit of lettable floor area in square feet or metres that a tenant will pay per annum as part of the lease contract. In the UK and many other countries, this value is obtained by the amount of floor space available and the number of tenants looking to rent that space (supply and demand).

Information on rental values per region for a specific developed floor space is available from different sources. In some countries, there is a statutory requirement to report property transactions, and this information is available in the public domain at no cost. In the UK, this information is available, but we have to pay for it through the Land Registry. The other main source of information on property transactions, and rental values, is through commercial agents. One way to ensure a reliable estimate of rental value is to employ the services of an RICS surveyor, either by way of a formal valuation or by appointing the valuer/agent as the letting agent.

As I have mentioned several times now, property development is a micro-economy by road, hence why the rental value varies markedly from one road to another, and from one property type to another.

For example, within Colchester, current best retail rents are around £300/m2 p.a; the best office rent is at around £215/m2; and the best industrial rents are around £85–95/m2. The rental values are location and specification-specific: a shop located outside the prime shopping street, perhaps only 100 metres from the highest value shop, may attract a rent of less than one-tenth of its more favourably-located competitor. A 30-year-old office in the prime office core of Colchester may attract a rent of perhaps half that of a modern building located nearby. This is simply an effect of image and user flexibility, which is so important to current office occupiers.

Other factors that affect the rental income value include:
- The terms of the lease, including all the small print lease clauses, and more importantly the length of the lease
- Maintenance costs: the UK standard leases are typically on what

is called Full Repairing and Insuring (FRI) terms. This means that leaseholders/tenants are liable for any repairs and maintenance, including structural and non-structural elements, throughout their tenancy agreement. The rent received by the landord is therefore not subject to any deductions for maintenance bills. On the off-chance that the building is maintained by the landlord, the rent will have to be higher than an equivalent building on FRI terms to allow for these extra costs.
- The value factors that influence the main property types have been considered previously.

In our case study, a rental value of £21 /m2 p.a. seems appropriate, given the specification of the building, its location and current market conditions. The building is assumed to have a net-to-gross floor area ratio of 80 per cent, which is conservative for a modern building.

Rental value allocated to car parking

There are other sources of income from a commercial building that will add to the value of the asset. These include items such as carparking spaces available to rent, storage space, advertisement billboards, telecommunication dishes, aerial sites, 'naming rights' (the ability of the lead tenant to attach their name to the building, eg. 'BigCo Tower'), and many others.

Car parking does not always produce a fixed return and, if the current trend of tax and fees continues, it may be that car spaces will be heavily taxed and, therefore, become a liability. A rental fee can only be charged when there are tenants willing to pay for it. This is usually in cases where parking is in short supply, such as in busy city centres. Parking is not usually rented out separately in business park-type locations; here, tenants expect the provision of parking spaces as a reason for selecting such a location and do not expect to pay an additional rent.

Investment yield

As we have demonstrated above, the investment yield is important in determining the present value of the income flow that an income-producing property generates.

The yield is determined by market forces representing the requirements of investors, in terms of return, for this class of property. This in itself is a

very complex issue; a number of factors intertwine to determine it. These include the following:
- The comparison between the Return On Investments (ROI) with other investments. This could be property or other asset classes such as cash deposits, government loan stocks of differing term lengths, home and overseas equities, etc. These in themselves are determined by the spectrum of interest rates in the economy as a whole, including the local bank base rate.
- The cost of money borrowed. For smaller developers/investors like us who finance a purchase partly with loaned money, it is often the lending rate that will determine the minimum yield that an investor can pay. For example, if a property is being purchased for £10 million, a bank or other financial institution would lend around 70 to 75 per cent of that sum, i.e. around £7 million. If the money that we borrow is, let's say, at eight per cent, this means that the property must produce at least £800,000 (i.e. a yield of eight per cent) to just cover the interest payments on an interest-only loan. This is outside the equity portion that the developer needs to come up with (typically 30 per cent of GDV) that sometimes can be even more expensive, such as mezzanine finance at 12 or 15 per cent p.a.
- The specific risks associated with a particular investment. Factors that affect the risk of an asset could be: an interruption of the income flow due to a force majeure, or circumstance, or a significant fall in the value of the property over time. This could be due to the layout configuration, age and location of the property, the asset class, the specification, the lease terms and length, and the quality of the tenant who occupies the space.
- Potential to gain value. Investments that have the greatest potential for growth in value also attract the lowest yields. The argument is that investors seeking growth are willing to accept lower returns in the short term in exchange for this growth which will, if realised, give them a higher overall return. For example, an office investment bought for a yield of seven per cent might expect to see annual growth rates of 10 per cent p.a over the long term, giving a total return of 17 per cent. A shop bought for a yield of eight per cent might see growth at four per cent p.a., giving a total return of 12 per cent.
- The amount of the same stock available in the marketplace. Investor sentiment and requirements can be very influential.

Sometimes, a particular type of investment is in short supply, but is one that investors have targeted because of its longer-term potential. This happened a while back with retail warehousing, where yields were driven down by the amount of supply.

There was a lot of competition between investors for an asset class that was felt to have huge growth potential, but likely to have a restricted future supply because of the changing government planning policy.

The result of the interactions of these factors is reflected in what investors pay for property investments in the marketplace.

These transaction prices are the best place to determine property yields. For example, if a commercial (B1A) property has been sold for £1 million and produces a rental income of £75,000 per year, then it is a straightforward investment yield calculation that the investor receives:

Purchase price of £1 million
Add
purchaser's acquisition costs
(Tax stamp duty fees, legal fees, etc) of £60,000
Total sum expended: £1,060,000

$$\frac{\text{Rental income £75,000}}{\text{Sum expended £1,060,000}} = 7\%$$

This yield can then be applied to the valuation of similar B1A offices in the vicinity, with appropriate adjustments where required for differences in, for example, the specification and quality of the location.

However, this analysis becomes more complex when the rental value of the property being valued has not been set recently. As we all have learnt, property prices have a degree of volatility and rental values can move in all directions.

Commercial property leases only allow for periodic adjustment of rent, usually every five years (sometimes shorter). Rents actually being paid on properties under the lease contract can frequently not be representative of what the property would let for if vacant and available for letting on the open market.

Investors factor this into their decisions about what to pay for investments.

For example, if the office example given above had been let five years prior to the sale and rental values had risen since letting, investors may accept a lower initial income return in return for the expected rise of rents at the rent review in two years.

To cement this concept, let's predict that the rental value of the property has risen by £10,000 p.a.

Purchase price - £1.2 million
Add
purchaser's acquisition costs
(stamp duty, legal fees and surveyor's fees) - £70,000
Total sum expended - £1,27 million

$$\frac{\text{Rental income - £85,000}}{\text{Sum expended £1.27m}} = 0.067 \text{ or } 6.7\%$$

The growth potential is reflected in the greater price paid for the investment (£1.2 million is based on a valuation of the long-term income stream based on the seven per cent yield suggested in the first analysis). The figure of 6.7 per cent is not a good indication of what newly-let properties would exchange for in the open market, but what this type of growth investment – called a reversionary investment – is producing for investors. This example is used as a cautionary indicator to the unwary as to how they can be misled by market evidence. When appraising a new income-producing investment, it is important, where possible, that the evidence should be derived from similar, newly-developed and newly-let properties.

In our example, market evidence suggests that a seven per cent yield is appropriate for this type of investment. In the next section, we will be using a live AFL project example so you will be able to understand this key concept even better.

Rental incentive

A rental incentive is a rent-free period given to a tenant as an inducement to sign a lease on the property. Incentives have always been given to tenants, although historically this amounted only to a few rent-free months, to allow the tenant time to fit out the premises before occupation. In previous decades, where supply of space greatly exceeded demand, the size and value of incentives grew enormously as developers fell over themselves to attract to the empty developments the few tenants that were available. These incentives included fit-outs free of charge, long rent-free periods, cash deposits, and freezes on rental increases. In the more 'normal' market conditions that have followed this period, incentives did not completely disappear.

The question that might be asked is why developers gave incentives rather than lowering the rent? And for this there are, in fact, many reasons, although these three are key:
- Diminishing rent damages the long-term cash flows and, therefore, the value of developments. The argument is that once, say, the two-year rent-free period on a development had expired, the "normal rent" would kick in and the property would be valued according to that high-income stream. If a lower rent had been agreed, it affects the property over at least the first five years of the rental cycle, and possibly longer.
- Landlords are keen to protect the value of existing properties that they own: bringing down the rent in new developments would have provided evidence of lower rents that could have been used in rent review negotiations.
- Tenants usually prefer the incentives offered as they give them short-term relief from cash flow problems suffered during the economic downturn, creating a win-win situation.

The reality is that rental incentives created huge issues for the property market, particularly for valuers and investors. The first two arguments used may also have been seen as being both over-simplistic and inaccurate. Whatever the case, incentives are still a feature of many markets. Let's assume that a 12-month rent-free period has been granted. This would then need to be counted as a cash deduction from the receipts.

As a result, it may be necessary to make a deduction from the value of the completed property as an alternative to this approach. Deducting cash rent-free and adjusting the valuation would be double counting.

Interest

The majority of property developers, including ourselves, use someone else's money in some way or another (I recommend you read my business partner's book Bricks and Mortar and Someone Else's Money) to carry out a development. This money will incur a cost, i.e. an interest rate paid to bank or an individual.

Even where developers are using internal sources of funds to carry out a scheme, the cost of money should still be allowed for.

This is because they have an 'opportunity cost'; money expended on a development scheme is money that could have been used elsewhere to gain return.

The opportunity cost is the highest return that has been given up by not investing in alternative investment mediums. Some large firms using their own funds to carry out developments use their own internally-assumed interest rate, which is often quite low.

Although this is legitimate in accounting terms, there is a strong argument that the interest rate used should be one that reflects the rate that would apply to a project with a similar risk profile to the development scheme, ie. the rate should be that which the firm would require if loaning it to another developer to carry out a similar scheme.

The perpetual discrepancy of the percentage of interest rates can be set aside in the majority of cases where money is borrowed. Interest rates are set competitively by lenders. The rate set will depend on factors such as the experience of the developer, the specific risk of the scheme, quality of tenants and, of course, the general tone of interest rates in the marketplace. Bank base rates, which have been around five to eight per cent previously but are currently at rock bottom, form the basis of the lender's calculation.

In a strong residential and commercial letting market, using a developer like us with a good track record of completing developments, and where there are quality tenants in place, and where the bank has the development (including the site), as collateral in case of default, the interest rate will be two to four per cent above base.

This may go up substantially if any of these characteristics are weakened. To give you an idea, for our first development we got eight per cent p.a. and nowadays we are getting between 5.5 to 6.5 per cent p.a. Historical interest rates can be found at www.bankofengland.co.uk

Three main finance factors must be taken into consideration:

Sometimes, there may be more than one loan in place at different rates of interest. For example, the site could have been acquired at a lower rate of interest than the funds used to pay for the actual construction costs. Similarly, developers sometimes find that they have a funding shortfall and need to acquire additional sources of finance, or mezzanine finance. This is usually available at much higher rates of interest, typically at around 12 to 15 per cent p.a. Banks are currently seeking to secure their money by requiring the developer to pay for the bank's own professionals fees, such a QS to be in place as additional overseers of the development progress.

In our case study below, we are considering a simple loan to us, as developers with a reasonable track record, and a low level of assessed risk as the number of units is below 20 and all are affordable, too.

At the time of writing, this would equate to an interest rate of between 6.5 and 7.5 per cent. For ease of demonstration of the calculation, an interest rate of 10 per cent will be used.

This completes the assumptions required to carry out the appraisal. The next chapter lays out a simple residual approach to the calculation of land value, then shows how each of the components is derived.

Chapter Ten

Case Study Six

Worked example: traditional residual approach

Here is the link to this project: www.instagram.com/stories/highlights/17868509599785068/

For this I am going to use a live project example, which is being built at the time of writing. The deal was brought to us by our star student Kevin Desouza. I met Kevin at one of our training events in London and had the pleasure to mentor him. Kevin is a doer. Once I trained him on how to find and analyse deals, he went and hunted for one until he found the below opportunity. Now, we are business partners and in the process of looking for our next deal to work together as a team.

My star pupil Kevin Desouza and I.

Property Metamorphosis

Kevin and I on top of one of our penthouses during one of our many project progress meetings.

Developer: Joint venture between Assets for Life and Springboard Renovations (Kevin's company)

Location: Loughton, Essex
- Loughton is a town and civil parish in the Epping Forest District of Essex
- It is located between 11 and 13 miles (21km) north east of central London
- Loughton is generally considered to be an affluent suburb, popular with commuters to the city on account of the town centre's Central Line underground station
- The subject property is in a town centre location, around 400m from the underground station

Chapter Ten

The car park corner brickwork that will be demolished to erect our new building

Access from High Road to site.

The development opportunity

- The subject property comprises a small development site on a back plot, formerly comprising the rear car park/storage to 165 High Road
- The site sits adjacent to the access road to the M&S Foodstore and the M&S car park and the rear of 165 High Road, a mixed-use retail, office and residential building
- The site benefits from planning permission to construct a new block comprising ground floor commercial space with A2 use, plus five upper floors of accommodation comprising 14 self-contained flats

Property Metamorphosis

- There is no on-site car parking and no 'affordable' (social) flats within the scheme
- Subsequent planning consent allows the commercial space to be split into two smaller units

Proposed accommodation

- Ground floor commercial – 157.35 sq m/1,694 sq ft
- Nine x one-bedroom flats, five x two-bedroom flats – Aggregate GIA: 900. sq m/9,688 sq ft
- GIA of whole building incl. common parts: 1,338sq m/14,402 sq ft
- Tenure - Freehold

Access

Access to the property is from High Road and an unnamed service road, both of which are fully adopted by the local authority.

Economic Overview

The following pages (p175-188) have been copied and pasted from the actual valuation carried out by our appointed project RICS surveyor Jeremy Mussett BSc Hons MRICS Director of Eddisons who has granted written permission for us to add this for your information.

The first estimate of GDP for Q3 2019 indicates an increase in output of 0.3 per cent, following a reduction of 0.2 per cent in the previous quarter. The all-important services sector was the main driver of this return to growth, showing a positive figure of 0.4 per cent compared to 0.1 per cent in Q2.

The production sector was flat in Q3, compared to a negative figure of 1.4 per cent in Q2, within this sector manufacturing was also flat overall, although there was an improvement in vehicle production. The construction sector has been volatile in 2019 and showed an increase of 0.6 per cent in Q3 compared to a reduction of 1.3 per cent in Q2.

The national annualised overall GDP growth rate is now 1.0 per cent. The HM Treasury compiles a monthly report which reviews the numerous market forecasts prepared by external organisations. The latest report dated October 2019 indicates an average forecast of 1.2 per cent GDP growth for 2019. For 2020, the average forecast is for 1 per cent growth.

The labour market remains strong and the unemployment rate was slightly lower at 3.8 per cent in the latest available figures to September 2019. The number of people in employment remains very close to an all-time high, being 32.75 million people or 76.0 per cent of the potential workforce aged between 16 and 64. The Treasury report mentioned above indicates that the unemployment rate is now forecast to be 4.0 per cent in 2019 (4.2 per cent in 2020). Wage growth has fallen back slightly to an annualised rate of 3.6 per cent and this may reflect a decrease in the number of job vacancies. These have fallen by 53,000 in the last year to a level of 800,000.

Inflationary pressures have reduced over recent months and the CPI index showed an increase of 1.5 per cent in the year to October 2019. The Treasury report indicates an average forecast for an increase in CPI of 1.9 per cent in 2019 and 2.1 per cent in 2020. The wage growth and reduction in CPI inflation (net wage growth after inflation 2.1 per cent) should lead to an increase in consumer spending power.

In July 2018, the Bank of England responded to the rise in inflation by signalling only the second rise in Base Rate in 10 years. The rise of 0.25 per cent took Base Rate up to 0.75 per cent, which still remains low by historic standards. There is considerable doubt as to the future path of interest rate movements and these will depend upon prevailing economic conditions.

Commercial Property Market

The 'Q3 2019 RICS UK Commercial Property Market Survey' results point to a deterioration in sentiment over the period, with 62 per cent of respondents now sensing the market is in the downturn phase of the property cycle. That said, notwithstanding the structural challenges across the retail sector, many contributors feel the Brexit impasse has become increasingly detrimental to market activity. As such, anecdotal evidence suggests a resolution to the uncertainty could potentially release some pent-up demand further ahead.

In the occupier market, tenant demand reportedly fell at the headline level once again, with the net balance slipping to -19 per cent, from -13 per cent previously. When disaggregated, the retail sector continues to drive much of the overall decline (net balance -60 per cent compared to -59 per cent in Q2). However, demand also fell in the office sector during Q3, albeit the net balance reading of -9 per cent is indicative of only a modest decline. Meanwhile, demand for industrial space continued to rise, although this increase was marginal, as the net balance came in at +9 per cent (down from +20 per cent in Q2).

Alongside this, the availability of leasable space was more or less unchanged across the industrial sector, marking a slight departure from the uninterrupted run of declining supply being reported since 2013. At the same time, vacancies are still rising sharply across the retail portion of the market, while availability of office space also ticked up again. This prompted another increase in incentive packages on offer to tenants in both instances.

Over the near term, industrial rents are still seen rising, even if growth may cool somewhat compared with earlier in the year. Projections remain steeped in negative territory across the retail sector, while office rents are expected to see very little change over the next three months.

Slightly further out, at the 12-month horizon, prime office rents are expected to increase, with a net balance of +28 per cent of respondents envisaging positive growth at the national level.

The outlook has turned marginally negative for secondary office rents however, driven by weakening expectations in London and a largely stagnant picture across the regions. By way of contrast, the industrial sector, particularly in prime locations, continues to return solid rental growth projections for the coming 12 months in all parts of the UK. Unsurprisingly, rents are foreseen falling further across the retail sector, both in prime and secondary locations, with expectations coming in even weaker than those returned in Q2 at the headline level.

On the investment side of the market, enquiries fell at a slightly faster pace than in Q2, in net balance terms, with 15 per cent more respondents reporting a decline (as opposed to an increase) in the latest figures. Overseas investment demand declined across all three sectors covered by the survey, and the headline net balance of -18 per cent represents the poorest reading since Q2 2016. The supply of property available on the sales market was relatively unchanged for a fourth straight quarter, although an increase in the retail sector was offset by falling supply in the office and industrial portions of the market.

Capital value expectations for the coming 12 months point to growth slowing across the industrial sector, but remaining solid for prime assets nonetheless.

Prime office values are seen rising modestly, although expectations are consistent with a slight dip in prices for secondary offices.

For the retail sector, the negative trends of recent quarters show no signs of easing and projections continue to signal a sharp decline in both prime and secondary retail values over the course of the next 12 months.

Reflecting a slightly more downbeat tone to the Q3 results, 62 per cent of survey participants are now of the opinion that the market is in the early to middle stages of a downturn. This is up from 53 per cent in the previous quarter and is the highest proportion sensing the market to be turning down since this series was introduced in 2015.

Furthermore, beneath the national level, a majority of contributors are taking this view across all of the 12 UK regions/countries covered.

That being said, all-sector average capital value expectations are only narrowly in negative territory for the year ahead, and longer term expectations depict a largely similar pattern at the three year horizon.

On that basis, the perceptions of respondents appear to point to the current 'downturn' being consistent with a relatively soft landing for the commercial real estate sector overall, even though the fallout for retail is altogether more severe.

Residential Property Market

The September 2019 RICS Residential Market Survey results suggest activity remains subdued across the sales market with headline indicators on buyer demand and supply slipping into negative territory. Much of the anecdotal commentary is pointing to heightened economic and political uncertainty as a contributing factor behind the sluggish picture. Significantly, forward looking metrics imply that the market is unlikely to gain impetus over the next three months, though sentiment over the 12-month horizon does appear to be a little more resilient.

Following three consecutive months of a largely stable trend in supply, the latest results point to a renewed decline in the volume of fresh listings coming on to the market.

Comments from contributors are suggesting that the Brexit impasse seems to be dissuading vendors. The new instructions net balance fell to -37 per cent, the weakest reading since June 2016. In light of this, average stock levels on estate agents' books remain near record lows. Furthermore, contributors are continuing to report that appraisals are down compared to a year earlier, indicating that there is little prospect of a pick-up in sales listings in the immediate future.

Alongside this, a more cautious approach from property purchasers is visible in the September results. After holding more or less steady in the last four months, the new buyer enquiries net balance fell to -15 per cent, pointing to a modest decline in buyer demand.

Unsurprisingly, the negative trend in demand and supply appears to be feeding through to the overall sales numbers. The RICS Newly Agreed Sales series edged down to -27 per cent (from -11 per cent previously) with activity reportedly slipping in virtually all parts of the UK.

As far as the near-term outlook is concerned, sales expectations stand at -9 per cent, indicating that survey participants anticipate activity to remain subdued in the coming three months. That said, contributors are expecting sales volumes to stabilise at the 12 month time frame.

Turning to prices, the headline price balance returned a reading of -2 per cent in September, little changed from -4 per cent in August. Overall, this indicator is consistent with a broadly flat trend in national house price inflation.

Nevertheless, as we have noted before, this headline gauge is being weighed down significantly by negative momentum in London and the South East whilst the price picture appears to be firmer across other areas of the UK. In particular, solid gains were reported in Northern Ireland, Scotland and the North West.

Looking ahead, price expectations for the coming three months stand at -16 per cent pointing to a modest decline in prices on a UK-wide basis. However, the 12-month outlook points to a turnaround with +18 per cent more respondents expecting prices to rise (rather than fall) over the coming year. Disaggregating the data, strong annual growth in prices is envisaged across eight out of the 12 regions covered in the survey led by the strongest price projections (in net balance terms) in Northern Ireland and Scotland. At the same time, a steadier price trend is seen emerging in London and the South East.

In the lettings market, the latest set of results (which form a part of non-seasonally adjusted series) are indicative of demand from prospective tenants rising firmly for an eighth month in a row (net balance of +22 per cent). Alongside this, landlord instructions remain in decline. With demand still outstripping supply, rent expectations for the coming three months remain positive (net balance of +24 per cent).

Further out, contributors are pencilling in rental growth of approximately 2 per cent over the coming 12 months. Significantly at the five-year horizon, the imbalance between demand and supply in the lettings market is expected to lead to an acceleration in rental growth, which is seen averaging to around 3 per cent per annum through to 2024. In comparison, average price growth projections stand at just over 2 per cent on the same basis.

Brexit

The nature of the future relationship between the UK and the EU remains very unclear with a number of possible outcomes still in play. Until the entire process has been competed, a significant element of uncertainty will continue to prevail. This situation should be carefully monitored by lenders and further advice should be sought from us if price volatility emerges.

Demand including timings for letting and sale

Rental demand for the proposed flats is expected to be good, on account of the brand new specification and proximity to Loughton Underground station. It may take up to six months to let all flats from completion. Once fully let, vacant flats are expected to be let within one to three months' marketing.

Rental demand for the commercial unit of 1,694 sq ft may be weaker. We consider there will be better tenant demand for two units of 850 sq ft and 798 sq ft respectively.

We expect the local planning authority to be receptive to reasonable changes in use class, thus rendering the units suitable to a wide range of potential tenants. However, we anticipate a marketing period of 9 to 15 months to secure new lettings.

The units could be let in shell condition or refurbished by the landlord, depending on lease negotiations. In either case, tenant incentives such as rent free periods may need to given.

Sales demand for the flats is expected to be reasonable, assuming sensible and competitive pricing. Asking prices which are too high will deter potential purchasers.

We note that the scheme will be registered with the Help to Buy scheme and this may boost sales demand. We assess typical purchasers to be first time buyers who may already be familiar with the local area. In our opinion it may take up to 15 months' marketing to sell all units. In mitigating circumstances, the completed block could be sold in a single transaction to an investor. However, an investor will require a discount of approximately 10 per cent to 20 per cent from the aggregate Market Values of the individual flats and commercial units.

Market Valuation and Loan Security

9.1 Valuation Approach
Methods Utilised
In preparing our advice we have primarily utilised the comparison and residual approach.

Our valuations have been undertaken in accordance with the RICS Valuation-Global Standards July 2017 incorporating IVSC International Valuation Standards. The conventional valuation methods are however dependent upon comparable evidence and where a lack of open market transactional activity causes uncertainty to exist throughout this process we have also relied upon our own market assessment/judgement based upon several considerations to include any marketing history, current equivalent sale processes, publicised indices, sector analysis, local factors and daily dialogue with the active agents.

Comparable Evidence

In undertaking our valuation we have had regard to comparable evidence. In some instances confidentiality prevents us from disclosing full details. Where there is a lack of available evidence regard has been given to valuer judgement. We have made this clear in our assessment where relevant.

Where the property has been subject to a recent transaction or a provisionally agreed price, enquiries have been made to ascertain the price agreed/realised and the effect of other factors including any marketing undertaken has been paid in this respect. We have also indicated the extent to which this information has been accepted as evidence of Market Value.

If our enquiries have not revealed such details or the agreed purchase price has changed and such information comes to light prior to the proposed loan being finalised, then this information should be referred back to us for further consideration.

Market Rent

The RICS definition of Market Rent is "the estimated amount for which a property would be leased on the valuation date between a willing lessor and a willing lessee on appropriate lease terms in an arm's length transaction, after proper marketing and where the parties had each acted knowledgeably, prudently and without compulsion."

We have considered the following market evidence:

Commercial property

Address: 165A High Road Loughton, IG10 4LF
Date: June 2017
Rent (pa): £47,000
Comments: A retail unit of some 136.56 sq m (1,470 sq ft) was let to a business tenant (Ginger Pig butchers). The unit was let on a new 10 year lease with a 5 year break clause, a rent review in the 5th year and a 5 months' rent free incentive. The rent achieved reflects £31.97 per sq ft overall and £54.00 per sq ft ITZA.

Address: 190 High Road, Loughton IG10 1DN
Date: November 2017
Rent (pa): £37,500
Comments: A retail unit of some 91.60 sq m (986 sq ft), with A1 use was let on a new 10 year lease with a 5 year break clause. The rent achieved reflects £38.03 per sq ft overall and £67.59 per sq ft ITZA.

Address: 267 High Road Loughton, IG10 1AH
Date: October 2017
Rent (pa): £32,250

Comments: A retail unit of some 164.4 sq m (1,770 sq ft), with an A1 user clause was let on a new 10 year lease, with a 5 year break clause. The rent achieved reflects £18.22 per sq ft overall and £54.67 per sq ft ITZA.

Address: 229 High Road Loughton, IG10 1AD
Date: March 2019
Rent (pa): £45,000
Comments: A retail unit of some 198.71 sq m. (2,139 sq ft), with an A1 user clause let on a new 15 year lease. The rent achieved equates to £21.03 overall and £55.48 per sq ft ITZA.

Residential property

Address: Flat 6, 213 High Road, Loughton, IG10 1BB
Date: August 2019
Rent (pa): £1,250
Comments: A one bedroom apartment comprising a luxury fitted kitchen and luxury bathroom. The property benefits from gas central heating and is in close proximity to Loughton Underground Station.

Address: Flat 2, 230a High Road Loughton, Essex, IG10 1EZ
Date: January 2019
Rent (pa): £950
Comments: A refurbished one bedroom, first floor apartment comprising a fully fitted kitchen and open plan kitchen/lounge. The property is in close proximity to Loughton Underground Station.

Address: 1 Algers Mead Loughton Essex, IG10 4NJ
Date: September 2019
Rent (pa): £1,275
Comments: A recently refurbished ground floor, two bedroom apartment of some 58 sq m (624 sq ft), benefits from a private rear garden. The property is close to the High Road and Loughton Underground Station.

Address: 8 Townview, 184-186 High Road, Loughton, Essex, IG10 1DF
Date: October 2019
Rent (pa): £1,275
Comments: A two bedroom top floor flat of some 60.85 sq m. (655 sq

ft) comprises a modern kitchen and bathroom. The property is in a town centre location and in close proximity to Loughton Underground Station.

Rental Value Analysis

Commercial

The commercial unit may be suitable for a variety of other uses including A1, B1 or D1, subject to obtaining consent for a change of use. The units will not have High Road frontage and rents will be lower than nearby A1 retail rents with prominent frontage. Demand is likely to greatest for A2, B1 or D2 users. We expect the commercial premises to be occupied within a 9 to 15 months' marketing period.

Retail rents fall within the range of £18.22 per sq ft to £39.81 per sq ft on an overall basis. Retail rates in terms of zone A (ITZA) for A1 and A2 use classes are within the range of £54.00 per sq ft ITZA and £67.59 per sq ft ITZA.

By way of comparison, the subject unit will be brand new on completion of the scheme, albeit with no High Road frontage. There may be limited rental demand for a single commercial unit of 1,694 sq ft and we apply a rate of £25.00 per sq ft, reflecting a Market Rent of £42,350 per annum.

If split to two units of 850 sq ft and 798 sq ft respectively, we apply the slightly higher rate of £27.50 per sq ft, reflecting £23,375 per annum for Unit 1 and £21,945 for Unit 2, an aggregate of £45,320 per annum. The figure of £45,320 per annum is reported as Market Rent as there is considered to be greater demand for two smaller units in this micro-location.

Residential

We anticipate good rental demand for the flats in the subject property. The flats will be well appointed upon completion, with a high standard of finish, brand new kitchens and bathrooms, notwithstanding the close proximity to the town centre and rail station. However, the absence of allocated parking and gardens will be more likely to attract young professionals, as opposed to growing families.

Having analysed the comparable evidence available, we apply monthly rates of £1,000 to the one bedroom flats and £1,250 to the two bedroom flats. We apply a slightly higher rate of £1,100 per calendar month to the two one bedroom penthouses, on account of their private roof terraces

This equates to an Aggregate Residential Market Rent of £15,200 per month / £182,400 per annum.

Summary

The aggregate Market Rent of the two commercial units and 14 approved flats (10 one bedroom flats and 4 two bedroom flats) is thus £227,720 per annum. Market Rent will increase to £229,520 per annum if planning consent is granted to reconfigure one of the fifth floor one bedroom flats into a two bedroom flat. Market Rent as reported is as per the existing approved consents at the date of valuation.

The rental income is a gross figure, i.e. it makes no allowance for periods when the flats may be vacant, the cost of managing the property, letting fees, building insurance, maintenance & decoration, replacement of fixtures & fittings, etc. It is therefore necessary to derive a net income. In the absence of audited accounts, an allowance of between 15% and 20% of the income should be made to derive a net income.

Market Value

The RICS definition of Market Value is "the estimated amount for which an asset or liability should exchange on the valuation date between a willing buyer and a willing seller in an arm's length transaction, after proper marketing where the parties had each acted knowledgeably, prudently and without compulsion." Market Value is understood as the value of an asset or liability estimated without regard to costs of sale or purchase, and without offset for any associate taxes.

We have considered the following market evidence:

Residential property

Address: Monroe House, 12-16 Church Hill, Loughton, Essex, IG10 1LA
Date: October 2019
Price: £350,000
Comments: A one double bedroom, first floor flat of some 53 sq m. (570 sq ft), built in 2012, benefits from an open plan kitchen/lounge and patio doors leading into a private balcony.

The property is at the north end of High Road Loughton. The achieved price equates to £614 per sq ft

Address: 26 Grange Court, Upper Park, Loughton, Essex, IG10 4QY
Date: October 2019
Price: £400,000
Comments: A two double bedroom, ground floor apartment of some 73 sq m (785 sq ft). The property affords gas central heating and is in close proximity to Loughton Underground station. The achieved price equates to £509 per sq ft

Address: 5 Roding Court, 2 Lower Park Road, Loughton, Essex, IG10 4NA
Date: September 2019
Price: £485,000
Comments: A two bedroom first floor apartment of some 75 sq m (807 sq ft) within a purpose built residential development. The property comprises a fully fitted kitchen, family bathroom, communal gardens and is in close proximity to Loughton Underground station. The achieved price equates to £600 per sq ft

Address: 19 Grange Court, Upper Park, Loughton, Essex, IG10 4QY
Date: September 2019
Price: £373,500
Comments: A two double bedroom first floor flat of some 69 sq m (743 sq ft) within close proximity of the High Road. The property benefits from a communal garden and modern bathroom facilities. The achieved price equates to £502 per sq ft

Gross Development Value

We have considered the Gross Development Value (GDV) on a comparison basis, having regard to sales of flats in the vicinity of the subject property. There is a scarcity of directly comparable evidence availability and, in these circumstances; we consider that wider than normal valuation tolerances should be anticipated.

The subject flats will be of average size by market standards and presented to a high specification.

The town centre location is very convenient for the Underground station which is just a few minutes' walk from the site.

However, the town centre location will not appeal to all purchasers, with many likely to opt for developments in quieter residential locations with parking and private gardens or communal grounds.

We have considered the comparable evidence available and apply Market Values to each flat, as demonstrated in the above table.

The commercial element is valued on an investment basis, whereby the estimated Market Rent as two units of £45,320 per annum is capitalised at an all risks yield of 7 per cent.

The yield reflects the fact that the unit will have vacant possession on completion and there may be a 9 to 15 months' marketing period to sell or let the premises. However, we also note that commercial units of this nature are well suited to owner occupiers and the private investor market.

The value of £6,030,000 is the estimate of GDV assuming that each element of the scheme is sold separately over a 12 to 15 months' marketing from practical completion. If the block was sold on completion in a single transaction to an investor or fund, we expect that the purchaser would require a block discount of approximately 15 per cent from the 'break up' value.

If planning is granted for Flat 13 to be extended and reconfigured as a two bedroom flat we increase the value of this unit to £440,000, resulting in a revised GDV of £6,100,000.

Existing Site Value

The existing site value is calculated by way of a residual valuation whereby the costs of development and a profit margin are deducted from the Gross Development Value. The GDV is fixed at £6,030,000.

We include acquisition costs in our appraisal as the valuation assumes that the site is sold to a third party on the date of valuation.

We have estimated build costs based on a rate of £160 per sq ft applied to the aggregate net sales area of the flats and a rate of £100 per sq ft to the common parts and commercial area. This reflects a basic build cost of £1,850,000.

We are advised by the lender's customer that there is no CIL liability. A Section 106 agreement stipulates a single payment of £704.

We assume that a contribution of £500 towards the Council's legal fees has already been paid. We include the cost of connection to utilities at £50,000.

We include NHBC/10 years' structural warranty and Building Regulations at a cost of £45,000. Finance costs are estimated assuming that 50% of GDV is borrowed at a rate of 7 per cent for 12 months.

Finally, a profit margin is included equal to 20 per cent of total costs, which is considered to be a reasonable return for local developers. Subject to these variables, the existing site value is noted to be £2,520,000.

If consent is granted for Flat 13 to be a two bedroom flat, GDV will increase to £6,100,000. However, construction costs also increase slightly, reflecting a marginal increase in site value to £2,555,000.

Special assumption valuations

You have requested our assessment of existing site value under the Special Assumption of a sale subject to a restricted marketing period of 90 days, although all other assumptions are unchanged.

This would be insufficient time in which to properly market the site and allow for potential purchaser's proper due diligence. To allow for this risk we reduce the value by 15 per cent as an incentive, reflecting a Market Value of £2,140,000 subject to a restricted marketing period of 90 days.

Appraisal summary commercial and residential

Location: Loughton, Essex
Developer: Joint venture between Assets for Life & Spring Board Renovations. All the below numbers are approximations.

Revenue

Area summary	m²	Rate m²	Gross
Office A1	157.35		£600,000
Valuation of commercial			
Market rent p.a.	X	YP@7%=	Gross asset value
£45,000	X	14.2857=	£600,000
Residential	860	£6,395	£5,500,000
Freehold sell			£164,700
Total			£6,264,700

Property Metamorphosis

Outlay acquisition costs

Residual price	£1,900,000
Stamp duty	£84,000
Surveys	£10,000
Legals	£7,500
Other costs	£85,500
Total	£2,087,000

Construction costs
Construction

	m²	Blend Rate	m² Cost	Total
Whole building in communal areas	1017	£1,819	£1,850,000	£1,850,000
Gross internal area split: Residential 860m2 Commercial 157m2 Communal 337m2				
Residual risk/project specific contingency 10%				£185,000
Car park demolition				£20,000
Total				**£2,037,000**

Professional fees

Architect approx	3%	55,000
Quantity surveyor approx	1.5%	28,000
Structural engineer approx	1.5%	28,000
Mech/elec engineer approx	1.5%	28,000
Project manager approx	5.5%	101,000
Party wall approx	1.5%	28,000
Other cost approx	3.5%	£65,000
Total		**£333,000**

Sales cost

Marketing	£15,000
Sales agent fee Sales	£65,000
Solicitors/ legal fee	£17,800
Total	**£97,800**

Finance cost
Senior funding (24 months)   £400,000
Equity loan (24 months)   £225,800
Total finance cost   **£625,800**
Total costs   **£5,180,600**
Expected net return/profit   **£1,084,100**

Analysis of the appraisal

The completed development appraisal suggests that a bid of up to around £1.9m for the land would be appropriate in order to meet the target for the net minimum return of £1,000,000.

How is that figure arrived at? It will be clear from the section below that the assumptions we have made strongly influence this estimate. Before examining the sensitivity of the appraisal, it is important to take some time to look at how this calculation was actually arrived at. Although many of the components are obvious, others are less so and need careful consideration as to how they were calculated. Each component will be considered in turn.

Revenue

Rental area summary office

The following two pages have been copied and pasted from the actual valuation carried out by our appointed project RICS surveyor Jeremy Mussett BSc Hons MRICS Director of Eddisons who has granted written permission for us to add this for your information.

"The commercial unit may be suitable for a variety of other uses including A1, B1 or D1, subject to obtaining consent for a change of use. The units will not have High Road frontage and rents will be lower than nearby A1 retail rents with prominent frontage. Demand is likely to greatest for A2, B1 or D2 users. We expect the commercial premises to be occupied within a 9 to 15 months' marketing period.

Retail rents fall within the range of £18.22 per sq ft to £39.81 per sq ft on an overall basis. Retail rates in terms of zone A (ITZA) for A1 and A2 use classes are within the range of £54.00 per sq ft ITZA and £67.59 per sq ft ITZA.

By way of comparison, the subject unit will be brand new on completion of the scheme, albeit with no High Road frontage. There may be limited rental demand for a single commercial unit of 1,694 sq ft and we apply a rate of £25.00 per sq ft, reflecting a Market Rent of £42,350 per annum.

If split to two units of 850 sq ft and 798 sq ft respectively, we apply the slightly higher rate of £27.50 per sq ft, reflecting £23,375 per annum for Unit 1 and £21,945 for Unit 2, an aggregate of £45,320 per annum.

The figure of £45,320 per annum is reported as Market Rent as there is considered to be greater demand for two smaller units in this micro-location.

The commercial element is valued on an investment basis, whereby the estimated Market Rent as two units of £45,320 per annum is capitalised at an all risks yield of 7 per cent. The yield reflects the fact that the unit will have vacant possession on completion and there may be a 9 to 15 months' marketing period to sell or let the premises. However, we also note that commercial units of this nature are well suited to owner occupiers and the private investor market and are often placed into a SIPP. This reflects a Market Value of £600,000.

As above, the first step in the valuation by the RICS surveyor is the calculation of the total rental roll of the investment. In this case, this comes from the rent from the offices (if we decide to split them, which makes perfect finance sense). This total income is capitalised using a single yield assuming an income flow into perpetuity, as is the norm with freehold investments. The figure of 14.286 is merely the inverse of seven per cent, giving the income multiplier or year's purchase (YP) figure.

In some circumstances, there may be the need to apply different yields to different parts of the income.

This may occur in a multi-type or mixed-use investment, or where the building is multi-let to different tenants of differing quality. In these cases, individual calculations of value for each component are calculated and then summed up to provide the total realisation.

The next step: calculating the gross development costs

From the sum calculated for the net return/realisation, the gross development costs need to be deducted. This becomes an accounting exercise, ticking off the value of each. Some of these costs are relatively straightforward to calculate, others not so much. The traditional residual model also incorporates peculiarities in the calculation of certain elements, particularly finance charges. These peculiarities are essentially shortcuts, or simplifications in calculation, dating from less technically-advanced times when calculation aids available to the appraiser were primitive. There is very little justification for the continued use of these shortcuts in the development appraisal model, other than that of familiarity, as they do not accurately calculate elements of the appraisal but give generally reasonable approximations of the true values. Most proprietary development appraisal software on the market gives the option of calculating these elements more accurately.

Construction costs

Construction costs are very straightforward. The basic principles have already been discussed in previous chapters. A lump sum has been calculated for demolition works and site preparation (£20,000). The cost of the new-build element has been calculated by applying an overall cost per square metre to the gross sellable area of the building. Some developers also split this value into gross internal area, including the communal areas and the sellable area. For simplicity in this case study, we have only used the sellable area.

Disclamer** Once more, this value is specific to every single project and varies immensely, so you need to make the necessary arrangements to ensure that this value is as accurate and as conservative as possible.

Finance on construction and demolition

While the construction cost element is a simple calculation, the calculation of finance charges is a bit complex. This represents the main area of simplification in calculation in the traditional residual model. It should be noted that, in the simplest of residual calculations, interest charges on a development may be calculated as a single, gross element rather than on a number of individual elements. Here, the interest calculation element has been divided into two: construction cost and professional fees. Each element has different cost/time profiles and this separation allows for a more accurate assessment of interest charges.

This calculation of interest charges should always be made, even when internal and unborrowed funds are used, in order that the true costs of development are assessed. Where borrowed money is used in the development, the cost is reflected in the interest charged by the lender. Even when internal sources of finance are used, this money has a cost, known as an opportunity cost. The money spent on the development could have been used elsewhere in order to obtain a return. The logic of this was discussed earlier, but it is worth underlining at this point. There is no such thing as 'free' money. Even I know that if you don't use your own money and you are using someone else's money, then you are paying them a fixed return fee. Some appraisals see own funds and borrowed funds dealt with separately, often at different rates. For simplicity, in this and in the majority of other appraisals, it is best to assume that all money used is borrowed.

When money is borrowed for a development scheme from an FCA-regulated institution, it is normally arranged through a loan facility which is then drawn down in tranches as the project proceeds and expenditure is made. It is only when the money is drawn down that the interest accrues.

In the construction phase, with traditional methods of procurement, the building contractor is paid in stages, usually on a monthly basis. The contractor carries out a valuation of works completed each month, which the client pays, normally after agreeing the sum using their own professional team to certify that the work has been carried out. The amount expended each month accumulates to the final contract sum, plus or minus any variations in work that have been agreed during the course of the work. This process means that the construction cost is only finally expended at the end of the contract and the average balance drawn down from the loan facility is typically rather less than the total.

If finance were calculated at our rate of 10 per cent on the entire balance, then there would be a gross over-calculation of the amount of interest accruing.

Initial work, ground preparation, excavation, foundations, etc. tend to be low-value/low-speed functions, depending on project. The rate of expenditure increases greatly as the expensive high-value components (frames, walls, etc) are installed. Towards the end of the construction period, the pace falls off again as finishing trades become involved. This work tends to be slow and often only one trade at a time can work; for example, electricians must finish before plasterers can complete the walls, which then have to dry before the decorating can start.

The normal assumption made in a simple residual appraisal is to simulate this process, albeit in a much-simplified way in the traditional models. The normal assumption is that, on average, half of the balance will be drawn down by halfway through the project.

The calculation thus assumes that 50 per cent of the money has been

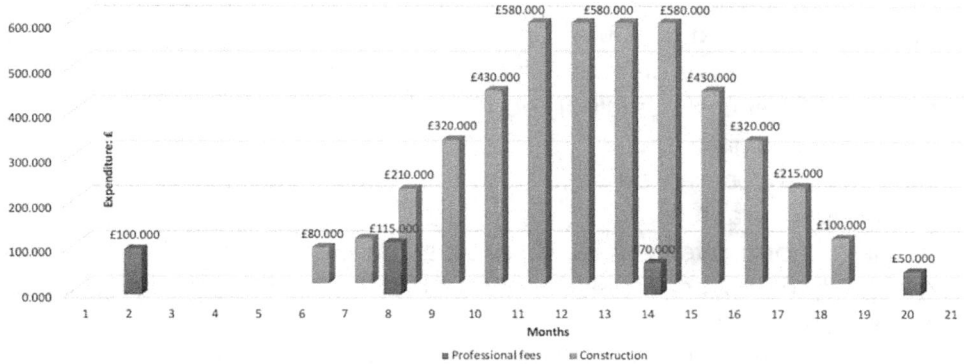

Expenditure patterns for construction fees

drawn down on average over the construction period. In our example, this would be £4,732,500+£473,250+£100,000+£236.6257/2=£2,771,187.50. Using the interest rate of 10 per cent p.a. this would equate to an interest charge of £277,118.75 for the construction period funding.

An alternative approach is to calculate the full cost of construction, but for only 50 per cent of the elapsed time (ie. £5,542,375 x [(1.100.5) − 1]). This produces exactly the same answer, although strictly speaking the logic behind taking this approach is rather suspect.

This assumption about 50 per cent of the expenditure is the biggest single source of inaccuracy in the traditional appraisal model. Ways of improving this problem are explored below, but it should be noted that the calculation in the appraisal above assumed level monthly expenditure and cost £271,364.

The derivation of the professional fees was discussed above. The calculation is simple, as it is normally calculated as a percentage of construction costs.

Finance on professional fees

The calculation of the finance charges on professional fees is similar to that of the calculation above for the charges on construction expenditure. The majority of development appraisals carried out at the early stage of development tend to see these two elements of finance calculated together.

It is preferable to separate the calculation in most cases, as the expenditure profile and thus the calculation of interest tends to be different between the two. The difference in the final appraisal is marginal, as fees tend to be a relatively small proportion of expenditure; but the sums involved can be significant.

The differences can be seen from the 'Expenditure patterns for construction fees' graph (left).

Construction professionals receive payment earlier than the contractor; indeed, the bulk of professional fees may be paid before construction work has advanced very far.

This should be reflected in the finance charge calculation.

Finance on void period

The third element of finance included in the calculation is the void period. This is the period from the end of construction (or practical completion) to the point where the development becomes a saleable investment (usually when the building is fully let in the UK).

It is virtually impossible to find a buyer for an empty investment building, except at 'fire sale' prices.

One that is partly let may be saleable, but at a sizeable discount to the full value. The sum obtainable is usually not sufficient to cover development costs, so this is usually a last resort for a desperate developer intent on a damage-limitation or time-buying exercise.

As a result of this, most developer traders tend to hold buildings until fully let, and this must be accounted for in the calculation. Similarly, an allowance for a void period should be included not just where a sale is involved.

The letting-up process reflects the transition of the building from development to mature standing investment, often from short-term debt finance secured on the site to longer-term mortgage finance secured on the building.

The void period on a speculative development is absolutely critical to the success or failure of the scheme. Finance charges quickly accumulate in this period because they are calculated on the full development costs. Interest charges accumulate on the development from day one, greatly increasing once construction starts.

However, around half of the interest charge on our development takes place after month 18, i.e. when construction has been completed.

The effect of compound interest is to give an exponential shape to the curve. Unless some of the principal debt can be paid off – which is unlikely – this phase has a critical effect on most developers, as this is where the greatest concentration exists on risk mitigation in development. The longer this void period exists, the greater the interest charge will be.

In an appraisal, the void period is the safety net and a financier will need to ascertain whether a sufficient allowance has been made.

Professional fees: Sales and letting

The costs we have incurred to date have in common the feature that they are assumed to occur at various times up to the end of the letting-up period, and are therefore time-critical. The timing and extent of expenditure on these items affects the calculation of the cost of finance.

The remaining items in the basic residual model usually take place at the end of the development period and thus have no effect on the interest calculation.

The traditional residual is an accumulative exercise. For the most part, it works forward, accumulating all the costs together, particularly the accumulated interest charges. The items that occur at the end of the period have no additional effect on the interest accumulated.

These are items such as marketing, letting and disposal fees and the developer's profit. These items are usually paid at the end of the development, or may even occur after the sale of the building.

Marketing

The marketing budget will tend to be expended earlier. In both residential and commercial schemes, it is not uncommon for advertising to take place before construction has started. Notwithstanding this, it is usually felt that it is not worth taking this early payment into account in a simple residual appraisal, as the sums involved are relatively small when compared with the development budget as a whole and, consequently, the impact on the appraisal of this inaccurate assumption is negligible.

Developer's profit

Developer's profit is also, effectively, a final stage payment. It is the hoped-for surplus after the sale and when all the costs have been accounted for.

Normally, this is taken as a percentage of development cost, or gross development value. At AFL, we take this last after we have paid all our investors; both senior funders and private funders.

The profit figures can be presented in a number of ways. Some of these are presented below.

While the raw sum of money that the project returns is important, it is often essential to present the figure as a percentage of costs expended, or of value, or in terms of the income return.

This is done to ensure that the return is sufficient to justify the development. Property development is risky; anyone embarking on it should ensure that they are sufficiently rewarded for taking this risk.

If an investor could get a return of say, 10 per cent, from investing in, for example, an industrial building let to a 'blue chip' manufacturer, they should seek at least 15 per cent (and probably 20 per cent) to invest in a development project to produce a new industrial building of the same specification. Why? Consider the risks inherent in each option.

There is risk with the existing investment that property values may decline, although they do tend to recover, and the tenant may go out of business.

However, even in this case, the building is still there and it can be re-let in time. The inherent risk is much, much lower than with a development where even a minor change in market conditions can cause a loss to be made, as we will see below. In order to assess whether the return is adequate, it is normal to see if certain benchmark figures are met. The most common figure is 20 per cent of costs, but this does vary from sector to sector (for example, development of houses in the UK does seem to work to lower profit figures). Three of the alternative methods used to measure profitability are given below. Other measures exist. The calculation method for each is as follows:

$$\text{Profit on cost} = \frac{\text{Residual profit figure}}{\text{All development costs}}$$

$$\text{Profit on net development value} = \frac{\text{Residual profit figure}}{\text{Net realisation}}$$

$$\text{Profit on gross development value} = \frac{\text{Residual profit figure}}{\text{Gross sales receipt}}$$

The above measures are simple expressions of profit as a percentage of something. Sometimes, developers and lenders wish to know how much time is available to let the building after completion. Two measures are often used: rent cover and interest cover. These formulas are below.

$$\text{Rent cover} = \frac{\text{Residual profit figure}}{\text{Annual rental value}}$$

$$\text{Profit erosion} = \frac{\text{Residual profit figure}}{\text{Initial monthly interest payments}}$$

Both of these are essentially benchmark measures, e.g. a lender may seek at least two years' rent cover as an indicator that the developer has surplus funds to cover outgoings before a risk of failure occurs.

In fact, neither calculation accurately predicts the duration of their respective period due to the compounding nature of the interest rate appreciation on the debt.

Inaccuracy in the traditional model

The traditional model does have a number of inaccuracies. Some of these have already been mentioned, and are classified into two different types of flaw: those that are general in all development appraisals, and those that are specific to the traditional model alone.

The general inaccuracies are connected with the extreme sensitivity of all development appraisal models to the value of the assumptions made in their construction. Even some very small changes in the values on some of the key variables can make enormous differences to the outcome being calculated, whether this be land value or profitability. These flaws will exist, regardless of what you do, but can be accounted for in the sensitivity analysis, which is covered below. The inaccuracies in the traditional models are related to the simplifications included in order to make the calculation easier.

From experience, the main issue with the residual models relates to the timing and extent of cash flows. These factors, in turn, affect the calculation of interest or finance. Let us look at the assumptions made in relation to construction expenditure. We assumed that the average balance owing was 50 per cent of the total budget, and this was the figure used in the interest rate calculation. This equated to a total interest rate calculation of £400,000 based on the 10 per cent effective rate. Be careful with this element of the calculation and make sure you calculations are as accurate as possible so you don't have any unwanted surprises.

Improving the appraisal

In order to improve the accuracy of the appraisal models, we need to step away from the simplicity of the residual model.

This does not mean that the residual approach should not be used. In fact, the speed and simplicity of the model is a huge advantage in the early stages of a development, i.e. in the initial feasibility stage to simply determine whether the project should go ahead before any real details about the development are known.

There is scope for improving the calculation accuracy of the residual model, although this does add to the complexity of the model, increasing the time needed to construct it. The key improvement is to move towards more explicit assumptions, as has been done with the construction expenditure in the previous section. As noted, most of the proprietary models have seen a shift towards more explicit calculation. These changes can be seen as a move towards cash flow approaches to appraisal.

Cash flow approaches to development appraisal

I am not going to cover this in detail on this book. In principle, moving to a complete cash flow approach for the appraisal of a development project is a major change. It is more time consuming and requires more detailed information, and the developer must make more explicit assumptions. As a consequence, the resulting appraisal model is harder to interpret at first glance. These models can be difficult to alter and it is quite easy to make mistakes. In moving from a traditional approach to a cash flow approach, it is very easy for the same developer to make very different assumptions about the project. So, given these huge drawbacks, why do people still use this method?

The truth is that some of these inaccuracies are also virtues. The need to be more explicit requires the developer to consider the project much more carefully. The goal, and major benefit, is accuracy. If the assumptions made are correct, then the appraisal will much more accurately reflect the actual financial outcome of the project. There are also additional benefits to a cash flow approach, the main one being project financial control and monitoring when the project actually goes ahead. Each projected cash flow period can be checked against actual expenditure, which can give valuable warnings of the development's progress and possible problems.

The traditional approach is clumsy and, as we have shown above, requires a number of approximations to be made in the calculation. Conversely, the cash flow model requires not only an estimation of the value of the individual variables, but also a future assessment of when the cash flow will happen at any given time.

Although this addresses the weaknesses in the traditional model, using a cash flow approach also requires a much greater degree of information about the development. Consequently, although cash flow appraisals can be done at the early feasibility stage, the value of doing so is questionable as the very nature of this stage is that details of the development are not finalised. The level of information available is low, likely to be sketchy, approximate, and incomplete. This logically points to an approach that is quick, flexible, and easy to apply and that itself relies on approximation rather than accuracy. As a result, I consider that the traditional residual approach is best suited to assess the viability of a scheme at this project phase. The fact is that using a cash flow approach would give the appearance of greater accuracy, but the assumptions made would be based on such unsubstantiated facts that it is unlikely that the outcome would be as reliable as that produced by the traditional approach, which also has the time advantage.

In my humble opinion, cash flows should only be used later in the appraisal stage when the data is more widely available and more reliable, and when the construction drawings are ready to go. From this point on, the benefits of greater accuracy will make the project run more smoothly.

There are two main forms of cash flow models used in development appraisal as per the book *Contemporary Property Development* by Dr Timothy Harvard (pages 213 and 216): full discounted cash flows (DCFs) and residual cash flows (RCFs). It is true that the two approaches represent alternative calculations to produce the same end result. In fact, I would argue that, in practical terms, the two approaches are distinct, particularly in that they are generally used for different purposes by developers.

The similarity of the two approaches is that both require the project to be broken down into a framework based on a time structure; and that all expenses and receipts be identified, quantified, and placed within this time structure. The residual cash flow is an accumulative cash flow, rolling forward the expenses and receipts as the development moves forward. The DCF is, by contrast, a discounting approach, in that the present-day value of each cash flow is calculated.

Sensitivity analysis calculation

Introduction

The basic appraisal models that we have mentioned briefly above are not the total picture of the full deal analysis of any development scheme. Deal analyses are extraordinarily sensitive to the input data used to construct them – any variable will impact on the result, which as well as going smoothly could go horribly wrong! As I always say "numbers have to be perfect"; we are only as good as our last project.

Any deal analysis, be it calculated traditionally or by way of cash flows, is just one set of assumptions that leads to a two outputs the cost of the land and the profit to be made. It is a prediction of how the future is going to pan out. Even though it may be the developer's best estimate of what may happen, it is just a forecast.

The assumptions made about the scheme can be wrong. If we don't have a ground investigation report available, the ground conditions may be different to those expected; building costs may rise; market conditions and tenants' requirements may change; and the economy may stall or boom. A typical residential scheme can take between one and two years, while a commercial scheme can take between one and five years. It is be certain that conditions when you are reading this book will be different in some way from the past and will differ, even if only in small ways, from the future. The question is, does this matter? The answer with development appraisals is almost invariably 'yes'. We will now look at the effect of changing just one figure: the rent achieved on letting. Let us assume that the rent achieved by the time the building came to the market was only £3,745 per square metre. This is a drop of just £150 per square metre, or a four per cent fall in values. This is not a major fall; it may just represent a mild slow-down in the economy. The effect on the appraisal, however, is quite striking. A four per cent drop in rent sees a drop in profits of nearly £23,100. This degree of sensitivity is not unusual. Because of this, it is essential that some sort of sensitivity analysis is carried out.

Sensitivity analysis methods

As per the book Contemporary Property Development by Dr Timothy Harvard (pages 218 and 219) there are various sensitivity analysis methods, with each having different uses. Each one also has a number of subtypes. The basic categories are:

1. Straightforward sensitivity analysis
   - single factor analysis – changing the factor by fixed amounts
   - single variable – break-even analysis calculation

2. Scenarios
   - basic scenario analysis
   - probability-linked scenario analysis

3. Simulation

Simple sensitivity analysis can be most useful in identifying areas of weakness; in terms of the appraisal and adverse movements in the market, or problems during construction. This also helps to ascertain the vulnerability of developments by looking at possible scenarios. The key is to have scenarios that are realistic, which examine the effects of movements in the assumed values of the pairs or groups of variables. Let's look at the way in which they can be used to assist us developers to make informed decisions.

Straightforward sensitivity analysis

Introduction

Straightforward sensitivity analysis should be the bare minimum in an appraisal. Even so, it is not very detailed. Straightforward sensitivity analysis examines the effect of changing one input factor at a time on the outcome of the appraisal, very much as was done in the example above.

Single variable analysis – fixed amounts

The traditional method of performing a sensitivity analysis is to alter the figures for each selected variable by a fixed percentage. For example, six key variables in our development have been selected and their values adjusted in the appraisal by plus or minus 10 percent. Subsequently, the effect on the overall profit level is calculated for each individual variable and the effect is measured.

Variable	Effect of changing variable on profit	
	+10%	-10%
Rental value	+62.4%	-62.4%
Interest rates	-6.0%	6.0%
Construction cost	-25.9%	+25.9%
Letting period	-7.6%	+7.5%
Land value	-18.6%	+18.6%

As the table above indicates, the factors that have the greatest impact on the profitability of a scheme are those concerned with its GDV. Factors such as interest rates usually have very little effect, at least not directly. Interest rate movements often indicate wider movements in the economy, which may have an impact on the key value variables.

A number of variations exist in the use of simple sensitivity analysis. Sometimes, monetary variations are used (for example, moving rents in £10/m2 intervals) although it is hard to achieve consistency between variables when this is done. A sensible approach is to create a table for each key variable, looking at the effect of possible different outcomes such as changes of three, seven and ten per cent on profitability or land value.

How to use sensitivity analysis in decision-making

The simple sensitivity analysis has considerable value to the developer. It enables them to identify the key variables in the development, i.e. those that have the greatest potential impact on the GDV, and therefore carry the most risks. It is down to the developer to quantify the degree of sensitivity to the variable; it is very important to ascertain how little or much the variable needs to move in value before serious consequences occur. Nevertheless, some variables such as rent very rarely move in isolation, and instead tend to move in complex ways with other variables. Hence, careful consideration needs to be taken on each variable. The best example is when rents falls: investors tend to become nervous about future rental growth prospects, and subsequently tend to adjust their yield requirements upwards. This, as a consequence, has a double effect on capital values, as previously discussed.

Single factor – profit evaporation or break-even analysis

A valuable variation on the single-point sensitivity analysis is to adjust the key factor until the profit produced from a development evaporates.

This is illustrated below:

Variable	Values required to reduce profitability to zero
Interest rates	28%
Construction cost	2,780 £/m²
Sales period after PC at 10% interest p.a. senior	36 months
Land value	£2,900,000

How to use this info for the developer decision-making process

Although this assessment does not appear different from simple sensitivity analysis, it does provide the appraiser with more invaluable information about the nature of the scheme.

The developer and their investors can identify exactly the point at which the scheme will fail to make a profit or brake even and the effect of key variables.

It can be seen that construction cost would only have to increase by between 45 and 55 per cent to extinguish the profits of the scheme.

In most market conditions, such a drop seems unlikely, but in extreme conditions this sort of movement can occur. The yield would only have to move from seven per cent to around eight point two five per cent to see this occur. Developers can ask themselves whether this is feasible. This sort of analysis adds considerably to the knowledge about the scheme.

Scenarios analysis

Introduction

All possible prediction scenarios, both positive and negative, are a must when analysing the sensitivity of the scheme. They address some of the problems that were identified earlier regarding the tendency of the individual variables to move together.

In simple terms, the analysis requires us developers to consider what might happen to the key variables in the scheme, such as construction cost, lower than predicted GDV etc. As projects sometimes take longer than expected, you should assume differing economic conditions ie higher or lower levels of economic growth than are currently being experienced.

Basic scenario analysis

This process is shown in table 10.1 below. The developer's best judgement of how the scheme will perform forms the basis of the analysis.

Two further outcomes have also been generated: one that assumes higher than average levels of growth (the optimistic forecast); and one that assumes a lower growth future (pessimistic).

The developer has formed judgements as to what would happen to the values of the key factor under each of these conditions, and the appraisal has been re-run to produce NPV and profit figures under each of these three possible views of the future.

Scenario summary	Expected values	Optimistic	Pessimistic
Changing variables:			
Residential sale	£5,500,000	£6000,000	£5,000,000
Commercial sale	£600,000	£6500,000	£500,000
Total dev costs	£5,198,159	£4,850,000	£5,5000,000
Result variables:			
Net Profit (NP)	£1,066,541	£1,800,000	0%
Profit on GDV	20%	37%	0%

Table 10.1

I am personally very risk-averse, hence in my view case scenarios are an essential additional step in understanding the specific risks of any particular scheme.

The pros

They are particularly useful in identifying more efficiency, the 'bottom line' or 'worst case' scenario, and equally the best possible outcome for the development compared with the simple approach.

Under the pessimistic scenario, it is assumed that the scheme could make a considerable loss. The developers could use this information to make a judgement about whether this is a risk worth taking or avoiding.

The cons

Scenarios of this form are still limited: they offer only two discrete views of the future, when we know that the future is more complex than that.

They also don't calculate the probability of each of the scenarios occurring. Similarly, the scenarios are only as good as the underlying constructional assumptions made within them.

Even though this is a very simplistic approach, scenarios are a vital part of the appraisal process and should really be the minimum that an appraiser ought to use in their assessment of financial risk.

Conclusion

It is absolutely essential that us property developers carry out some kind of sensitivity analysis on each feasibility study we perform.

Development appraisals are inherently unstable and unreliable, as they are based on predominately optimistic predictions.

The profit estimate, or land/site value, may represent the appraiser's best prediction as to how the development will perform, but it is likely that the outcome will differ from each specific projected scenario because of the length of time involved in the development process and the degree of inherent sensitivity to key variables within the process.

I strongly recommend that a simple sensitivity analysis should be done as the bare minimum.

As stated above, it is unlikely in reality that each single variable will change in isolation. It is therefore recommended that scenario building is undertaken for all deal analyses.

Time invested in exploring the different financial outcomes of the project can protect the developer from later losses.

Development appraisals are very important to the development process. They are not simply calculations; they represent an examination of the outcome of bringing together the development's components. This process is complex; the components can be fitted together in a number of ways and many assumptions have to be made.

These assumptions that the developer/appraiser makes about an uncertain future must be soundly based; it is easy to be misled and over-optimistic, and the highly sensitive nature of the financial appraisal can lead people into disaster. All developers should spend time gaining a full understanding of both the process and mechanisms of the appraisal process, and develop a feeling for what the outcome of the process actually means.

As I mentioned before "the numbers have to be perfect", and "we are only as good as our last project"; our reputation is our biggest asset, especially when we are working with someone else's money.

Development Execution

Introduction

In many respects, to a developer, the bulk of time and effort involved in carrying out a development is in the stage prior to the construction. The actual execution of the scheme is, however, the whole purpose of the development and should be treated with the requisite care. This chapter examines how development schemes are taken from existing only in the minds of their promoters, to their physical completion.

General principles

Having myself worn a contractor, designer and now a developer hat, I believe there should be a number of general guiding principles that us developers should follow when executing a development. These are very simple: prepare and plan ahead, and then plan and prepare again each week during the project execution! It is vitally important for the success of the development that the pre-construction and enabling works are carried out before the scheme commences, and that all the key components necessary to execute the development are in place at the time you hit the ground. According to the book *Contemporary Property Development* by Dr Timothy Havard, these include the following steps:

a) Appoint carefully your power team/development team. They must have the relevant and appropriate skills and knowledge to complete the scheme.

b) After this team has been appointed, two important matters need to be agreed before the relationship can develop and the scheme can proceed:
- Written contract of engagement must be signed, between the power team members and the developer. This document details the scope of the works, roles, responsibilities, duties, and timescales required of the development team members. These documents are vitally

important and must be consistent.
- Professional liability (PL) and professional indemnity (PI) letters from insurance providers should be sent to the developer for each member of the professional team. The level of cover should be commensurate with the level of risk (construction, design cost, etc), The PL and PI insurances are an essential safety net for the developer to ensure that, if a member of the development team fails to meet their professional requirements, any cost as a consequence will be covered. Property development involves high risks. For example, let's assume that a structural engineer, made a mistake on their calculation and, as a consequence, costly multimillion pound structural alterations need to be carried out. An individual or partnership will probably not have the resources to cover such a claim, and it is essential therefore to have adequate insurance in place.

(c) A detailed programme of works, with all actives and all the project's key goals, timescales, and milestones must be established. Good planning is essential to ensure that the project is successfully completed on time and on budget, although the need for flexibility must be incorporated into the team's thinking, in order to be able to accommodate unforeseen events.

(d) All the necessary preliminary activities to facilitate the construction of the scheme need to be in place before the physical on-site work commences. In an ideal set of circumstances, to minimise the risk to the developer, the key elements should be in place even before the land is purchased. These key project components / risks are:
- Senior and junior finance risks: it is impossible to proceed to the contract stage unless the finance is in place to pay for all the parties involved in the design of the scheme and the construction work. To do so would risk trading fraudulently.
- Planning consent risks.
- Legal risks: proof of the resolution of any legal matters, such as adjacent ransom strips, ownerships, leases, rights of way, etc.
- Archaeological risks: some areas of the UK, and many other countries, have a long history of occupation. In many areas, even in so-called up-and-coming towns, there may be an impact on archaeological remains. In historic towns, it is almost inevitable that works in the ground, or even alterations of existing older structures, will

subsequently have heritage consequences. The solution to this is carrying out reports from the local archaeological unit as early and as promptly as possible.
- Ground contamination risks: similarly, it is wise, given the level of contaminated sites in the UK, to commission a specialist report on potential contamination of the site, both above and below ground.
- Geo-technical risk: a report on the soil strata and ground conditions on the site. As this has a major impact on the design, this is a key report for most developments and should be carried out as soon as possible.

Other key components that should be in place prior to breaking any ground include:

- Detailed construction design, including drawings and specification of the building and all its components.
- Detailed cash flow costings and projections.
- Building regulations approval: construction work in the UK requires several stages of approval from the local authorities. This is in addition to the planning consent. Local authorities are charged with ensuring that construction is carried out safely; that the buildings are structurally sound; and that they meet all health and safety requirements. This is in terms of both design and construction. The building control office of the local authority will therefore need to approve the plans of the scheme prior to commencement, and will need to approve the construction elements of the work as it progresses. They will also certify the final building. Nowadays, we are also allowed to use private companies for this service, but extra time should be allowed as the local council needs to be notified of such intention.
- Detailed cost plan and bill of quantities.
- Written contracts.

If these items are not in place, then expensive delays or interruptions to the project may be experienced.

- (e) A competent contractor should be appointed to be able to successfully complete the work within the specified time period.

- (f) The most appropriate designer and contractor procurement method should be chosen for the project.
- (g) The most appropriate contract for the project should be selected.

The list does not end here. Once these above key components have been put into place, further items are required:

- Tender analysis report: if applicable, this is the report prepared by the cost consultant/quantity surveyor on the tenders received (depending on the contract procurement route chosen).
- Programme.
- Collateral warranties from main contractor, suppliers, and sub-contractors with the relevant design liability. Collateral warranties are legally-binding documents that enable subsequent users or owners of a building to be protected against latent defects in the design or construction of the building.

Parties to a contract are protected; there is a duty of care from professionals that they will do their work properly for their client. No such duty is owed to third parties, such as subsequent tenants or owners of the building. Collateral warranties give that contractual comfort, albeit of a generally weaker nature.

Nowadays, there is an insurance product to cover for this eventuality – decennial insurance, so named because it offers cover for a period of 10 years.

- Insurances: all risks covered for the works, endorsement of the existing building policy (if applicable), third party, and loss of liquidated damages.

The power development team

Our AFL power development team is made up of a group of professionals with very different backgrounds, attitudes and outlooks. It has taken us a long time to build this team, as it is important to find companies that share the same values and principles in order to create a meaningful, and what we call a long-term win-win value create relationship.

The power team can be divided into five loose categories: legal, project and development management, design, construction and others. We will examine each group in turn, focusing on identifying the key member of each one, and outlining their main roles and responsibilities. I will also try to identify the qualities that us developers should seek when appointing each member of the team.

I will also define the working characteristics of the main members of each of the groups. This process is useful to appreciate some of the dynamics of working with such a diverse group of professionals; though, this diversity of backgrounds can potentially lead to conflict. Each sub-team member has a different role to play during the project. Sometimes, there is a requirement to change personnel as these roles change. All of this can make building the team very difficult; without careful management, it can lead to conflict.

Legal Team

The legal team is paramount at feasibility stage, making sure there are no legal issues before you purchase the site and when it comes to selling or renting the units at the end of the project. Your power team must have extensive experience of advising other clients in specific projects; this could be housing, commercial and retail infrastructure, transport, renewable energy, etc. They can also help us carry out due diligence work for development or project financiers.

Reliable legal support is essential to ensure that our business is protected and that our project is delivered on budget and on time. Legal advice on what needs to be reflected in the project documents from the outset is key. Prevention is always better, and cheaper, than cure.

They are also essential when disputes arise. Their knowledge and experience help us resolve them, whatever their type and size, in the quickest and most cost-effective way.

Whether this is through advising in the background, negotiation, adjudication or litigation, we ensure that our business is placed in the strongest possible position to achieve the best result.

Development management

The high level of risks, the diverse nature of the power team members, and the complexity and duration of most development projects mean that some kind of project manager is required.

In the past, it was the architect who acted as the project manager; but with time, this has changed. It is still quite common for us developers to be the project manager, should the budget be limited.

We are after all, the entrepreneur and catalyst for the project, and it is always us developers who have the vivid vision of the end product and how the project is to be completed and executed.

This structure is only feasible for small projects and with smaller developers, due to the considerable time devoted by the developer to overseeing the project on a day-to-day basis. In other circumstances, where a number of schemes are involved, or are being undertaken simultaneously, or where the project is large and complex, it is not feasible for the developer to be able to devote sufficient time to adequately supervise the project.

In these circumstances, it is best to appoint a specialist delivery or project manager to be the overall coordinator and planner.

Development and project management is a discipline which has developed greatly over the past 30 years. It is used in many aspects of business, as well as in construction and other development fields.

Project managers are professionals in their own right, and many universities have started to run post-graduate programmes in the discipline. In the UK, the Institution of Civil Engineers (ICE), of which I am a corporate member, has set up a separate project management faculty in the last two decades.

The development, or project, manager fulfils the coordination and planning role that used to be undertaken by architects. Although there is an additional fee to be accounted for in the development budget, most large projects find it essential to employ a project manager.

Design

A number of key designers are involved in the development process. These are:
- architects
- space planners and interior designers
- landscape architects
- structural and civil engineers
- services engineers
- mechanical and electrical engineers

Architects

Here we have a link to one of our videos where we interview one of our architects: https://youtu.be/ZvFlu1ODw1Y

Architects are key members of the power team, they are in charge of shaping the concept and idea of the client into the final scheme.

They are in charge of the teams that produce the drawings and specification for pricing the scheme and for the construction of the building.

The architect's traditional method of working is to take the concept, as defined by the commissioning client, from an overall outline as to how the building should look and how it should function, to concrete designs as more information becomes available, and as the client's ideas materialise. Another important role of the architect is to provide a record of what has actually been constructed, something that is essential for future management of the building and for carrying out future alterations.

A summary of the key roles of the architect in the development can be seen in the Royal Institute of British Architects' (RIBA) 'Outline Plan of Works'which lays out the role of the architect at each stage of a scheme.

Stages of the RIBA Plan of Work 2020
- 0 – Strategic definition
- 1 – Preparation and brief
- 2 – Concept design
- 3 – Developed design
- 4 – Technical design
- 5 – Manufacturing and construction
- 6 – Handover and close out
- 7 – Use

For different types of procurement, the roles may differ. The choice of procurement method may be as important as other, more obvious, factors, such as the amount of work to be done, the client's tendering requirements, risks associated with third party approvals or funding, etc.

Key attributes

The key attributes to look for when selecting an architect really depend on the type of the development project to be carried out. The majority of architects are trained to have artistic flair, a feel for space utilisation, and the ability to translate and interpret ideas into reality.

I must say that is your responsibility as a developer to guide them on what you want and need.

At the end, the desired outcome comes from your end users / customers (renters or buyers) should you do rent to build or rent to sell strategy.

There are many different types of architects with different levels of training and skill and different fortes.

From personal experience, some architects are very good at aesthetics and design, but less efficient at producing practical buildable solutions to meet the needs of our costumers. If the project requires strong design and a striking appearance then it is essential to select an architect with flair and imagination. If, however, the project requires a practical solution within a tight budget for first time buyers like us, then it is very important to appoint a pragmatic, experienced professional who is used to working within such limitations. Sometimes to appoint a 'flair', architect in these circumstances can be a recipe for disaster. It's well worth taking the time to talk over ideas with a range of architects, and also to consult with their previous clients before you move forward.

Challenges working with some architects

A number of potential challenges exist in working with architects of which as developer you should be made aware. Here are a few:
- Buildability issues – it is often the case that architects design buildings and details that cannot practically be constructed on site. Then as a result there are extra scheme iterations with other team members such a structural engineers.
- Expensive designs - with architects, costs tend to be secondary to aesthetics;
- Sustainability - Environment and commercial requirements and market requirements are secondary to design considerations in some architects' minds.

Members of the development team specially the structural engineers often find that the architect is the most difficult member to work with and to understand.

This is largely as a result of different backgrounds and different outlooks; after all it is only the architect, of the whole within the development team, who has a background in humanities rather than construction, engineering, or economics.

Interior designers

Predominantly the design of the interior of buildings is carried out by the project architect. On larger schemes or high end residential and commercial projects a specialist is sometimes hired. Nevertheless, is rare for a developer to carry out a fit-out of a commercial building. This is normally left to the tenant. There will be occasions, however, when the developer is working to a brief, produced by the client and will need to employ such skills.

Landscape architects

Landscape architects are a specialist, as the name implies, who deal with the external environment of the development.

Where the development has fairly minimal external works, the planning and layout of the hard and soft landscaping can be carried out by the lead architect.

However, with buildings such as office parks, a much higher level of landscaping is required and a specialist landscape architect is essential.

Civil /Structural engineers - permanent and temporary works

Here is a link to one of our videos where I interviewed one of our structural engineers and shared some valuable information with you:
https://youtu.be/PkiY7K03xNM
https://youtu.be/dmklR3_nb10

The Civil and structural engineer, has a paramount role in the project (not because I was once filling those steel cap site boots!) They are specialists in the design of the structural elements of the building both permanent and temporary works (during construction). Normally, the architect will design the general layout of the building, but then pass the responsibility for the structural elements to the structural engineer.

The engineer will be responsible for the design, for example, the drainage, and the structural frame of a building.

They calculate things such as dead and live loads, wind loadings of the structure based on the end user and type of structure. Architects have very limited knowledge and qualification in these areas.

The second key role that structural engineers play in the development is in monitoring and checking progress on site.

Engineers will make regular site visits to the site to check calculations provided by the contractor and to inspect and approve the installation of the structural elements.

Key attributes

A good structural engineer will ideally be chartered with a sound level of experience in the type of development being undertaken. They will need to have an established track record in producing practical solutions to engineering challenges.

Structural engineers are a vital part of the development team. Ideally, you would need to appoint an experienced chartered structural engineer that is a corporate member of the Institution of Civil Engineers (ICE) and/or Institution of Structural Engineers (ISE).

Although education is changing, engineers have a strong background in calculation and mathematics, but with little emphasis on financial and management skills. Although some have financial awareness, some may not. A developer should be mindful of this aspect.

The actions of civil engineers may be in conflict with the financial aims of the project. Another characteristic which can be applied to engineers is that they tend to be cautious and over-design some elements of their responsibility. This, too, can have detrimental financial implications. The best example of this is when a permanent works engineer does not have temporary works experience and, as a result, they overkill the design and the developer ends up paying for the extra cost.

Mechanical and electric engineers

These engineers design elements such as lifts, air conditioning, heating, lighting and other service elements. The work of these engineers quite frequently overlaps.

Key attributes

Many of the key skills and characteristics of services and mechanical and electrical engineers are similar to those for civil and structural engineers. In particular, it is vitally important in complex buildings that these engineers have relevant, practical experience of the type of project concerned.

Project finances

There are a number of professionals who work in this area, most being related to the quantity surveying or construction economist professions. The two main types are quantity surveyors and value engineering managers.

Quantity surveyors

Key attributes

In simple bullet points the key attributes to look for on quantity surveyors are the ability to do the following efficiently:
- Whole project cost forecasting
- Whole project cost planning
- Whole project cost control /monitoring
- Whole project cost saving

At the initial feasibility stage the quantity surveyor will produce the initial budget and whole project cost control forecast.

At the outline design stage, this forecast will be updated, and more detail will be supplied by the client. Then at the detailed design stage, the quantity surveyor will prepare a much more detailed cost forecast and estimate.

This should in principle include a month-by-month projection of future costs and cash flow – this is essential for us the client, in order to maintain an understanding of the viability of the project and the effect of any changes.

This information is also vital in budgeting and arranging future finance.

In the conventional procurement route, one of the main tasks of the QS quantity surveyor is to prepare a Bill Of Quantities (BOQ).

The BOQ, is a key document where all the amounts and quantities of materials and construction elements of the proposed building are measured and described using standardised terms.

The BOQ has several functions in the construction phase:
- One of key functions is that the BOQ can be used as tender document. Once this document is produced by a QS or estimator is the supplied to the main contractors, along with the drawings and specification of the building. The contractors then enter their prices against the measured quantities. This enables a rapid estimate of the total lump sum cost, to be deduced.
- Once the overall building contract has been agreed and the work is awarded to the successful main contractor, the BOQ, tendered and priced up by the successful contractor, becomes one the main methods of development monitoring and payment for the main con-

tractor. Each month or fortnight , or whatever the appropriate interval between payments happens to be, the amount of work done will be assessed against each items noted in the BOQ. A percentage estimate of the amount of work completed is then calculated. This allows the rapid calculation of stage payments. It also allows variations to be calculated relatively quickly using the rates supplied by the contractor in the document.

This will be further described in the alternative methods of procurement below, in which the BOQ is only really applied in the traditional methods of procurement. When other methods are used by the developer, although the QS is still a vital member of the development team, their role of the quantity surveyor is somewhat different, although still vital. They still have the same areas of responsibility as before, but the method of working has to be adapted to suit the procurement route chosen.

Further key attributes contributions

Other key contributions by the QS include:

- Tender preparation, scrutiny, and checking – despite the presence of the BOQ, when we get us humans involved in the process it is common for mistakes to be made by contractors when pricing work. The quantity surveyor's role is to audit the contractors' bids and to identify errors. These are usually brought to the attention of the contractor, who is given the opportunity to either stand by their original estimate, alter it, or withdraw. Another role of the quantity surveyor is to assess the accuracy viability of the estimates submitted. Although it is normal to take the lowest estimate, it is sometimes obvious that contractors have underestimated the work for which it cannot be done for the sum submitted. In these circumstances it may be best to take a more viable tender from an alternative contractor.
- Quantity surveyors are also in charge for stage payments under the majority of building contracts. This normally requires the QS to undertake monthly valuations of work completed on site. These valuations are supplied either to the clients's project administrator, architect, project manager, or whoever is responsible for approving payments.
- From experience one of the main duties for which that I employed a

quantity surveyor QS for is for scrutinising and pricing of any variations by main contractors and subcontractors. These are changes in design, quantity, or timing of the construction work, for which the main contractor will require additional payment. From experience, us developers need to be very careful at appointing main contractors as sometimes they spot areas where they can hit the developer with numerous variations that could sometimes be well overpriced. Then the developer is held to ransom as the main contractor argues that not other trades can be brought to the project, for work guarantee proposes and us developer ends up paying for the overpriced variations.
- QS also have the responsibility of agreeing to the final account with the main contractor.
- In addition to the initial forecast and cost estimate, the QS provides regular updates of the forecast and monitors the expenditure on a week-by-week basis, this is an essential tool of project development management.

In certain circumstances, the QS can also act as the project manager but I strongly recommend that you appoint the QS as PM but only if they have the relevant experience.

It is essential that the developer appoints an excellent QS with relevant experience of the nature of your project and someone that is thoroughly diligent. Their main role should be a focus on saving money and time, at any project phase. This can conflict with the aims of the development as a whole. Another skill of QS should be conflict avoidance and as a last resort, management with contractors.

Contractors also employ their own in-house QS, whose role it is to carry out the financial side of the contract process, on behalf of the contractors. This includes agreeing to monthly valuations with the developer's surveyor, and also preparing and calculating claims for variations, which are subsequently negotiated with the developer's surveyor.

All of the above QS skills and functions of the quantity surveyor do tend to be confrontational and this can spill over into other working relationships. In summary, the QS is an essential element of the development team.

It will be very difficult to undertake any development work and to manage a large project, without their services.

Value engineering managers

A key team member is a VEM who deals with the cost and time efficiency of our development. VEM would scrutinise a design before it goes to the tender stage in order to determine whether costs can be saved, i.e. whether the design is efficient or if some alternative, better solution can be found.

Value engineering management has been increasingly used in the UK to save costs in construction. It is, however, rare to make use of this in commercial investment developments.

During my chartered engineering career, I was able to help several projects come up with outside-the-box solutions. Developers can still benefit after we have tendered for works in the sense of asking the contractors to come up with any more cost-effective solutions that can be put forward in their tender and can be used to benefit their part of the work. In this way, the client (us developers) can use their ideas to save money and/or time.

Construction

Main contractors

Having completed several projects now I know that if we have a good contractor on board depending on the complexity of the project it can be plane sailing. My view is that one of the biggest risks is appointing the wrong contractor for the job.

The reality is that development team needs the acquired skills, knowledge, and experience of the main contractor to complete the project on time and budget. In many scenarios the status of the contractor could can be ambiguous. In conventional contractual arrangements the contractor is almost a third party; an outsider, perhaps even considered to be the in opposition to the development team. This is because in traditional developments the contractor is not part of the design team but is the last element of the team, brought in at later stage and sometime seen as the enemy which is totally wrong if you want a successful outcome.

If we decide to go for the traditional procurement route (i.e. clients and designers both appointed by client separately) The contractor's position is quite separate from the rest of the team. This is something that the construction and development team have long considered to have undesirable characteristics, not least of which is that this arrangement lends itself to conflict. It also means that the contractors' invaluable input into the design process are is limited; a good contractor can suggest valued engineers solutions to the design, or alternative methods of construction. It is because of this, that as a result, alternative methods of procurement have been developed, which will be reviewed later in this section, integrating the contractor into the development, at an earlier stage. We will also explore why these alternatives have had a limited impact on many types of development.

We cannot generalise and assumed that all contractors can perform to a high level - not all contractors are the same, even at the larger end of the market. The large contractors have different strengths, and it is worth reviewing the type of contracts they have recently undertaken to see where their experience really lies with in relation to your specific project. Smaller contractors are far more variable in terms of their skills, experience, and resources.

Taking the latter as a factor, many of the problems that exist at the domestic and smaller commercial-type end of the market, in terms of,for example delayed completion and intermittent progress, is are due to the fact that during booming periods contractors may be taking on too many projects that they are not able to handle and as a result, they being late on all of them!

Contractors usually refuse to turn work down work, out of fear of not being considered for future works; this therefore, can sometimes lead to irrational decisions about the workloads. Even though most building contracts such as Joint Contracts Tribunal (JCT) and NEC Engineering Contract (NEC) contain provision for imposing penalties for late completions (LADS), these penalties are mostly the majority of the time very difficult to enforce and take loads of time and solicitors fees to pursue, and usually give inadequate compensation for the true impact on the developer of late delivery on the developer. Late completion of a project means the loss of a tenant or large compensations to them or a even the loss of sales. It is best to do as much as possible to avoid these problems before the contract is placed.

Similarly over-optimism is also frequent with regard to skills. The skill requirements for a contractor will vary from development to development. It is important for the developer to identify exactly what the critical skills are for the scheme, and match these requirements against the list of potential main contractors and their subcontractors.

When we are dealing with complex projects, it is worth talking to other members of the development team, particularly the QS, architect, structural and M&E engineers. They often have prior knowledge from previous schemes and may know key contractors or subcontractors in the marketplace. Even if no direct prior experience has been gained, the members of the development team are often able to use their contacts with professional colleagues in other organisations, to obtain this information.

It is paramount that the best contractor is appointed for any specific job. Selecting a contractor or subcontractor blindly without prior research is like playing Russian roulette. Usually for small projects we may be able to get away with it, but the consequences of making an incorrect selection can be catastrophic for small and medium size projects. The building industry has a bad reputation, and with good reason.

Choosing a big name contractor will usually give some guarantees. Therefore, taking up references and doing plenty of research is absolutely essential. Remember that appointing the main contractor is our highest risk and we are only as good as our last project.

Key responsibilities

The big role of the contractor is to complete the project on budget and on time as per the written contract agreement. They will some time have the inhouse human resources staff to deliver the project or alternatively need to employ subcontractors and any other skilled labour and hire equipment to carryout the agreed works. How they perform their duties is largely up to the contractor as long as they fulfil the terms of the contract. Once we clients/developers have signed a legally binding contract, we have only limited powers to influence the way the contractor actually conducts the development.

Key attributes

We clients developers should be systematic and spend considerable time and effort scrutinising the contractors we select to go on the tender list (assuming this is part of the procurement strategy). We need to be 100 per cent sure that they have sufficient experience and sufficient resources to complete the project to the required scope of works and within the time frame.

Subcontractors

Subcontractors are contractors to contractors, employed by the main contractor to do elements of work. Many large contractors do not retain many staff directly but instead operate essentially as management shells employing personnel and equipment as required. Many tradesmen and labourers are 'labour only subcontractors'.

Main contractors also employ smaller firms to carry out specific or specialist tasks. It is these bodies which tender for work from the main contractor and which then find their contract sums reduced by negotiation. These organisations have little power and are open to manipulation.

Depending on the property cycle, many contractors acquire work with low or sometimes minimal profit mar-gins.

The reason for this is simply to capture turnover in competition with other firms. Of course, they then need to find a profit margin. They do so in a number of ways.

Diminishing subcontractors' margins

Contractors tent to pay subcontractors on time,There is a tendency for contractors to delay paying subcontractors even though the work has been done and the main contractor paid by the developer. This enables the main contractor to leave the money in the bank and get extra interest and credit on these funds.

Although neither of the above practices is illegal or strictly the concern of the developer, these practices can cause bad working relations on site and also force subcontractors to take short cuts and reduce the quality of the finished product.

A wise developer / client would put pressure on the main contractor not to follow these practices. Personally as a developer I always ask to have a say on choosing the relevant subcontractors and try to negotiate with them directly which could be another way to bring the cost of project down.

Lessons learnt from previous projects

Link to our videos

1. https://www.youtube.com/watch?v=s98yrfqwB4Q

If the contractor had a small margin then a popular way to compensate is the use of variations and disputes. This is perhaps the most popular of the methods employed by contractors. Contractors also employ quantity surveyors whose main role is to negotiate interim and final payments for the contractors and also to negotiate variations. Variations, as we have seen, arise out of things such as extra work need, design changes. Another common source of income for them is making claims on "errors" in the contract documentation that sometimes are only coming to light after they have been appointed. These include items such as misdescription or mis-measurement of work or mistakes on specification and drawings.

Once the contract documentation is received, the contractors QS quantity surveyor and PM project manager scour the specification and drawings for errors. Some contractors are more litigious than others, this can be determined at the pre-tender selection enquiry stage and also speaking to previous clients which I strongly recommend you do as developer.

Here is a link for further nuggets: https://youtu.be/Zk_raMHRb1k

Other key members of the development team

These other parties of our power team have a significant impact on the design, cost and execution of the project, if appointed correctly. Just because some members of the team fall into this category does not downgrade their importance. A number of bodies fall into these categories, but two of the key ones are property agents/consultants and planning consultants.

Various types of property consultants are used by developers. The roles of many will be considered later in the post-construction section, but with respect to the development process, some of the roles will be considered below.

Agents and consultants

Here is a link to our videos: https://youtu.be/zxf3klOrTc8

- Residential estate agents – used in the marketing of residential property, as well as, in the design process and make up of the development. They do know our customers better than we do so we must tap into their knowledge for any layout advice even if we appoint the an architect
- Residential and commercial land sources agents – we have several as part of our AFL familia. They specialise in the identification, sometimes assessment (if they are trained) and acquisition of land, with or without planning consent, for residential and commercial development. Specialist knowledge is required to successfully fulfil this role, particularly carrying out the deal analysis and the sometimes occasionally difficult approach of the planning authorities.

- RICS Valuation surveyor – used during the process mainly to value the site for loan security purposes. At AFL we have also used them to come up with win-win JV structures where we need impartial valuation assessments
- RICS development surveyors – these are members of the QS quantity surveyor profession who specialise in development work. They are multi-skilled in terms of the tasks that they can undertake, which range from valuation and appraisal work, to advice on development and design, marketing of the completed scheme, and planning advice and applications.

Commercial agency surveyors

They are also power team member in commercial schemes. Their main roles are:

- To find and secure an acceptable tenant for a scheme. Once the structure is build the real assets are our tenants.
- To negotiate on our behalf the heads of terms with the occupiers, particularly the rental level and the outline lease terms (period term) of the lease, rent review details, user clause, repairs, rent free period if applicable and maintenance, etc)
- To advise us developers on current market requirements and trends at all stages of the development. The play a vital role at the feasibility stage, final design, pre-tender stage, and also during the course of the development. Getting these professionals involved at an early stage of a development will pay dividends, avoid costly design mistakes, and avoid any late costly changes in our design. They are a key interface between the market and the production team.
- Commercial investment agents – these professionals do not play the same vital roll as commercial letting agents. They contribute in a different way and have different skills set. Commercial investment agents tend to be rather more technically adroit and numerate than letting agents, as they have to deal with financial analysis and investment appraisal. Their main roles are:
- To advise us developers on the market requirements of the investors
- If we are not going to keep the asset for life, to secure the sale of the investment interest in the scheme at an acceptable rate and within an acceptable time period.

Key attributes to look for

The main potential challenge with property consultants is their tendency to be over-optimistic about sales and rent prices and, therefore, the prospects for development. An important function of an agent is to 'test up' the markets, in order to maintain confidence. This will enable turnover and activity in the market to be maintained. This can be easily overdone, which can increase the tendency for property markets to go belly up, by allowing unsustainable values and prices to be maintained for too long. Hence, be careful of where you are in the property cycle and learn from the past, as I have already taught you in this book.

Planning consultants

Planning consultants are vital and play a key role in development. They are the private sector that work on our side of the planning profession. Traditionally, planners were only employed by the public sector to fulfil the standard planning role of urban and economic development of an area. But, over the past five decades in particular, planners have crossed over to our side to assist in the navigation of schemes through the planning process. Just as agents give invaluable input about market and requirements into the design process early on, similarly, planning consultants perform the function of advising the planning authorities on what is and what is not acceptable.

The main roles of planning consultants are:
• Conduct schemes through the initial application process, including pre-planning applications, leading negotiations and consultation with the local planning authorities.
• Assist in the preparation of reports supporting planning applications.
• Prepare and argue the case for development during planning appeals.

I don't believe there is a single large scheme where a private planning consultant is not involved. The current trend is for local authorities and other public bodies to also employ planning consultants, to counter the arguments of developers' consultants, particularly when a planning application is rejected and an appeal is made. Other professionals employed by medium and large developers include environmental assessment consultants, archaeologists, and market researchers.

'Clockwork' power team work during development

The development power team should work as a clock, if any component fail, the projects gets delayed or end up over budget. An indication of how some of the key members of the development team take part at any given point of the development process is shown in Figure 5.4 overleaf. This a great visual summary of a typical project clockwork components.

Procurement routes

Before we carry out the work, we need to think about an efficient method for procuring the building work, i.e. the process of physically carrying out the development. There are numerous ways of achieving this, the choice being dependent on a number of factors related to the objectives of the developer. The key factors include:
1. Time
2. Cost
3. Quality
4. Complexity
5. Level of control
6. Risk allocation

All of the methods of procurement have different levels related to these variables. Some are good for reducing cost; some allow the development to retain a high level of control, etc. Which one is chosen depends on the nature of the individual contract or development and sometimes even on the personal preferences of the developer involved. To give an example of this, many institutional investors prefer the conventional methods of procurement. The conventional methods of procurement see the separation of the design and build elements of the project. In such cases, the contractor is placed outside the development team, as we have seen, leading to a more adversarial and confrontational relationship. Institutions need to have both certainty and control, something provided by the traditional methods, despite their other, acknowledged flaws. The conventional method also has the benefit of familiarity and, even though it is heavily criticised, it continues to be used.

The main three methods of procurement can be summarised as follows:

- 1. Conventional methods
- — single-stage selective tendering
- — two-stage selective tendering

PROJECT STAGES	Appraisal	Design Brief	Concept	Design Development	Technical Design	Production Information	Tender Documentation	Tender Action	Mobilisation	Construction to Practical Completion	Post Practical Completion	Letting and/or sale
	PREPARATION			DESIGN			PRE-CONSTRUCTION		CONSTRUCTION		USE	LETTING
ARCHITECT'S ROLE	CLIENT BRIEFING PERIOD		SKETCH PLANNING PERIOD		WORKING PLAN PERIOD LEADING TO PREPARATION OF FINAL DESIGN				SITE OPERATIONS PERIOD			Post completion
	Outline sketches		Revisals	Scheme Design plans	Detail design		Contract drawings issued		Monitor/late - revisions/issue of details	Certificate of practical completion	"As built" drawings issued	Certification of final completion
QUANTITY SURVEYOR'S ROLE					COST PLANNING PERIOD					COST CONTROL PERIOD	COST RECONCILIATION PERIOD	FINAL ACCOUNT
	Initial cost limits set		Cost limits finalised		Cost checks	Outline cost plan finalised	Bills of quantity prepared		Cost monitoring and preparation of periodic valuations for stage payment of contactor		Preparation of final accounts	Release of retention
	INITIAL APPRAISAL				FINAL APPRAISAL AND MARKET FOCUS			Cost checks	Cost analysis	MARKETING		
AGENT/ PROPERTY CONSULTANT'S ROLE	Briefing by client	Preliminary valuation advice	On-going valuation and marketing advice as the scheme develops					Final valuation and market advice before commitment to build made	On-going valuation and marketing advice as the scheme develops	Marketing and letting programme begins	Negotiations with occupiers and investors	Agreement of sale and/or leasing
		Market analysis			Monitoring of market				Monitoring of market			

Figure 5.4

- — Earlier contractor involvement negotiation

- 2. Integrated procurement systems
- — design and build
- — package deals
- — turnkey method
- — develop and construct

- 3. Management-orientated procurement systems
- — management contracting
- — construction management
- — design and manage.

Traditional procurement methods

The main difference between all the contracts is the separation of the design from the construction element. The detail layout design is completed by an architect, who is also assisted by other specialist designers such as civil, structural, mechanical, and electrical engineers, and prior to the on-site work commencing.

The detail design work (construction drawings) is usually completed prior to tendering. The contractor's main role is managing the project rather than assisting with the design, giving little scope for the designers and contractors to become involved in each other's activities.

The traditional method tends to be a sequential process involving the following phases:
- concept design by client's architect
- detailed design by client architect and rest of design team
- preparation and obtaining of tenders by client's development team
- construction by client's main contractor

Concept design

The client/developer, with the help of their architect, establishes the concept design of the type of building that has been visualised. With most developers like us, this is in response to our customer's needs. There are certain times when this process involves working directly with the intended occupier.

This process will establish, or at least outline, their requirements. An architect and/or development manager is appointed to draft the outline of the building required, to establish the feasibility of the scheme.

Detailed Design

The main outcome of this phase is having a detailed design that meets the needs of the client's customers. This phase must be carried out before going out to tender or commencing work on site. It is essential for the detailed design to be completed before site work commences, unless it is emergency civil infrastructure work.

It is in this area where the traditional approach lacks efficiency. There is a lack of consultation and involvement between the design team and the contractors that perform the work. This is due to the following factors:

- The client usually chooses to retain control of design, sometimes to be able to control quality.
- A list of tenders is not usually available until the design is completed.
- There is no opportunity for the main contractor to come up with valued engineering options that would otherwise save time and/or money at feasibility stage.
- The contractor's identity is not finalised at this stage; different contractors being involved at this stage are likely to give different input, which may end up altering the design and generating a cost increase.
- Once the on-site work has commenced, it is really too late to alter the scheme design. Any input from the contractor changing the design will cause increases in cost and delays.

Preparation of tender documents and obtaining tenders

After a final the layout has been determined by the developer/ client, the detailed design is then subsequently completed. This comprises construction drawings, specifications, and Bill Of Quantities or schedule of works. Sometimes, for smaller projects, the BOQ is dispensed with, and the tender documentation consists only of construction drawings and specification.

This documentation needs to be as accurate as possible, as tenders are prepared using these materials. Changes made later and mistakes corrected will be expensive.

For my projects, I make a list of ten competent contractors and send a pre-qualification document that is based on the project level of expertise required. Based on their responses, I shortlist between four and six contractors, and invite them to prepare a tender. These tenders usually consist of sealed bids prepared without collusion, and to be submitted in a specific timeframe.

Construction

This stage is the actual execution of the physical works. This is frequently carried out under a bespoke or standard building contract, usually prepared by the Joint Contracts Tribunal (JCT), such as JCT 2016.

These contracts include items such as time to complete, payment methods, detailed scope of works, specifications, relevant authorities during construction and also methods of dispute resolution.

It should be noted that, during the contract, the con-tractor is responsible for the site and issues such as health and safety, and therefore can stop anyone entering the site, including the client.

Pros and cons of this procurement method

Cost

When the design is fully developed and a BOQ or schedule of works is prepared, the tendering cost risks are reduced for contractors.

Once there are detail construction drawings, there is also a clear definition of the scope, complexity and character of the works to be carried out. This greatly reduces uncertainty and gives a level playing field for true competition between contractors.

In other methods, the contractor has to interpret far more, increasing the level of risk and giving rise to costly differences between tenders. On the downside, preparation costs for the client are higher, and the design must be frozen earlier.

Time

From experience, as part of this method of procurement, there are two elements involved when considering the time characteristics: the pre-contract and on-site works. There is no real difference between this method and others for the on-site work, although the methods and sequence of working may be more strictly defined than with other methods.

The main difference is in the pre-contract preparation work, making this one of the slowest methods of procurement, and as result not the most efficient.

Quality and control

On the plus side, this method of procurement gives the highest degree of control over the detail design i.e. the finished product. It is for this reason that this method continues to be the most preferred by investment clients.

Other key advantages

- Familiarity: this method is well understood by most members of the team; it has the clear attraction of familiarity.
- Output control: the main advantage has to be the ability of the client to control the output of the development process very closely.
- Design team selection: the developer is able to select the design team to suit the needs of the development.
- Time: the developer has the ability to decide when to commit to the contract.

Disadvantages

- Speed: this is the main disadvantage. This is generally regarded as the slowest of the procurement methods.
- Value engineering limitation: it is not a good method for achieving cost savings.
- Design changes: it is difficult to deal with later design changes that may be required in the scheme.
- Contractor limitations: the contractor is remote, and has very little opportunity to influence the project, make an impact, or have an input into the design and other aspects of the scheme until a very late stage.

In my opinion, this method is full of clear disadvantages, particularly for complex projects, but continues to be used. This is because many clients find that the advantages greatly outweigh the disadvantages. It is particularly true of investment clients, where control is far more important than, for example, cost saving. Many members of the construction team, particularly those concerned with cost, find this a difficult concept to understand. If, however, the relative impact of changing cost and changing values in an appraisal are investigated, in the great majority of cases, it is the latter which has a much greater impact.

For this reason, control of the output is the major requirement of procurement methods used for the construction of investment properties.

Other alternative options

Two-stage selective tendering

This method involves two distinct stages of the tender process. I have personal used this method as a contractor. It is used in a number of circumstances: where the design is not finalised; where the control of the finished product by the client is not as critical as in the above scenario; and where the building is complex, like in my personal experience, and more input, in terms of design and advice from the contractor, is required.

In the first stage of the tender process, outline sketch drawings (tender drawings) and bills of approximate quantities are sent out to between four and ten contractors, who are then invited to submit tenders.

Once the tenders are received, the clients shortlist and interview two contractors, and then picks one to move forward with. The successful tenderer is then notified of the client's intention to enter into a binding contract, subject to the client's conditions. An acceptable final tender figure is agreed between the client and the potential contractor. The chosen contractor then agrees to provide what we call "early contractor input" and cooperate with the design team. From there, they give advice on issues such as buildability, materials, costs, programming, and the detailed design.

Pros

This approach is worthwhile where the project is complex and where experience exists among contractors, which will assist in the design and construction.

Cons

The disadvantage of this approach is that the competitive element is lost after the first stage of the tender process, as the contractor is then able to submit costly variations if he wishes to.

Earlier contractor involvement and negotiated contracts

The steps are exactly the same as the conventional single-stage tender process, at least until after the outline design stage.

At the detailed design stage, or prior to the final design iteration, a contractor is appointed.

The appointment is based on the contractor's past expertise and past record of similar projects, and possibly value for money.

This type of contract is most effective in unusual, innovative, or complex projects such the ones with which was personally involved as the main contractor in central London, where the contractor's prior experience of similar situations allows their advice to be provided at the critical design stage.

This helped with buildability issues, such as temporary works, timing of work, and programming, as well as cost forecasting.

There are a number of ways of appointing the contractor, including interviewing a range of suitable candidates, and negotiation with a single contractor who is known to the design team or who has worked with the developer previously.

Pros

This method of procurement saves time and reduces risk.

Cons

This method can be more expensive as the competitive element is reduced.

Continuity contract

These types of contract are used when a number of phases are involved. For example, a residential project with two or more similar phases may see the first phase of the contract awarded using a single-stage selective process, as per the traditional approach, then the second and/or third phase of the contract being negotiated based on the previous phase, if agreed. This usually involves modifying or updating the first set of priced tender documents.

Pros

This approach reduces the time required by the developer's team, and the cost of preparing a second tender process.

Cons

There are disadvantages with the approach, given that the competitive element is reduced.

Furthermore, there is no guarantee (if not agreed) that a contractor, having behaved well in the first contract, will do so in the second or subsequent contracts, particularly if there is no further work to consider in the future.

A contractor remaining in the second phase of the work might divert labour and machinery to other contracts, which has happened to me personally as a developer. And what might seem a sensible approach to the developer may in fact go badly wrong and lose precious time and money in the process.

Serial contracts

I have limited personal experience with these, but in essence they are similar to the ones mentioned above with the difference being there is a series of contracts, some consecutive and some occurring simultaneously. In these cases, the best possible approach for all parties is to work to a master bill of quantities.

This document contains the rates for a series of activities across the various contracts.

Cost reimbursement contracts, with my personal twist

There are a number of types of cost reimbursement contract with which I don't have experience; one is the cost-plus approach. Here, the contractor tenders for work at an agreed cost and rate, supplied by the client's quantity surveyor. The contractor, as part of the tendering process, just adds a percentage for overheads and profit as required. The contract is usually awarded to the lowest percentage bid.

A second type of cost reimbursement contract, which at time of writing I am trying to establish with a long-term contractor that I have been working with, is called the target cost procurement method.

Here, the contractor is given a target cost, and any savings actually achieved are subsequently shared as an additional profit between contractor and client at an agreed percentage (in our scenario, 50/50).

There are challenges with this approach, the principal one being that, if the contract goes wrong and the target cost is exceeded, then the contractor may lose motivation to complete the project on time.

To address this, we are in the process of agreeing that 15 per cent of the total gain at the end of the project will be awarded to the contractor, creating a win-win situation.

Integrated procurement systems

This is so-called because the design and construction elements are the responsibility of a single organisation, usually the main contractor. I personally don't have experience of this, but these methods have increased in popularity over the past 50 to 60 years.

The impetus has come from two sources: first, contractors who feel that greater and earlier input into the design and development process will increase the efficiency and reduce costs; and, second, the wish of some clients to reduce both costs and time.

Although these methods give distinct advantages, the use of the conventional methods still continues, much to the chagrin, and sometimes bewilderment, of academics, government and contractors.

The reasons for the continuing use of the conventional methods have been mentioned above, namely the issues of controlling the project's output, and familiarity.

Sometimes, control rather than cost is the key element in many investment projects. In addition, investment banks and fund managers are cautious, risk-averse people. Conventional contracts are a known entity, with relatively low levels of risk to the client. Their argument, which is sometimes valid is, why bother taking on more risk to save a relatively small amount of money?

As a way of kinaesthetic learning, we will examine a typical investment project:

Project values
End value	£6,000,000
Cost of land	£2,000,000
Cost of construction	£2,000,000
Professional fees	£500,000
Finance cost	£500,000
Profit	**£1,000,000**

Taking a non-conventional route may save five per cent of the construction costs. There may also, however, be the risk of losing five per cent of the value due to not quite meeting the requirements of the market. As we have seen, these methods do not allow the client the same degree of control. If we examine the impact of this on the project viability, we can see the type of risk that the client is running:

Project values

End value	£5,700,000
Cost of land	£2,000,000
Cost of construction	£1,900,000
Professional fees	£475,000
Finance cost	£500,000
Profit	**£825,000**

In this scenario, although the costs are reduced, profits have fallen because of the impact on the end value.

Of course, this will not always occur, but why take the risk?

Why should investors give up their control? Contractors are not in touch with the market and do not normally share in profits, so why should they worry?

This factor does not rule out the use of these methods, nor do these problems occur with every type of project; however, the developer should carefully consider the potential downside risk before adopting these methods of procurement.

We will consider four main types of integrated procurement systems:
- design and build
- package deals
- turnkey method
- develop and construct
-

Design and build

I have several years' experience in this field and consider it to be one of the best ones out there. Furthermore, this is one of the best known and most popular of the integrated procurement systems.

In this approach, the client develops a detailed brief, or advanced detailed design, as to the type of building required. This brief, or design, needs to be clearly presented in the same way as during a tender process, with drawings and specification with regard to what is required. Also it needs to be sufficiently comprehensive for tender bids to be prepared on a competitive basis. The contractor then bids a lump sum to cover for the remaining design element and the construction of the building, based on the information supplied. The bid is on a fixed-price basis, i.e. it cannot change unless there is a substantial change in a requirement from the client. The process produces a simplified contract and functional relationship. The contractor who is successful commences the detailed design in consultation with the client.

Pros
- As long as the drawings and specification provided by the developer is comprehensive and accurate, it is possible to achieve a level of cost and programme certainty in the project.
- Time and, therefore, cost is saved as the contractor is also responsible for the design. This means that the contractor has full control of the design team and is not waiting for details. It is therefore possible to overlap elements of the design and construction due to the integration of the two processes.
- Enables a closer working relationship between the developer and the main contractor.

Cons
- The major disadvantage of this approach for the developer is that we lose detailed control of the finished product. However, this can be agreed at the start of the project if necessary.
- If there is not a QOB, the pricing of any variations to the contract can be very difficult.
- Quality could sometimes be compromised using this procurement method. The contractor is primarily concerned with cost reduction and maintaining, or increasing, the margin between actual costs and the agreed tender sum, which can therefore have an impact on the end product.

There are other points of which to be aware when using this procurement method. An important factor to establish prior to the appointment of the contractor is whether the organisation has sufficient knowledge and expertise in the design to adequately complete the work to the developer's satisfaction. There are contractors with in-house design teams which possess the requisite know-how and depth of experience in designing and building, and indeed are designing and building specialists. But there are also many other organisations which do not specialise in this field. Many contractors have gone down the design and build route to obtain work, then buy the design expertise by employing outside firms of architects. In this situation, the advantages of design and construction integration are largely lost. There is little real advantage over the traditional approaches, other than potential cost savings.

Off-the-shelf package deals

Package deals are very similar to the above; however, a bespoke design is not produced. This works well on large housing developments. In simple terms, the contractor, instead of carrying out a detailed design, uses an 'off-the-shelf' solution, i.e. a design used elsewhere in another project. Using a ready-to go design should be both cheaper and a lower-risk option, in that any technical defects should have been eradicated in the previous attempts and therefore you are guaranteed fewer costly design iterations. The main downside of this approach is that the product may not fully satisfy the developer's expectation and needs.

Turnkey method

This is a car factory and chauffeur approach to the production of a building. Effectively, it involves the full design, construction and facilities management of the building, including installation and commissioning of all operational, civil and M&E equipment, and sometimes goes as far as recruiting and training staff to run the facility. The PFI/PPP approaches are extensions of this.

The approach allows a rapid use of the facility by the user. It is therefore particularly useful in complex buildings, such as advanced manufacturing or medical facilities. I have not been involved in such developments and, as I understand, It has not been widely used in mainstream investment-type properties, usually because the end user has often not been identified prior to the development commencing, and also due to a lack of demand by end users for these types of services.

Develop and construct

This is another variation on the same theme car and chauffeur approach. In this case the developers' consultants are provided with a brief from the concept drawings and an indicative site layout is produced. Contractors, as part of the tender process, develop the initial design, producing detailed drawings and specifications, in turn submitting this as part of their bid. The contractor then effectively becomes the developer, coordinating the scheme as a traditional developer would do; sometimes including the arranging of finance and employing other contractors.

I was involved in such procurement method working as main contractor and solving a never-ending leak problem at St Thomas hospital in the heart of London.

Construction management procurement routes

This section outlines a group of procurement methods that sees the main contractor acting as more of a construction manager of the project, rather than as a direct contractor.

Management contracting

In simple terms, the management contractor (construction manager) does none of the construction work; instead, they play the role of a manager and coordinator of already procured specialist subcontractors. This service is provided on a fixed-fee basis as part of the developer's management team.

The management contractor provides and maintains all the necessary site equipment such as offices, storerooms, roads, etc., and is appointed either because of previous relationships with the developer, or because of bids on a competitive fee basis for the managing contract.

The management contractor then takes all the steps necessary to complete the building to the client's requirement, specification and budget. They are then commissioned to employ a series of specialist subcontractors to carry out the various sub-tasks for the building.

Pros
- Potential cost savings as there isn't a main contractor as such looking for a share of the profits.
- Particularly for large projects, time will be saved by overlapping elements of design and construction.
- The subcontractors can potentially become part of the development team, adding valuable, practical knowledge and input to the planning of works and design process.
- It is a useful method when the details of the works are not finalised at the time of the initial tender.
- Splitting up the works into component parts and subcontracting them out allows the early work to be completed without hold up, while the plans for the later stages are defined.

Cons

- Development banks, and therefore senior development finance, are not familiar with this procurement method, hence it may limit the developer's funding options if external funds are needed.
- There is a level of cost uncertainty as the final cost of the project is not known until the final contracts are placed.
- The method's flexibility invites costly variations in design to be made and can cause issues later on. This can lead to problems with keeping costs under control for us developers and may lead to variation claims from individual subcontractors due to design changes in other parts of the works.

Construction management

Construction management is not a procurement route. Instead, it refers to the service offered to the developer by a professional construction manager, who is often, but not always, working for a major contracting organisation.

The service offered is very similar to the situation described in the management contracting section above.

Design and management

Design and management is a variation on the same theme. The main difference is that the construction manager, or management contractor, also procures the design of the building, either on an in-house basis or, more commonly, with the architect/designer as a further subcontractor.

The main advantages are related to fewer design iterations and the closer integration of the construction process into the management of the development. Having the input of the construction professional upfront will save time, particularly with regard to the more rapid identification of practical problems and with the opportunity for design and construction to proceed in parallel. Conversely, there will be challenges due to the number of subcontractors involved (instead of just one main contractor), and this sometimes can cause friction and delays due to space allocation and programme interdependence. This causes to the developer a lack of certainty about the project cost, until later on in the process.

Summary and conclusions

Several procurement methods are available to us developers and there are no limits on being creative in mixing and matching to suit the project needs, as we have for several of our projects at AFL. Each has its own strengths and weaknesses. We should aim to match our goals with the appropriate procurement strategy. For example, if speed and cost minimisation is the goal, then one of the integrated procurement systems should be followed. If certainty of output is required, then the choice should be one of the traditional methods. From experience, the private construction investment industry in the UK has mostly tended to support and fund the traditional methods, which seem to confirm that certainty and familiarity are more highly valued. There has been some movement towards more contemporary methods of procurement, in the investment and speculative market; however, this tends to happen when the buildings produced across the market are similar, and where the profit margins are made thin by relatively low rents. This tends to be the situation with the decentralised office market and the industrial market. It seems that the preference for design and build in higher value situations, such as city centres, will be maintained due to the complexity of such developments.

Contracts and contracting

Our final piece of the puzzle in the execution of the project is the contract itself. This is a specialised area and one that the professional team, particularly the quantity surveyor, will advise the developer on. I will be including a brief summary of the main types of contracts, based on my own experience.

It is worth making sure that we understand the overall purpose of the contract, as this often gets missed in the detail. The purpose of the building contract is simply to ensure that the developer obtains the asset or structure that they desire at the cost agreed, and that the contractor is able to provide this and receive payment for this work, either in stages, as the works proceed, or as a final lump sum.

The contract should be as clear as possible and a legally-binding document that avoids any ambiguity between all parties involved. In summary, it will outline the following:
- The work to be done.
- The information to be provided by each party.
- The responsibilities of each party.
- The money to be paid and the basis on which the money is to be released.

- The procedures and processes to be followed, in the event that there is any dispute.

All of this is a well-worn path for many in the construction field. Essentially, it means that, although individual bespoke contracts for work can be drawn up by a developer, they would be very unwise to do so. For this reason, it is far better to use standard forms of contract.

Standard forms of building contracts

Most building contracts in the UK involve the Joint Contracts Tribunal (JCT). Using a standard contract form has to be the recommended path. It provides consistency for all parties and also provides a reliable framework for dispute resolution.

Source: https://www.jctltd.co.uk

The JCT was established in 1931 and has produced standard forms of contracts, guidance notes and other standard documentation for use in the construction industry ever since. In 1998, the JCT became incorporated as a company limited by guarantee.

The company is responsible for producing suites of contract documents and for operating the JCT Council. From 2016, the JCT started to issue a revised series of contracts under the blanket title of JCT 2016. The JCT 2016 contracts available are:

- **Standard Building Contract (SBC)**
- SBC/AQ Standard Building Contract With Approximate Quantities
- SBC/Q Standard Building Contract With Quantities
- SBC/XQ Standard Building Contract Without Quantities
- **SBC Sub-Contracts**
- SBCSub/A Standard Building Sub-Contract Agreement
- SBCSub/C Standard Building Sub-Contract Conditions
- SBCSub/D/A Standard Building Sub-Contract with sub-contractor's design

- **Agreement**
- SBCSub/D/C Standard Building Sub-Contract with sub-contractor's design

- **Conditions**
- Short Form of Sub-Contract (ShortSub)

- Sub-Subcontract (SubSub)

- **Intermediate Building Contract (IC)**
- C Intermediate Building Contract
- ICD Intermediate Building Contract with contractor's design

- **IC Sub-Contracts**
- ICSub/A Intermediate Sub-Contract Agreement
- ICSub/C Intermediate Sub-Contract Conditions
- ICSub/D/A Intermediate Sub-Contract with sub-contractor's design Agreement
- ICSub/D/C Intermediate Sub-Contract with sub-contractor's design Conditions
- ICSub/NAM Intermediate Named Sub-Contract Tender and Agreement
- ICsub/NAM/C Intermediate Named Sub-Contract Conditions
- ICSub/NAM/E Intermediate Named Sub-Contractor/Employer Agreement
- Short Form of Sub-contract (ShortSub)
- Sub-Subcontract (SubSub)

- **Minor Works Building Contract (MW)**
- Minor Works Building Contract (MV)
- Minor Works Building Contract with contractor's design (MWD)
- Minor Works Sub-Contract with sub-contractor's design (MWSub/D)

- **Design and Build Contract families**
- Design and Build Contract (DB)
- Design and Build Contract Guide (DB/G)
  - Design and Build Sub-Contract conditions (DBSub/C)
  - Design and Build Sub-Contract Guide (DBSub/G)
  - Short form of Sub-contract (Shortdub)
- Design and build contract (DB) Tracked change Document
-

An excellent guide to selecting the appropriate contract is available from the JCT's website (www.jctltd.co.uk).

For more in-depth guidance on the main groups of the JCT 2016 contracts, it is worth referring the excellent series of contract guides written by RIBA Publishing (source www.ribapublishing.com).

The JCT standard forms of contract are meant to be comprehensive, but they can be amended by the parties.

Amendments are common, and are often successful, but they are also often a source of litigation and should be avoided where possible or, at least, very carefully considered.

Conclusions

The works execution stage of the project represents the culmination of what is often a long, difficult process.

It is a stage where the project's vivid vision becomes a reality. In order for the completed project to realise the developer's vivid vision, this stage must be carefully planned.

It is a stage that rewards attention to detail and careful preparation. If this is not done properly, considerable delays can result, costs can mount, and the end product may not be that required by either the developer or the market.

Of all the areas in this phase of the project, it is perhaps those concerned with the personnel elements that are the most critical.

Time taken to assemble the right power team, with the right experience, knowledge and skills, will be well spent.

The right team will greatly ease the burden on the developer and ensure that all the requisite pieces of the development jigsaw are put into place.

Post completion phase

Introduction

A successful development is one in which all the people involved are free of any health and safety issues and which makes financial gains. The process after completion of the project is an important part of this success.

Activities involved in the post-completion phase

There are several options at the end of the development process.

These include:

1. To sell the whole asset to owner/occupier(s).
2. To rent or lease the whole building to an occupier(s), and sell the freehold investment interest to a third party.
3. To lease or rent the building to an occupier(s), and retain the freehold as an investment.
4. To sell a few units to pay back investors and refinance others to keep as rental units (assets for life).

A number of variations on these options exist, but these are the fundamental choices. Each requires different activities to be carried out by the development team in the post-development phase.

- Option (1) requires marketing and advertising to be carried out to find occupiers and/or purchasers for the completed scheme.
- Option (2) requires:
- The same as option (1) above, plus the setting up of an acceptable special purchase vehicle (SPV) that will be suitable for occupiers and acceptable to investors, or find a mortgage for each individual unit to repay all investors.
- Marketing and advertising to find occupiers; and/or
- Marketing and advertising to find investors willing to purchase.
- Options (3)and (4) require (1) and (2), as above, and also the creation of an ongoing management system. This is necessary to service the property as an investment. This system will need to cover income collection, tenant monitoring, assessment of maintenance, etc. These are all factors necessary to maintain the value of the investment in the future.

These activities and processes should not be tacked on as an afterthought, but must be integrated into the project exits strategies as well as funding, design and planning process

Key responsibilities post-completion phase

The key items mentioned above would need to be delegated by the developer to a good chartered surveying firm and also, budget permitting, a separate marketing consultancy may need to be employed for specialist advice. Even where this is the case, it is best to coordinate this through a partnership with an estate agent that is fully conversant with the Help to Buy scheme at the time of writing, and/or a commercial agent.

As we have seen in the development team construction, surveyors are an integral part of the team, which is why it is important that they are involved at the design stage. The list of the functional specialisations of surveyors involved in the process is quite extensive.

Although, in general practice, surveyors can technically carry out work in all these areas, usually specialisation occurs. If the development is complex and requires many different areas of work in the post-completion phase, then it is worthwhile ensuring that the firm employed can service all of the areas required.

The level of fees charged by each function is rather complex. There is also no centrally agreed scale of fees; instead, each rate is agreed by negotiation.

Each of the main functions needed in the post-completion phase will be examined in turn.

Residential letting	Typically 10–15% of gross rental value At AFL we use 15% of net rental income below 90% occupancy and 20% of net rental income for 100% occupancy
Commercial letting	Approximately 10% of annual rent (excluding advertisements, marketing fees and disbursements) although more complex structures can be used to incentivise an agent
Sale to owner occupier	Typically 1–2% of capital value (commercial)
Sale to owner occupier	Typically 1–3% of capital value (residential)
Sale to investors	Typically 1–2% of capital value
Management fee	Either a lump sum is agreed or a percentage of annual rent is taken
Rent reviews/ lease renewals	A typical figure is 10% of the new rent or a percentage of the uplift or a fixed fee with coverage over a certain figure or a fixed fee
Valuation	Varies from a lump sum to 0.25–0.75% of the capital value

Although general practice surveyors can technically carry out work in all these areas, usually specialisation occurs. If the development is complex and requires many different areas of work in the post-completion phase, then it is worthwhile ensuring that the firm employed can service all of the areas required.

The level of fees charged by each function is rather complex. There is also no centrally agreed scale of fees; instead, each rate is agreed by negotiation. The above table gives an idea of the level of fees involved in some of the key functions.

Each of the main functions needed in the post-completion phase will be examined in turn.

Sales and lettings

This is one of the most important areas of residential and commercial schemes. The timing and amount of rent achieved per unit can make a huge difference in the success or failure of the scheme. If you don't have the in-house staff, the company that you appoint must have the right blend of experience, specific to the type of development being undertaken.

The commercial and residential agents you choose must have the adequate (number and training) human resources to meet your needs. Efficient agents are like gold dust. They are typically well-organised, well-motivated, great at persuasion and influencing, with good contacts in both the offices of potential occupiers and also other firms who may act for potential occupiers. They should have a big list of potential buyers for your residential units.

This type of data makes our life much easier compared with using firms that are less experienced or less respected, and who rely far more on 'cold calling' or people that are new in the neighbourhood. In many aspects of the property development and investment, it is who you know, and building up a network of contacts is an asset for life.

Property development and investment is a journey by a group of people with a leader; he or she requires a melding of technical skill and knowledge with a gregarious nature that stresses the importance of good oral and written communication, as well as, percolation, persuasion and influencing.

Remember once again that these agents are the ones that should have had the greatest input into the design and planning of our projects. This allows the application of information on current market requirements and future trends. They can also give advice on timing issues, e.g. when the developer should aim to finish the scheme in order to capture the greatest interest from potential buyers, both buy-to-let or owner occupiers.

Marketing

Timing is essential.; When to start the marketing phase, as well as the staff involved, and what form the marketing of the property should take, depends on the nature and size of the project being undertaken.

Residential

With residential property, to eliminate or mitigate projects risk, it is essential that the developer is prepared to 'sell off-plan'. Usually, projects start with an initial announcement being made; often this is when site works commence.

This is not usually done earlier because of the risk that an image problem that might be created if the project was abandoned for some reason. This most frequently occurs due to market conditions changing; for example, if the economy went into a period of recession, or if there was a marked rise in the cost of borrowing. It is only practical to stop a development before the building works commences. Normally, only an extreme situation, such as bankruptcy, will stop a project when it is on site.

Once the on-site work has started, then advertisements are placed in local newspapers. Quite frequently, a marketing suite is placed on site.

For this, I recommend that the agent should be able to sell the scheme through Help to Buy and should be familiar with the time and paperwork needed. I also recommend you choose an agent that has the power team in place to make sure that the sales price is followed up on a daily basis, as once the conveyances teams get involved the paperwork can take forever.

Commercial

The critical decision of when to commence marketing is virtually the same for both commercial and residential developments. In a challenging market, or one that follows a downturn, there is effectively no option but to try to secure at least an agreement to lease (pre-letting) or an agreement to buy (pre-sale), perhaps even prior to the site purchase.

As we have discussed previously, for large projects, especially high-end, the developer will not be able to obtain funding for a speculative scheme without these agreements when the market is weak, or where financial bodies have suffered recent losses, possibly in the event of a market downturn.

In a rising, strong market, the initial marketing may occur at the beginning of the project in order to attract expressions of interest. I personally do this, and it is important to develop 3D-modelling that reflect the quality of end product. Most developers, sadly, will wait until the end of the construction phase before the main marketing is undertaken, taking a risk of losing potential buyers for their schemes.

On the other hand, if you are happy to wait until the end of project, wish to capture any rise in market values, and do not want to enter into a premature agreement which may be at a lower rental level than could be achieved, then it is a valid strategy to consider.

In this scenario, early marketing expenditure may be premature and could be wasted as it would need to be redone at the end of project.

Types of marketing

There are several types of marketing that can be used for the different types of developments. A brief explanation of these methods is given below, separated into residential and commercial types of project.

Marketing residential developments

The preparation of brochures 'selling a lifestyle rather than a house' requires a description of the project, a layout of the site, the types of houses and flats being built, the numbers of each type, a floor plan and 3D rendering with outline specifications and a price schedule.

Many developers have found that feature hoardings, with an artist's impression of the completed project on or near the site, one of the more useful types of marketing that targets the core market for the project.

Advertisements can be placed in local newspapers and magazines outlining the type of building being produced (sizes, layout, quality) and also indicative prices.

An on-site marketing presence comprises of either a temporary marketing suite, or a completed unit within the development manned by a representative of the developer. This key member of your team can introduce the scheme to prospective buyers, take details of their requirements and ensure that follow-up calls are made as the scheme approaches completion. This approach requires good promotional literature to be available for distribution to callers.

A local agent or agents who will promote the scheme through their offices should be appointed.

Web-based advertising has become far more important over the past decades, given the number of people who initially search for new property on the internet. For larger schemes, it is worth having a dedicated website; for smaller schemes, advertising through some of the more general residential sales sites like Rightmove, Zoopla, etc may be enough. Most schemes now have electronic versions of their marketing brochures, including interactive PDF, 360-degree walk around viewings and drone flyovers.

Marketing developments

The first step in marketing is to appoint a suitable agent. This may be a single or joint agency, ideally a national one.

There are a number of advantages in this. These agents will prepare the following marketing material:
- A brochure with 3D renders including an artist's impression, initially giving a brief specification.
- During construction, space permitting, a hoarding will be erected, usually containing an artist's impression and an outline of the floor areas and specification of the building.
- A one- or two-page flier for posting to potential occupiers, other agents and
- or purchasers; this will give outlined details of the development, which will then hopefully translate into further interest on contact with the appointed agent.
- A detailed technical specification should be drawn up for parties displaying serious interest; this can be a limited print run.
- If the property is to be leased and sold to investors, it is useful to prepare a lease with outlined 'heads of terms' indicated by your trusted solicitor.
- As with residential development, web-based advertising such as Rightmove, Zoopla and the like has become increasingly important. Again, for larger schemes, it is worth having a dedicated website with 3D renders and, now, virtual reality; while for smaller schemes, advertising through some of the more general commercial sites may suffice. Many schemes have electronic PDF versions of their brochures which can be viewed, downloaded, or printed by prospec-

- tive purchasers or tenants.
- For larger projects, other advertising media may be considered. A number of schemes with which I have been involved have had their own Instagram page and a memory stick containing the brochure material presented in a more interactive way. This may be the same material in the web advertisement but may also include, for example, animations or films of the scheme and 'walk through' virtual reality and/or three-dimensional design material.

The appointed agent will prepare mailshot lists of potential occupiers or purchasers who are known to have a requirement, or other agents who are known to act for such parties. Agents will tend to prepare a telephone contact list to follow up these parties.

If the scheme is large enough, you may agree with the agent to place advertisements in the trade press. There are two main national property publications in the UK (Estates Gazette and Property Week, both published frequently), along with a number of smaller, sometimes regional, publications.

Both have websites offering the opportunity to advertise schemes. Advertisements for commercial schemes are not always required, depending on location. Targeted marketing via mailshot and telephone is usually far more effective, and, certainly for the very large schemes, press advertising is almost seen as an admission of failure. With smaller schemes that appeal to local markets, this approach may, however, tease out occupiers who had not registered interest with agents and who may not have even considered moving prior to becoming aware of the scheme. In these cases, advertising in the local press and local trade magazines may prove useful. Very occasionally, radio or even TV advertising may also be undertaken.

At AFL, during construction, we celebrate by carrying out a 'topping out' ceremony. This is a builders' ritual, traditionally held when the last beam is placed on top of a structure. Nowadays, the ceremony is turned into a media/public relations event.

Here is a link to our project top out ceremony
https://www.instagram.com/tv/CEZp3MpFDMP/?utm_source=ig_web_button_share_sheet

Later in the development process of a speculative building, the agent may promote a launch party. This is usually held on completion of the scheme, where part or all of the building remains vacant. The launch party should invite local businesses, potential occupiers and their agents. These events are popular with agents in particular, and are useful in getting the development known in the marketplace, but these events can be expensive.

Agents and deal sources

Now let's explain the difference between agent and deal sources. Agents are those employed directly by the developer or investment client. In this case, they are retained to secure a successful selling or letting of the scheme, and will be paid a fee by the client when they do so. Occupiers searching for space can also retain agents to find space on their behalf. These agents are paid a fee by their own clients when they successfully fulfil their instructions, but not by the developer.

There are also deal sources, or free agents, who operate somewhere in the middle ground; they are not under instruction by any party, or are sometimes under an exclusivity agreement. What these agents try to do is bring together two parties who are not aware of each other. They will try to introduce an occupier to a building. If the sale of letting proceeds, they will try to obtain a fee from one or the other of the parties involved. It is, at times, a precarious existence, but one in which many agents survive and thrive. These agents receive the protection of the law for the introductions they make, even if they do no more than get verbal confirmation over the telephone.

Whatever the type of property, or the approach on which we decide to embark, time taken to establish a coherent marketing strategy with a good firm of agents, early in the development scheme, will pay dividends later on. Rapid leasing or sale of the scheme does more than anything to save money and maximise profitability.

Marketing for investment sales

Previously, we have covered selling each individual unit; now, let's cover preparing the entire development for sale as an investment. This is not usually carried out by the same team which deals with the leasing of the property, or selling all the units individually. This is not simply because firms aim to make multiple fees out of the same property instruction, but really because investment agents have different skills and contacts to those possessed by letting agents. The marketing approach depends on the nature of the scheme. An investment-grade building will only appeal to a relatively narrow range of potential buyers, and as a result needs only a relatively limited marketing programme. This will effectively involve personal contact between the retained agent, and the investors and their agents.

For smaller projects that may have wider appeal, a marketing programme similar to that outlined above for commercial and residential letting may be required.

Disposing of development projects – sell or lease

Most developments will involve some kind of sell or lease disposal process. Properties for sale to owner occupiers, whether they are residential or commercial, require the sale of the occupational freehold or long leasehold interests. Investment properties will involve at least the disposal of the occupational interest on a lease. If the investment is not retained, the freehold reversionary interest will also require disposal. This is another way to generate income for any project. In the next section, we will cover the methods of disposal and provide you with a basic guide to the processes and procedures involved.

Sales of freehold and long leasehold interests

For the purposes of this book, sales of these two types of interest will be considered to be the same. As a brief explanation, 'fee simple absolute' (freehold in Scotland) or freehold interests are the highest bundle of rights that can be held in the UK, below the Crown.

Leaseholds, or 'term of years absolute', are a lesser interest created out of freeholds where a consideration passes from the leaseholder to the freeholder (or higher landlord as tiers of leaseholds can also be created) in return for a grant of lease, giving the rights to occupy the property for a given term of years.

Long leaseholds are those created for a period usually in excess of 99 years.

Long leaseholds can be created for several reasons, but the two commonest are:
- Development leases where the landowner wishes to retain overall control of the site.

- In properties of multiple occupation, such as residential flats.

In the latter case, this approach is required due to the peculiarities of UK common law, which does not allow the enforcement of positive covenants such as to repair or to provide support.

The lease contract is enforceable; hence, at present, all flats for owner occupation should be leasehold. The consideration, or the rent, is usually nominal in the cases that we are considering here, and the interest for sale is taken to be a virtual freehold.

There are a number of ways of achieving sales, although in the UK one dominates. The three main types are sale by tender, auction and private treaty.

The three types of sale

Sale by tender

The vendor wishing to dispose of the asset asks for 'best bids', and sometimes a best and final bid by a set deadline. Usually, these are submitted sealed, and then opened at a given time.

Tenders are widely used for selling sites where developers are competing for the opportunity to build.

They are very rarely used for the sale of completed developments, unless there is a property type that has strong demand, in which case it can be used in favour of the developer to get the best price for the asset.

Sale by auction

If I am wearing the buyer's shoes, I would not go for this option due to the time pressure. The property is offered for sale at a specific date and time and will be sold at this time unless a previously set reserve has not been reached.

Auctions have an odd reputation in the UK market. In other parts of the world, auctions are a sensible and widely used method of selling. In the UK, there is a cultural stigma with auctions. Auctions are viewed as a last resort to sell problem property such as repossessed homes, secondary investment properties, and student houses. Despite this stigma, auctions are widely used in the UK and good prices can be achieved. Several of the leading surveying practices run auctions in which some good quality property is sold. Once again, if you are buying make sure you have a power team that can deliver within the time limitations imposed by auctions.

Private treaty

This is my favourite, as there is no fixed date of sale for buyers. This avoids the time pressure of an auction, where a buyer can end up losing their deposit if they are not able to complete in 30 or so days after the hammer goes down at auction. The property is marketed as described in the text and the price is agreed by private negotiation. This is one of the most popular types of sale in the UK.

With private treaty sales, and sometimes following the receipt of tender bids, the client's agent will normally negotiate the terms of the sale with the prospective purchaser, with the ultimate approval of the instructing client. These 'heads of terms' will then be passed to the parties' solicitors for agreement of the detailed contract of sale and the final conveyancing of title.

Lettings

If one of the exit strategies is to keep the asset for life i.e. build to rent or lease, typically your appointed agent identifies prospective occupiers and deals with general enquiries arising from other sources. The agent will arrange viewings and will supply information to the potential clients. Where the party is interested, the agent will lead the negotiations based on the parameters laid down by the client. If the negotiations proceed to a point where the party agrees to take space, then the agent will agree Heads Of Terms (HOT). These will usually include:

- The initial rental level agreed.
- The total area and layout of the property and a clear definition of what is actually being let under the lease.
- The term of the lease (its length).
- Key details, such as the period and mode of the rent review clause, the alienation clause, repairs and maintenance responsibilities, etc.
- Any special features of the deal, such as rent-free periods given at the start of the lease, or fitting out contributions paid for by the landlord, break clauses, etc.

Once the above is agreed, these terms will be passed to the other parties' solicitors for the full preparation of the lease document. The basic lease documentation will be prepared by us, or the developer's solicitor, but its final form will be developed in an iterative process between the parties. This involves the lease being passed between each side, with alterations being made until agreement is reached as to the final form of the contract. Depending on the size of the project, this can take several months.

It is important to highlight that, in multi-let properties that are to become investment properties, the lease terms should be kept as similar as possible across the building. Variations in lease terms, particular key clauses such as rental values, rent review clauses, terms, and the repairing clause, will impact on the overall value of the investment; investors seeking a discount from the management can lead to problems.

The letting management and investment performance of the property are closely related. The properties' characteristics in these areas must be set up correctly from the beginning, otherwise the problems will persist over most of the investment life of the building.

One of the other key roles of your agent is to find out the quality of the potential occupiers. Your tenant-to-be is the real asset here, and the agent will need to ensure that the tenant will:
- Be able to afford the rent both now and in the future,
- Be honest and conscientious, obey the lease covenants and look after the building.

This, again, is where the agency, management, and investment requirements meet. Although the agent will want to let the property as quickly as possible to secure their fee, developers and our investment and management departments will need the best possible quality of tenant, to maintain and increase the value of our investment.

Long term, the value of a cash flow is not strictly dependent on the amount of money, but also on the quality of that income flow, i.e. the quality of the party that is paying it.

A local company with little track record in business may be able to pay the same rent as a large corporation, but the cash flow from the latter will be worth more because it is more secure. A managing agent will not want a tenant to fall into arrears, or fail to maintain a property, or to use it in breach of the terms of the lease, as this will create additional time and management costs and problems, for example with neighbouring tenants. All of this means that good quality, long-established tenants (good covenants) are to be preferred, even if they pay us less rent.

The careful investigations that our agents should be performing on our behalf will depend on the identity of the proposed tenant. With larger corporations, little investigation is needed, although it is worthwhile to check whether the lease is with the parent company or a subsidiary, the former naturally being preferred.

With smaller companies, our agent should be looking into at least the past three or four years' trading accounts where possible. This should give information as to the solvency of the company.

Larger companies can be investigated using credit rating and long-established company analysis agencies such as Dun & Bradstreet and Standard & Poor's. Dun & Bradstreet is a corporation that offers information on commercial credit, as well as reports on businesses. Most notably, Dun & Bradstreet is recognisable for its Data Universal Numbering System (DUNS numbers); these generate business information reports for more than 100 million companies around the globe. Dun & Bradstreet was established as the result of a merger in the 1930s between R.G. Dun & Co. and the Bradstreet Cos.

References should be obtained from previous landlords where possible and the companies' accountants and bankers. Many of these references are often too general to be of any use for us. Decisions over tenants, both for residential and commercial, often become a matter of personal judgement. Where there is doubt, it may be possible to obtain additional security using things such as guarantors, upfront rent payments, performance bonds, simple deposits, or personal guarantees from the directors of the companies signing the lease.

Key successful management factors for investment properties

These are mostly aimed at developers who intend to retain their investment properties as an asset for life.

However, with property for sale, as we have seen from the preceding section, there is a strong interrelationship between investment performance and the management structure.

I can write a whole book on this subject, but for this section I will only give you an outline of good management practice with regard to commercial and residential property.

We will focus on the key factors that affect the performance of commercial investment property. It is these areas that us developers should concentrate on getting right at the start of the investment life of the project, as it makes the transition from the development phase.

It is absolutely essential that a good quality managing agent is hired to help you with this.

If you are not able to find such a team then forget it, you won't be able to make any money whatsoever! These agents must have relevant experience and the systems in place to ensure the smooth operation of the property during its life.

When looking at how to manage commercial and residential property, the following should be considered:

- lease/rent period
- covenant strength
- service charges fees
- repair and maintenance responsibilities
- rent review clause
- user clause
- alienation clause
- alterations and improvements
- other relevant clauses.

What we are looking at, essentially, is the structure of a commercial lease. It is the lease that is at the heart of good management practice with commercial property. It is the document that must be correctly constructed at the beginning, in order to ensure smooth management in the future. It is very important to get advice from the management surveyor when these leases are being constructed.

Quality of income factors

As with many other investments, cash flow from a property investment is the thing that gives it value. As we have already seen, this value is related to both the quantum of the cash flow and also its quality. Quantum issues are partly a question of management; often, they are determined by market forces. Quality, however, is mainly determined by management decisions, although these, of course, are also heavily influenced by market conditions. The two main areas that affect the quality of the cash flow are the lease length and the covenant strength of the tenant.

Lease length

One of the key issues with regard to leases is the period of the agreement, in other words its length. The lease length must both satisfy occupier requirements and also be long enough to suit investors. Commercial tenants want both flexibility and security.

This is slightly ambiguous: security comes from having a long lease. A long lease, however, is frequently inflexible. An ideal situation for tenants is to have the ability to give up the lease with no penalty, but also to have the option of continuing occupation if so required. Developers and investors, on the other hand, value the certainty that comes from a long lease. The requirements of both sides of the letting equation have been in conflict for many years in the UK, and across the globe.

The strengths of each party vary according to market conditions, which change across time as I explained in my property cycles chapter. Effectively, the market is considered to be a 'landlord' or a 'tenant' market. The former exists where there is strong competition for space and the latter when there is an oversupply in the market. The situation is made more complex by the intervention of the government in the operation of a free market.

There is a substantial amount of landlord and tenant legislation that exists and which us developers, investors and occupiers need to take into consideration. Some of this legislation affects this issue of security of tenure and flexibility in the actions of occupiers and landlords.

As noted, this is a very complex area. Some of the issues require particular attention. I have highlighted a few below for you to consider: .
- Most business tenancies in England and Wales have an automatic right to renew their leases under Part II of the Landlord and Tenant Act 1954. The landlord has only limited grounds to oppose the grant of a new lease and therefore even a short lease taken out by a business tenant can be extended. In many respects this gives the best of all worlds to business tenants.
- Looking at the past, the market in the early 1990s in the UK was very unstable. The UK saw a reduction in the length of leases from 25 years to 10–15 years at the prime end of the market. These are effectively the leases that would be granted on investment-grade property. Even following the recovery in the market in the second half of the decade, the trend for shorter leases has been maintained.
- Another feature of the market at this time was the fact that break-in clauses for commercial leases became far more frequently applied. These break-in clauses were invariably in the tenant's favour. This allowed far more tenants to terminate their leases early.
- Changes in legislation in the 1990s in England and Wales further

altered the balance in favour of the tenant. The Landlord and Tenant (Covenants) Act 1995 ended something called 'privity of contract' for leases granted after 1 January 1996. If the tenant wants to dispose of a lease, they effectively have two choices. One is to sublet the property. This creates a lower level of interest below the tenant's lease. The other alternative is to assign the lease.

This is effectively the sale of the lease with, in theory, the original tenant dropping out of the picture and the obligations under the lease being taken on by the incoming purchaser. This was naturally the favoured option for tenants who no longer wished to have the liability of the premises. However, prior to the 1995 Act, although the original tenant was no longer in occupation, nor paid the rent, and usually the lease had actually been altered to note the change in occupier, the original tenant still had the residual responsibility for the premises.

This was due to the original landlord and tenant alone having been party to the contract negotiations and agreement. As a result of this, the landlord could revert to the original tenant if the assignee defaulted or breached a lease clause at some point in the future. In normal circumstances, therefore, it did not really matter if a PLC covenant assigned their lease to a much weaker tenant, as the privity of contract acted as a virtual 'back stop' in the case of future default by the new tenant. This situation was felt to be onerous on tenants and much lobbying was done in the early 1990s, which resulted in the legislative change.

All of the above factors have made it much more difficult for us property developers/investors to secure a good tenant on a long lease.

The developer has to be much more conscious than in the past in the creation of the investment vehicle in order to ensure that its value is maintained. Some of the steps that we can take with regard to future security of income are listed below for you. Once again, this is a key subject and you must have the right power team members appointed to help you get this right.

- The insertion of authorised guarantee agreements in the lease: these agreements arose out of the 1995 Covenants Act and are intended to mitigate the effect of the loss of primitive contract. They allow the landlord to require the initial tenant to offer limited guarantees as to the future payment of rent if they choose in the future to assign the lease to a third party.

- A tighter alienation clause now can be included in the lease, requiring the landlord to give written approval of any assignee and granting the landlord the right to reject the tenant on the grounds of quality. Prior to the 1995 Act, such clauses were illegal.

It is still possible to jointly agree to operate the lease of the commercial property outside the terms of the 1954 Act, i.e. giving the tenant no security of tenure. This has to be done by joint application of the parties to the courts.

This may seem biased, in that it can swing the power of negotiation to the landlord if the tenant has no security at the end of the lease. Nevertheless, the system has worked very successfully in Scotland, where the 1954 Act provisions do not apply.

Leaseholder quality

The main issue with regard to the management of an investment property is to ensure that the highest quality tenant possible is signed up to the lease. This may sometimes mean accepting a lower rent from a better quality tenant to ensure that the investment value of the property is maintained.

Where we cannot secure such tenants, there are mechanisms that can be put into place which can mitigate the effect of a weak tenant. Two ways of achieving this are:
- The developer/landlord requests that the tenant sign a personal or third-party guarantee agreement. This is a legally-binding document and is particularly useful where the business signing up for lease is of dubious quality, or where the business has not been running for many years. As there is a separate identity to a limited business and its directors, without a guarantee a default on business debt cannot be corrected if the business goes belly up or otherwise fails. Where a personal guarantee or a guarantee from a solvent third party exists, the property owner can at least recover some of the costs and unpaid rent from this source.
- A similar strategy can be achieved by asking the incoming tenant to take out a bond with a financial institution. The bond is effectively an insurance policy for which the tenant pays a one-off, or annual, premium. The bond is made in favour of the landlord, who can only access it if the tenant is in serious default.

Commercial leases: important clauses

The following clauses in commercial leases should be very carefully considered in order to maintain the value of the asset.

Maintenance and repairs

It is paramount that the buildings and its surroundings are well maintained, and are returned to the owner in a good condition. In most cases, investors in the UK seek to pass all of the costs of maintaining and repairing a building on to the tenant. In a single-let building this is done by way of the repairing clause; in multi-let buildings, this is done using service charges.

The majority of leases in the UK are what is well-known as 'full repairing and insuring' (FRI). This is a description of what has been shared previously; namely, that the tenant is responsible for all outgoing costs including those of insuring the building. Most leases also require tenants to carry out periodic redecoration to maintain the image of the building. These maintenance clauses state the normal number of years to pass between redecorating internally and externally.

The repairing clause normally defines the condition in which the building is to return to the owner at the end of the lease. It is good practice not to be too strict, or create too onerous repairing clauses. If the clause is too onerous, it will make the premises difficult to let, and reduce the value of the asset in the long term.

Service charges

Without service charges, the asset will decay, and therefore they are essential in multi-let buildings. A basic requirement of UK investors is that rents should be net rents, i.e. no deduction for repairing, maintaining, heating, or lighting a building should be made from the rent. In a single-let building, this is generally covered in the repairing clause, which makes the tenant responsible for all repairs both inside and outside the building. In a multi-let building, however, the work needs to be done by a central agency to ensure that it is carried out without fail.

The work must also be managed by the landlord's representative. To ensure that the rent received on the property is still a net rent, the costs of all of the work required to the building should be recovered from occupiers.

This is done by way of a service charge. There should be no shortfall on the service charge, otherwise the investment value of the building will be reduced.

There are various ways of calculating a service charge and constructing it for the actual recovery of work undertaken. This varies from an estimate of the annual or quarterly costs of maintaining the building with an upfront payment, and mechanisms for additional recovery or repayment if required, to actual recovery of costs as the work proceeds.

The service charge clause needs to be accurately constructed. From experience, it should also not be too onerous as this can reduce the attractiveness of the property in the market and impact on its investment value.

There is a tendency to make service charge provisions too clever. Some allow almost unlimited recovery of cost as the landlord sees fit, up to and including the complete rebuilding and redevelopment of the building. This can be especially true of residential buildings. As we have seen, multi-let residential buildings are leasehold.

There must, however, be an overriding freehold interest.

The leaseholders normally only pay a nominal rent to the freeholder; it is the freeholder who is responsible for the maintenance of the building. The main source of trouble is connected with the quality of leases in residential property. They are often very loosely constructed compared with a commercial lease. They are therefore rather easily exploited by the unscrupulous.

There are numerous examples of residential leaseholders finding themselves facing excessive bills under the service charge, and making their investment lose value as a result.

Rent review clause

The rent review clause is one of the critical areas of the lease and it will directly affect the value of your asset, although its importance has waned as leases have become shorter.

The rent review clause is the mechanism that allows periodic reviews of the rent to take place. This is normally every 12 months for residential property and also for poorer quality commercial property; every three years for secondary commercial property; and normally every five years for top quality property lets on longer leases (10–15 years).

There are various ways, in theory, of constructing a rent review clause. For example:

- An adjustment of the rent using an index (inflation, retail price index, building cost, etc)
- Fixed rate increases (e.g. three to seven per cent p.a.)
- Frequent comparison of the rent with the current market rental value of similar properties on the market at the time of the rent review.

All three are viable methods on paper, but it is only the last one which is actually acceptable in UK practice. While simple in theory, it is in practice very difficult to successfully carry out. The reason is that it requires a set of circumstances to be clearly defined, so that each party knows exactly what is being valued.

Effectively, what the parties are asked to do in rent reviews is to assume that the premises are vacant and available to let at the time of the review. What, then, would this property let for in the open market to an occupier acting with normal business motives in mind? This sounds straightforward, and indeed the original rent review clauses were very simple.

When things are considered more carefully, however, they become much more complex: what term of the new lease is to be considered? What state of repair is the demised property assumed to be in?

Should incentives that are being given to tenants in the open market at the time of the review be taken into account in the calculation of the new rent? Should any improvements made to the asset that have been undertaken by the tenant be included in the calculation of the new rent?

These, and a whole host of other questions, have to be addressed in the clause. Modern rent review clauses attempt to cover all of these questions comprehensively. They lay down assumptions that the parties should make at the time of the review. The rent review clause is perhaps the single most important clause for investors and should be carefully considered.

Rent review clauses in the UK do not normally allow the rent to fall at review. Inaccurately, these clauses are referred to as being 'upward only', whereas in fact they are ratchet clauses whose normal wording is that the rent on review should be the higher than the current market rent, or the existing rent passing on the property.

The government instigated a review of the workings of the property market, which recommended in 2005 that no changes be made. As a result, these clauses are almost universal in the marketplace and would only be at risk from future legislation, or from changes in the landlord/tenant balance of power, as occurred in the early 1990s.

Although, on the surface, they appear onerous, they are in fact only an issue where market rents have fallen severely and rapidly. In the UK, this situation has only occurred twice in the post-war period, and then only for a fairly limited time.

They do, however, provide investors with considerable security and are highly valued by the investment community.

The detailed construction of the rent review clause should be left to a rent review surveyor and solicitor working in tandem. The review clause should have a timetable, and also must have some mechanism for dispute resolution by a third party, either by determination of an independent expert or by arbitrator. The timetable should not be strictly construed, otherwise the lease will be deemed too onerous.

User clauses

The use of assets or buildings can be defined in two ways: fundamentally, by the land use planning system, and also by the user clause that exists in the lease.

What is the main reason that a landlord needs to regulate the use of its asset? The answer is to do with long-term asset management. In a residential building, the landlord would need to ensure that no commercial use occurs that would interfere with other occupants in the building. In retail property, the mix between tenants is important in order to ensure that a wide range of shoppers will visit the shopping centre.

With office property, landlords would not want an undesirable use to upset the other tenants. For example, an office building occupied by a top-quality accounting firm, which relies on regular client contact, would not wish for a funeral office to occupy the same building. Without any wish to be disrespectful to funeral businesses, this is an issue of image, and the image conflict is clear. The tenants in the building would not tolerate the situation and would almost certainly move out.

The user clause enables the building owner to maintain a balance between tenants.

All user clauses, however, should not be 'closed', allowing no other use than the one defined. This also applies to all other clauses. Normally, clauses should be constructed to permit other uses to be considered on written application to the landlord. It should be written into the lease that the landlord's consent 'should not be unreasonably withheld'. These five magic words should be applied to many of the clauses in the lease, as they allow the landlord to keep reasonable control, but permit the tenant some leeway and flexibility.

Alterations to layout

Layout alterations are normally allowed if they do not include structural alterations, e.g. work to internal partitioning, for which additional permission from the landlord is needed.

All other alterations should require consent, particularly if they involve the alterations of the substructure (foundations), pipework and wiring, the movement of fixtures and fittings or any work that involves any element of the superstructure of the building.

The reason for this is to ensure the safety of other tenants, the structural integrity of the building and, indeed, the value of the building. While the landlord should retain an absolute right to prevent such structural changes to the building, any other work should require the landlord's consent, which is not to be unreasonably withheld.

Other important lease clauses

Other clauses to include in the lease are access rights, dispute resolution and issues to do with the landlord's interest disposal. They should also define the landlord's responsibilities.

Commercial leases in particular are very thorough documents, with a typical one sometimes being in excess of 150 pages long.

Nevertheless, from experience, developers and landlords should avoid the temptation to make leases too onerous, as this tends to have a significant impact on value.

Summary and conclusions

Once the asset/property is built, the real income generation comes from the quality of the tenant and the management team that we decide to appoint. For this, there are some simple rules which affect the management of investment property:

- Good management and good investments go hand-in-hand. If you don't have the right management team, you won't be making any money!
- The asset value is essentially determined by the quality of the income that the asset generates day in, day out. This is only partly determined by the quality of the building and its specific location.

- A very important element is the quality of the leaseholder/tenant and the terms under which they occupy the premises, i.e. the lease. Each clause in the lease is important, and the whole should be carefully scrutinised by both investors and occupiers.
- After the lease is signed by all parties, it is too late to amend it, at least in practical terms. Every effort should be made to get the lease structure correct, even before the first draft is delivered to a prospective tenant's solicitor. Sometimes a 'plain English version' to start with is the best way forward.
- Selection of potential tenants, and careful vetting of them, is paramount to ensure that the building will be properly maintained, and that the income flow will have as few interruptions as possible.

If these rules are followed, then the management should be straightforward and the investment performance of the building should go smoothly.

Do we always get this right? The answer may be found in the fact that there is still money to be made in the secondary property market by property companies who purchase older investments and work on them. By work, we mean refurbishment and remodelling (layout is king), but it can often mean correcting errors in leases and problems in occupation, therefore adding back 'lost' value.

Admittedly, part of this opportunity arises out of the passage of time, and the changing market practices, but a proportion is due to the errors made when the building was first let.

The message is: to be successful, get the right SPV (specific purchase value) from the beginning!

Congratulations!!!

You made it happen!

If you are reading this, then you have reached the end of your old journey, and now is the beginning of your new property development metamorphosis journey. Trust me, it will be life-changing, but only if you expand and apply all the knowledge I have passed on to you.

Now is the time to follow the step-by-step process I have given you, and focus your energy on your new priorities. Then you will be able to transform your life and the lives of the ones you love.

Take a leap of faith and grab this opportunity to start your own property metamorphosis. It will change your life, and that of many others in the process, like it did to me five years ago when I decided to go for it.

I do hope that, in reading this book, you found your 'satori' moment; where you clearly see your past (old you), the present (this precise moment) and future (a vivid vision of you) align into one. Now, you should feel more than ready to be a successful protagonist of your own property metamorphosis.

Kilonewtons of love!

Bibliography

1. Wilkinson, S. & Reed, R. Forward by Prof Cadman, D. (2008). *Property Development, Fifth Edition*. Routledge.

2. Dr Harvard, T. (2008). *Contemporary Property Development, Second Edition*. RIBA Publishing.

3. Hill, N. (2015). *Think and Grow Rich*. Mindpower Press.

4. Dalio, R. (2017). *Principles: Life and Work.* Simon & Schuster.

5. Womack, J.W. (2012). *Your Best Just Got Better: Work Smarter, Think Bigger, Achieve More*. John Wiley & Sons.

6. Morgan, S. (2017) *Seven Mindsets Of Success: What You Really Need to Do to Achieve Rapid, Top-Level Success*. Morgan James Publishing.

7. Santarelli, M. (2020) *Passive Real Estate Investing*. Online.

8. Snow, S. (2018). *Dream Teams: Working Together Without Falling Apart*. Portfolio.

9. Baker, T. (2018). *The 1% Rule: How to Fall in Love with the Process and Achieve Your Wildest Dreams.* Archangel Ink.

10. Holiday, R. (2014). *The Obstacle is the Way: The Ancient Art of Turning Adversity to Advantage*. Profile Books.

11. *Herold, C. (2018). Vivid Vision: A Remarkable Tool For Aligning Your Business Around a Shared Vision of the Future*. Lioncrest.

12. Schulhof, A. *Look Before You Leap. An Insider's Guide to Profitable Real Estate Investing*.

13. Munoz, J. (2018). *My AFL Journey*. Amazon.

www.ingramcontent.com/pod-product-compliance
Lightning Source LLC
Chambersburg PA
CBHW070619220526
45466CB00001B/53